Edited by Robert Arp

TATTOOS

PHILOSOPHY FOR EVERYONE

I Ink, Therefore I Am

Foreword by Rocky Rakovic

⊛WILEY-BLACKWELL

A John Wiley & Sons, Ltd., Publication

This edition first published 2012
© 2012 John Wiley & Sons, Inc.

Wiley-Blackwell is an imprint of John Wiley & Sons, formed by the merger of
Wiley's global Scientific, Technical and Medical business with Blackwell Publishing.

Registered Office
John Wiley & Sons, Ltd, The Atrium, Southern Gate, Chichester, West Sussex,
PO19 8SQ, UK

Editorial Offices
350 Main Street, Malden, MA 02148-5020, USA
9600 Garsington Road, Oxford, OX4 2DQ, UK
The Atrium, Southern Gate, Chichester, West Sussex, PO19 8SQ, UK

For details of our global editorial offices, for customer services, and for information
about how to apply for permission to reuse the copyright material in this book please
see our website at www.wiley.com/wiley-blackwell.

The right of Robert Arp to be identified as the author of the editorial material in this
work has been asserted in accordance with the UK Copyright, Designs and
Patents Act 1988.

Library of Congress Cataloging-in-Publication Data
Tattoos : philosophy for everyone : I ink, therefore I am /
   edited by Robert Arp. – 1st ed.
      p.   cm. – (Philosophy for everyone ; 50)
   Includes bibliographical references and index.
   ISBN 978-0-470-67206-8 (pbk.)
1. Tattooing. I. Arp, Robert.
   GN419.3.T375 2012
   391.6'5–dc23

                                                        2011044950

A catalogue record for this book is available from the British Library.

Set in 10/12.5pt Plantin by SPi Publisher Services, Pondicherry, India
Printed in Singapore by Ho Printing Singapore Pte Ltd

1   2012

VOLUME EDITOR

ROBERT ARP has taught and published in many areas of philosophy and ontology in the information science sense. He also has done a lot of work in the philosophy and popular culture realm, and has regularly flashed his half smiley face, half skull tattoo (located on his right arm, thank goodness!) to make a point about the distinction between appearance and reality in 'introduction to philosophy' courses.

SERIES EDITOR

FRITZ ALLHOFF is an associate professor in the philosophy department at Western Michigan University, as well as a senior research fellow at the Australian National University's Centre for Applied Philosophy and Public Ethics. In addition to editing the *Philosophy for Everyone* series, he is also the volume editor or co-editor for several titles, including *Wine & Philosophy* (Wiley-Blackwell, 2007), *Whiskey & Philosophy* (with Marcus P. Adams, Wiley, 2009), and *Food & Philosophy* (with Dave Monroe, Wiley-Blackwell, 2007). His academic research interests engage various facets of applied ethics, ethical theory, and the history and philosophy of science.

PHILOSOPHY FOR EVERYONE

Series editor: Fritz Allhoff

Not so much a subject matter, philosophy is a way of thinking. Thinking not just about the Big Questions, but about little ones too. This series invites everyone to ponder things they care about, big or small, significant, serious… or just curious.

This book is dedicated to Susan, Zoe, and Lexi Arp, and Bill Drake.

CONTENTS

I INK, THEREFORE I FOREWORD

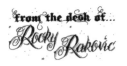 Tattoos were a harbinger of Twitter. If I were to tweet that message, it wouldn't reach the right audience. Twitterers have opinions (lots!), but for someone to see my tweet they would have to follow me, and you mostly follow people whose opinions you share. Also, there are those who don't get tattoos or tweets; for instance, my mother is not on Twitter.

'You're what?' was my mom's response when I told her I was leaving my job at a major publication to take editorial control of *Inked* – a tattoo lifestyle magazine. If this were a sitcom I would have just repeated myself, but it wasn't, so I paused to give her a moment to reflect on my decision. 'I don't like tattoos,' she continued (though that phrase could use an exclamation point, my mother doesn't exclaim; at times like this her voice inflects a loving worry and there's no punctuation mark for that). 'Do you have tattoos?'

When I told my former journalism professor, Amy Kiste Nyberg, she mused, 'What can you write about tattoos?' Indeed, tattoos evoke questions that can be mundane, or even deeply philosophical. When I was in college, that same professor hammered home the journalistic maxim, 'in a city of eight million people there are eight million stories.' So, the simplistic response to her question was that in a city of eight million people who each have two tattoos there are sixteen million stories. Ink is that important to the wearer. The marks on their skin signify an important time in their life – even if someone just got a tattoo on a whim because they were 'young and crazy,' that's an entry point into talking about what else they did when they were reckless.

To answer my mother's first question, the timing was right for both myself and for tattooing. She was born in the first half of the twentieth century – a time when the only people who got inked were sailors and scofflaws. Now we see tattoos on a few doctors, mayors, priests, and even academics such as those who have contributed to this book.

For older generations, the American Dream was to conform. The goal in life included a nine-to-five job, khakis, two-point-five kids, a golden retriever, and ambrosia salad. Anyone who deviated – the hipsters, hippies, mods, punks, and then a different iteration of hipsters – was labeled as weird. But suburban fatigue set in, and, when a younger generation was told that they could be anything they wanted to be when they grow up, they no longer aspired to be businessmen or lawyers – they wanted to be themselves.

At that time, the tattoo landscape was dangerous, filthy, and devoid of talent. Most shops were strategically located a beer-bottle's throw from the skeeviest dive bars, the insides resembled Soviet-era doctors' offices, and the purveyors either looked like or were the kind of guys you'd meet in prison. The tattoo parlor was a hangout for the usual suspects, where you could easily score drugs or a girl for hire. Naturally, in the tear-down-the-picket-fence era, this lifestyle attracted throngs of young talent. Creative teenagers who before had the choice of being a starving artist or selling their soul by going into advertising now had a third choice: become a tattoo *artist*. Akin to being a commissioned painter, tattooing offered a variety in projects, though it is arguable that ink has a steadier stream of customers. But, most importantly, tattooing was lucrative: it was, and still is, a cash-in-hand business (i.e., 'If the IRS wants their money they can come down here and try to take it from us'). This new crop was not interested in tracing stencils of staid hearts and hula girls – they wanted to create their own designs. With their deft hands, they perfected composition, color schemes, and shading in the medium. Before, tattooists were people who could operate a piece of machinery – mere craftsmen. *Now* they were artisans.

Maybe it was the new guard, or perhaps it was the AIDS hysteria, but tattoo shops started cleaning up their act. Back in the day, your crude skull tattoo might have come with a bonus of hepatitis or something else off dirty needles. Now, hygiene was as much a crusade as the movement to progress the art form, with the buzz around the autoclave being that they would never expand their clientele if it weren't safe to get inked. One shop gets a customer sick and the rest of the shops in the city lose. Some tattoo artists even implored their local governments to enact health codes and inspections, and because, as you remember, the government didn't often step foot into shops, some tattooers even helped write the codes.

With new, interesting art and a sterile environment, the free-from-conformity youth at large began exploring the idea of getting tattoos. One of the pillars of individualism is fashion; when prisoners are stripped of almost all of their rights and freedoms, the moment they are able to make a free decision, they pick out their own clothes. In the new 'be yourself' environment, what was Dockers' loss became tattoos' gain. Fundamentally, ink is fashion: you pick it out, it's worn on you, and it tells people something about you. At first, a brazen few started altering their look with tattoos; those early adopters were looked at with envy by their peers, as well as with flippant distain by the mainstream. The style went through the same periods of cultural introduction and acceptance that women's makeup and then hair dye had earlier in the century, only tattoos seemed stranger and more severe due to their permanence (confounding those who see it as a passing fad). And, though tattoos weren't alone in the brave new world of body alteration thanks to the rise in nose jobs, face lifts, tummy tucks, and breast implants, those procedures were meant to make a person fit in (well, maybe not in the case of some extreme breast implants), while the only purpose of tattoos was to make one stand out.

Again, at first it was the edgy, bombastic youth who tried out tattoos; but then Kat Von D, the face that launched a thousand tramp stamps, became Middle America's liaison to the tattoo world. Kat's shows – TLC's *Miami Ink* and *LA Ink* – took the tattoo shop experience and beamed it into the homes of soccer moms in Ohio. The nuclear family that would have never dared peek into the window of a tattoo parlor could safely play a fly on the wall thanks to reality television. Not only did they like what they saw, they wanted in – they wanted ink. The producers of the *Ink* programs made shrewd choices in casting not only charming, personable tattooers but also some of the best working artists. Had they gone with the scary, crusty old guard of workman-like inkers, tattooing would have never embedded itself into the skin of the mainstream.

I don't believe that tattooing is *underground* – it's not even a subculture any more. Numbers vary, but most of the hard data agree with a 2006 Pew Research poll that found that forty percent of Americans between the ages of twenty-six and forty are tattooed. That means that there are more people with tattoos then there are blondes in the United States. Let that sink in. And, speaking of the popularity of tattoo art, in a highly

ROCKY RAKOVIC

unscientific study, conducted by yours truly, I cold called a bunch of phone numbers in Lebanon, Kansas, the geographic center of mainland America. I asked the person who picked up on the other end if they could identify any of the following artists: Jeff Koons, Shepard Fairey, and Kat Von D. Guess which name they knew?

Tattoos and reality television – two celebrations of everyman individualism – have helped each other grow to prominence. The rise of these two have occurred thanks to people who were told they were special, told they could be themselves: the 'me generation.' The people of our generation wanted to scream their identity on their skin and shout their opinions from the rooftops. When the craft of tattooing bettered itself through aesthetics, safety, and public relations, we went under the tattoo gun. Then, when technology finally caught up with our need to self-express, we logged onto Twitter.

When Robert Arp, the editor of this book, contacted me about the project, I was a little shaky about the idea, despite the fact that the book is loaded with readable and thought-provoking chapters. I know that Joe Sixpack likes tattoos and will pick up a publication to read about them, but it wasn't clear to me that the philosophers, academics, and more 'thoughtful' people would appreciate, or even want, ink on ink. These thinkers seem to float above pop culture, not in it: do they perceive tattoos to be nothing more than the mark of a deviant?

During my mulling-over period, I received an email from my old professor, who wanted to send me one her brightest students to intern at *Inked*. Well, this indicated to me that, by her sending a future bright light of journalism to cover tattoos, a part of the intellectual elite was investing in the culture's relevance. In order to reach a more highbrow audience about my belief that tattooing is the new modern art, as well as an important symbol of my generation, I concluded that the message should be in this heady book rather than tweeted to my circle. The only other question I had was whether I was right person to write this Foreword. I wasn't sure whether my immersion in the tattoo scene had tainted my perspective of the current acceptance of ink. Damn the Pew numbers – were tattoos still perceived as scary and weird?

Then my mother called. She started, 'You should see this woman at my job, she has the niftiest tattoo.'

I AM, THEREFORE I INK

An Introduction to *Tattoos – Philosophy for Everyone:*
I Ink, Therefore I Am

Can you imagine yourself without your own body? Can you conceive of yourself existing in someone else's body? Go ahead and take a moment to try. If you have a tattoo, and you think it's something that defines who you are, then chances are you'll find it a little more difficult to perform these above thought experiments. Why? Probably because your inner self is revealed for the world to see *through* your tattoo, and you need your body in order to do the revealing. Your tattoo on your body expresses *your* thoughts, *your* beliefs, *your* experiences, *your* feelings, and *your* past – all of which make up who you are at a fundamental level. Even if your tattoo represents something else, or someone else's thoughts, beliefs, and the like, it's still on your body as *your* statement of your thoughts or beliefs *about* someone else's thoughts, beliefs, and the like. The same goes for those tattoos that you may have been forced or coerced to get, or got when you were (perhaps) drunk or high, but have decided to keep anyway. Who would you be without your tattoos, which are indelibly marked into the skin of your body?

The above thought experiments are serious questions that René Descartes (1596–1650) posed in his *Meditations on First Philosophy* (1641). In this work, Descartes claims that, because he can clearly and distinctly understand that he has a mind – with thoughts and perceptions – and can be deceived and think, there must be *something* that is doing the thinking, perceiving, and even being deceived (the deception is possibly by virtue of some evil, genius, god-like thing). Descartes viewed his own existence as a non-bodily *thinking thing*, or mind, as the 'something' that does the thinking, as well moving the body around. Thus, Descartes claims that, if he is thinking, he is existing as a thinking thing/mind to do the thinking in the first place, and that's where we get what has come to be known as the 'I think, therefore I am' dictum associated with this famous French philosopher. The argument itself can be laid out in simple *modus ponens* format like this:

- *First premise*: If I think, then I am (existing as a non-bodily *thinking thing*, or mind, to do the thinking in the first place).
- *Second premise*: I think.
- *Conclusion*: Therefore, I am (existing as a non-bodily *thinking thing*, or mind, to do the thinking in the first place).

The argument is valid (the conclusion follows necessarily from the premises), but I will leave it to you to take the further step and decide whether the argument is sound by determining whether the premises are true or not with evidence and further argumentation.

In the *Meditations*, Descartes also goes on to distinguish the thinking thing part of himself from his bodily part. One argument Descartes puts forward has to do with the idea that he can conceive of himself as a thinking thing distinct from his own body extended in space and time, but cannot conceive of himself as distinct from his own mind as a thinking thing. Thus, claims Descartes, the body is distinct from the mind in fundamental ways. The argument can be laid out like this:

- *First premise*: I can conceive of myself as a thinking thing (mind) distinct from my body as a thing in space and time.
- *Second premise*: I cannot conceive of myself as distinct from my own mind as a thinking thing.
- *Conclusion*: Hence, my body is distinct from my mind (given that the two, body and mind, have different qualities).

Again, I'll leave it to you to evaluate the argument by deciding whether the conclusion follows from the premises and whether all of the premises are true (these are the two general steps to take in evaluating whether an argument is a good one or not). Here's one possible problem, though: it may be that Descartes is assuming in his premises that mind and body are distinct, which is what he's actually trying to prove in the conclusion! Such a fallacious move (if in fact he's making it) is an example of bad reasoning called 'begging the question.'

In the history of Western philosophy since Descartes, these two arguments have been influential in not only driving a wedge between the body and the mind but also in getting people to think that the fundamental and defining part of a person is her/his mind and mental capacities. So, people have used these arguments (and others) to answer the questions 'What is a person fundamentally?' and 'What makes you be who you are in essence?' by claiming that a person's essential nature and identity is some kind of mind or collection of mental capacities (experiences or memories, for example). There is a whole area of philosophy known as the *philosophy of the person* that investigates these questions (areas of *philosophy of mind* investigate these matters, too) and researchers in this area offer numerous arguments for and against taking the thinking thing as a person's basic essence. But here I just want to call attention to the fact that positing a person's identity as *solely* a mind would probably be called into question by the tattoo person, again, given that the *bodily-based* tattoo is such a strong form of self-expression. 'My tattoos express who I am' is a mantra that can be consistently heard out of the mouths of tattoo persons, as well as found in numerous articles, books, and blogs in virtually every language on the planet. And one's body is necessary for that expression.

Now, I want to take Descartes' famous dictum of 'I think, therefore I am,' reconstitute the ideas a bit (as well as do some wordplay), and maintain that the tattoo person would probably feel comfortable saying 'I am, therefore I *ink*.' What I mean by this is that the person with a tattoo

1   Realizes not only that s/he is intimately tied to her/his body but also that bodily expression is a fundamental way of communicating to others (this is the 'I *am*' part) and
2   Utilizes the intimate connection with the body to express innermost thoughts, beliefs, experiences, and the like by indelibly marking the body for all to see (this is the 'therefore I *ink*' part).

In other words, the tattoo person might say something like '*I am* a person intimately tied to my body in a community of persons who express themselves bodily; *therefore I ink* to express my innermost thoughts, beliefs, experiences, feelings, and the like to this community of persons.' Again, it's not the same kind of reasoning utilized by Descartes, and I'm word-play-ing a bit, too – but you get the picture.

It sometimes happens that people are forced to get tattoos, in concentration or internment camps, or they are coerced through peer pressure to get a tattoo (maybe in the military), or they get a tattoo while completely drunk, stoned, or high on something. Even in these situations, unless you get the tattoo removed, almost everyone who has (or keeps) a tattoo probably thinks of the tattoo as a constant visual reminder of who they are and/or what they have experienced, whether the experience is a positive or negative one. In an email correspondence with me during the construction of this introduction, one of the contributors in this volume, Adam Barkman, emphasized the experiential nature of the tattoo by wisely noting:

> Tattoos are a part of our personal histories and as such are valuable, even sacred in a sense. We all are faced with a choice as to whether we will grow or merely change. Growth is what a tree does – it adds new layers, but never denies or replaces the other layers. So should we (and our tattoos ought to), like the rings of a tree, represent our past, a part of us that will always be us, in some respect.

It should be clear by now that I have underscored the fact that tattoos are a form of self-expression and, given the intimate tie between a person's bodily-based tattoos and who they are, numerous philosophical questions arise regarding personal identity. So, in this introduction we have already done a bit of philosophical reflection on tattoos from the perspective of the philosophy of the person, which is usually a branch of philosophy under metaphysics. A few of the chapters in this book investigate issues concerning what constitutes self-expression, personal identity, and identity over time. But there's more philosophizing to be found associated with tattoos: tattoos and the tattooing arts are fertile ground for both Western and Eastern philosophical ideas and analysis, and this book offers many valuable 'seedlings' in the form of chapters devoted to several central topics in Western and Eastern philosophy. In case you're wondering what the areas of Western philosophy in general might be, see Figure I.1 for short descriptions.

★

As an editor, I have never seen such enthusiasm expressed by contributors in their emails as was expressed by these authors when submitting abstract ideas for this book. Virtually everyone who submitted

Philosophy:
The systematic study of reality using good reasoning in order to clarify difficult questions, solve significant problems, and enrich human lives. There are five major branches of philosophy, and those branches themselves have sub-branches.

Metaphysics:	Epistemology:	Logic:	Political philosophy:	Moral philosophy:
The study of the nature of existence, including the kinds of things that exist.	The study of knowledge, including how we come to know things, the justification for knowledge, and types of truth.	The study of the principles of correct reasoning, including argument identification, formation, and analysis.	The study of the justification for organizing human interaction in social settings, which includes defining and justifying rights, laws, justice, and appropriate forms of government.	The study of human actions that affect beings capable of being harmed in some way (definitely humans, as well as many animal species) and the principles that people appeal to when they act.

FIGURE I.I   Branches in Western philosophy.

an abstract said something along the lines of: 'I am so excited to see someone doing a book like this!' or 'It's about time a book like this was written!' or 'What a great idea!' This volume, thus, *enthusiastically* presents chapters that touch upon many areas in Western and Eastern philosophy with the goal not only of enlightening people concerning the nature of tattoos and the tattooing arts but also of bringing philosophical ideas to non-philosophers, and vice versa.

Besides philosophical questions regarding personal identity like the ones I have presented above, in this book you'll first find a chapter on the history and nature of tattoos and the tattooing arts, TATTOOS AND THE TATTOOING ARTS IN PERSPECTIVE, which seems to be a sensible way to start the discussion. However, as Charles Taliaferro and Mark Odden note, the 'historical progression, meaning, and significance of tattoos and the tattooing arts are neither smooth nor unified, and actually can be considered as varied and *punctured* as the skin on which the tattoo is placed.' Many will find it fascinating to learn that the word 'tattoo' is derived from the Tahitian word *tatau* (which means 'marking something') as well as the Polynesian word *ta* (which means 'striking something'). By the end of this chapter, not only will you have a basic understanding of the history, cultural meaning, individual meaning, and self-expression associated with tattoos, but you will also be able to think about whether you agree or disagree with the intriguing 'double skin' theory that Taliaferro and Odden put forward.

In HOW TO READ A TATTOO, AND OTHER PERILOUS QUESTS, Juniper Ellis quite cleverly shows how several different personal tattoo experiences throughout history yield their own 'I ink, therefore I am' claims. For example, the great critic of tattoos and tattooed people, Adolf Loos (1870–1933), likely would have claimed, 'I ink, therefore I will commit murder,' while one of the first Christians, St. Paul of Tarsus, might have been comfortable saying something like, 'I ink, therefore I am saved by God.' In point of fact, Ellis has written her own book on tattoos – specifically tattoos from the Pacific – and her expertise shines through in her writing. After completing her chapter, you'll likely agree with her comment that 'within and beyond the Pacific, a tattoo's proclamation reverberates in both the most secular and sacred realms.'

The third chapter, ARE TATTOOS ART?, begins a discussion, running throughout the volume, of whether or not tattoos can be considered forms of art. As Nicolas Michaud notes, it's important to get at a definition of art since people go around saying of certain things they see, 'What cool artwork!' or 'That's not art!' And, we wouldn't want to call just any old thing we see (or experience with one of the five senses) art – for example, some chewing gum on the sidewalk that has been stepped on. But, do we *determine* what counts as art? Or is art what it is, and then we have to conform to it when we create things like sculptures, paintings, or tattoos? After presenting four popular theories of art – namely, art world theory, formalism, expressionism, and performance art – Michaud goes on to consider whether tattoos could appropriately fit into one or more of them. In the end, he argues that tattoos might best be considered examples of performance art, adding: 'the fact that a tattoo is placed on a person adds a significant layer of context and potential meaning that makes tattoos a fertile ground for aesthetic experience.'

Continuing the art of tattoos discussion, in the fourth chapter, FLESHY CANVAS, Kimberly Baltzer-Jaray and Tanya Rodriguez maintain: 'It seems that the only thing that distinguishes tattooing from other fine arts is the fleshy canvas its content appears on.' They back this claim up with a discussion of feminist and hermeneutical aesthetics ('aesthetics' is the branch of philosophy that concerns the definition and nature of art, beauty, and taste). Feminist aesthetics adds a personal, individually willed, *redefinition* of a tattoo as art that exists on the 'female fleshy canvas,' while hermeneutical aesthetics – inspired by Hans-Georg

Gadamer (1900–2002) – imbues the female fleshy canvas with the possibility of a variety of interpretive perspectives of that tattoo. A tattoo is a personal statement, as well as a public display of that personal statement, which is bolstered by Baltzer-Jaray and Rodriguez's following observation: 'As much as art has a very intimate, individuating aspect, it is also a way in which the witness to art participates in something beyond themselves, something communal.'

All of us need to be reminded of the fact that, throughout human history, there have existed male-dominated social, philosophical, and scientific spheres, among others, in a variety of cultures all over the world. Numerous women have tattoos, and the feminist philosophical perspective not only offers valuable insights into tattoos and the tattooing arts but also sheds light on these male-dominated spheres. FEMALE TATTOOS AND GRAFFITI is the fifth chapter of the book, and in it Thorsten Botz-Bornstein suggests that tattoos can help us rethink, as well as break down, stereotypes associated with women and men. He puts forward the interesting argument not only that contemporary female tattoos have created a new social space that is multidimensional but also that the female tattooed body acts as 'a wall on which multiple desires are projected.' 'In this sense,' claims Botz-Bornstein, 'tattoos have become graffiti.' Whereas a landscape offers one the visible features of the land before one's eyes, and this landscape can include graffiti, Botz-Bornstein speaks of a 'skinscape' that offers one the visible features of the human skin (here, specifically, female skin) before all of society's eyes, and this can include the female tattoo expressive of a 'women's own economy of thought, will, and/or desire.'

'Popular portrayals of feminism often use simple, sensational terms such as 'man-haters,' 'penis-enviers,' or 'closet lesbians' to depict proponents of this 'f-word.' These misogynistic stereotypes and attitudes fundamentally overlook the diversity and complexity of feminist history and philosophy.' So begins Nancy Kang's thoughtful piece, PAINTED FETTERS, which is the sixth chapter of the book. She notes that, while there are a variety of different feminist perspectives (for example, radical feminism, Marxist feminism, liberal feminism, and corporeal feminism), what they all have in common is the desire to rectify a world in which women are assumed to be inferior to men, and, hence, do not enjoy the same kinds of rights, benefits, and privileges as their male counterparts. One thing Kang seeks to establish in her chapter is that female tattoos act as a way to 'accentuate' and 'amplify' this unjust, differential treatment of women. Another is the fact that 'both tattooing and feminism elicit powerful emotional responses, often in the forms of hasty judgments about a person's moral character.' Kang mentions Michelle 'Bombshell' McGee (who, by the way, endorsed this book) and how people probably thought she was all the more a 'home wrecker' of the relationship between Sandra Bullock and Jesse James precisely *because* she dons many a tattoo. Such an example, Kang maintains, is important to mention because 'it is a feminist imperative to question, deconstruct, and critique any bias against women based on physical appearance.'

The next three chapters of the book all deal with what I started to write about at the beginning of this introduction; namely, tattoos and personal identity. In the seventh chapter, TATTOO YOU, Kyle Fruh and Emily Thomas focus on two questions: 'What does it take for a person to maintain their identity over time?' and 'Who am I?' In response to the first question, although the majority of folks think that it's some aspect of your mental capacities that makes you be *you* over time (as I mentioned above, too), Fruh and Thomas seriously consider the possibility that it is your body – complete, possibly, with tattoos – is what constitutes your identity over time. In response to the second question, they cleverly utilize the metaphor of an anchor (with the pun on the classic anchor tattoo intended) to argue for one's identity as a kind of ongoing narrative. The final line of their chapter speaks volumes: 'When you get a tattoo, you tattoo you.'

'Tattoos are forever,' claims Rachel C. Falkenstern in the first line of the eighth chapter, ILLUSIONS OF PERMANENCE. 'Yet, tattoos are *not* forever,' she claims a little later. Why? It's not only the obvious fact that our tattoos are connected to a body and the body will disintegrate with time; it's also the fact that any self-identification with our minds *or* bodies (complete with tattoos on them) is illusory in the end. Why? Because our selves are intimately tied to our environments, which are constantly in flux: 'We come into being, develop, and interact with our environments as embodied beings; the world shapes us and we shape the world.' Falkenstern backs up this claim utilizing ideas and arguments from Maurice Merleau-Ponty (1908–1961), the aesthetic theories of early German Romanticism and German Idealism (late eighteenth to the early nineteenth century), and the Pragmatism of American philosopher John Dewey (1859–1952). After reading this chapter, you'll never look at yourself in the mirror again without wondering, 'Is this really me I'm seeing in the reflection?'

One way to think about yourself as being the same self through all time has to do with your memories. You know you're the same you who went to Disney World at age seven, had your first cup of coffee at age twelve, and had a sip of alcohol at twenty-one, precisely because you *remember* those events. And those events seem permanently burned into your mind. But, are those memories really as permanent as you think they are? In the ninth chapter, MY TATTOO MAY BE PERMANENT, BUT MY MEMORY OF IT ISN'T, using arguments from Marcel Proust (1871–1922) and St. Augustine (354–430), Clancy Smith claims that, although his tattoo seems to be permanent, 'as soon as I begin to reflect on the static, unchanging nature of the ink, I realize that my memories have nothing of the immutable nature of the tattoos themselves.' After reading this chapter, you'll never look at yourself in the mirror again, *then walk away*, without wondering, 'Was that really the same me I now *remember* seeing in the reflection?'

Tattoos can express a person's decision to do whatever s/he wants with her/his body, and, in the case of tattoos forced upon persons in concentration camps, they can represent a person's radical enslavement – thus, tattoos naturally raise various issues in the philosophy of freedom (a branch of philosophy under metaphysics). Am I really free to get my tattoos, or am I compelled or determined by forces beyond my control when I walk into the parlor? Also, *should we* be free to do whatever we want to our body, possibly covering most of it with tattoos? In the tenth chapter, TATTOOS ARE FOREVER, Felipe Carvalho addresses not only the freedom to get a tattoo but also what might be good reasons to choose to get a tattoo in the first place. He offers us a sensible solution: don't be overly impulsive and don't be overly rational when you make a decision to get a tattoo, or make any other decision for that matter. Of course, you might always want to err on the side of being rational, as being impulsive about tattoos can lead to something like getting a tattoo when you were younger that says, 'I Love Becky … Forever and Ever!' when you may later marry a woman named Mary!

According to Jonathan Heaps in BEARING THE MARKS, the eleventh chapter, you may think that you are free to go to a tattoo artist and get a tattoo. However:

> Doesn't my *nature* – in terms of genes causing me to act one way or another – determine my character, beliefs, opinions, motivations, intentions, and actions? … Further, I had no control over the circumstances into which I was born, and the people who raised me and influenced my life growing up (parents, guardians, teachers, role models, and the like). All of this environmental influence and pressure surely has had a direct effect upon my character, beliefs, opinions, motivations, intentions, and actions. So, it's not just my nature, but doesn't my *nurture* (the environment and its lasting effect upon me) also determine who I am? And hasn't that nurture

further determined how I have acted, do in fact act now, and will act in the future? How can I be the thing freely choosing my actions, given the determining influence of *both* nature *and* nurture?

Heaps does have a response, though, and it has to do with the fact that nature is really a system of statistical laws – not necessary laws that wholly *determine* everything – and the probability associated with these laws allows for the possibility of free choices. This offers a clever solution to the problem of being determined to get a tattoo, or perform any human action, actually.

In the twelfth chapter, NEVER MERELY 'THERE,' Wendy Lynne Lee begins a discussion of experiences and stories surrounding tattoos. All of us who have been inked probably remember the experience quite vividly, and even the time before and after entering the parlor. For me, getting ink was an experience laced with pain (obviously), fear, doubt, and anticipation. I got my tattoos in the late eighties, when it was still considered pretty counter-cultural to get them. Lee maintains that there is an 'intimate relationship between a tattooed subject and her or his embodied experience' that cannot be placed into words *completely*; and this seems correct for almost any highly charged, emotional experience. Yet, she tries to put the tattoo experience into words by telling us a few 'stories' – including her own – noting that 'Whatever else is true about tattooing, tattoos are never "merely there."'

'There's something really the matter with most people who wear tattoos … I know from experience there's something terribly flawed about people who are tattooed above the little something Johnny had done in the Navy, even though that's also a bad sign.' Kevin Decker utilizes this quotation from Truman Capote in the thirteenth chapter of the book, SOMETHING TERRIBLY FLAWED, noting that it's an example of a hasty generalization. Of course, everyone contributing to this book would agree that a statement such as this one is an unwarranted generalization. Decker does something really neat in his chapter: he takes two famous stories by the American literary giant, Ray Bradbury – namely, 'The Illustrated Man' and 'The Illustrated Woman' – and offers us a few significant bits of philosophical reflection surrounding tattoos. This illustrated pair are donned with many a tattoo, and not only does Decker give us enough of these two interesting stories to rival Cliff's Notes (a good thing, actually) but he also links tattoos to a few issues in the philosophy of human nature. 'As a form of social creativity,' Decker tells us, 'tattooing has a deeply philosophical significance inscribed, as it were, in its flesh.'

The possible unsightliness and stigma associated with tattoos gets us to start thinking about issues in ethics/moral philosophy and political philosophy. Do we jump to the conclusion that tattooed people are immoral or unethical? Can we get too many tattoos, such that we're addicted to getting them like one might be addicted to drugs? Should we shun people with tattoos, or think less of them? Is there any connection whatsoever between tattoos and a criminal lifestyle? In the fourteenth chapter, THE VICE OF THE TOUGH TATTOO, Jennifer Baker begins to address these above questions with an interesting argument from the perspective of a general moral position dating back to the Ancient Greeks (and at least to Confucius in the East) known as 'virtue ethics.' Unlike ethical positions that focus on the act itself, the principles associated with the act, or the consequences of an act, the virtue ethicist concentrates on the moral character of the person committing the act, asking the question 'What kind of person – virtuous or vicious – am I, or am I becoming, as a result of this act I'm about to perform.' Her argument is simple and direct: Getting a certain kind of 'tough' tattoo contributes to an unhealthy subculture, and a 'good person should want no part of this subculture.' 'In fact,' she maintains, 'getting a tough tattoo contributes to a vicious, rather than a virtuous, psyche.' And we wouldn't want to cultivate vices for ourselves, for our communities, or for our world.

Even though Daniel Miori claims that he doesn't know his 'ass from first base,' he's a seasoned physician's assistant who works in palliative care, a field that deals with end-of-life situations on a regular basis. So, he's often around doctors, and he knows his bioethics (the branch of applied ethics in which philosophical positions are actually put into practice when making decisions concerning matters such as physician-assisted suicide, abortion, contraception, usage of animals for research, and others in the realms of biology, medicine, and clinical practice). In the fifteenth chapter of the book, TO INK, OR NOT TO INK, after some introductory material regarding bioethics and some key players on the field today, Miori ultimately argues that, before getting a tattoo, you should certainly weigh the risks and the benefits associated with getting inked. Obviously, if getting a tattoo will be bad for you (in either the short term or the long term), in your particular set of circumstances, then you shouldn't get one. This risk/benefit analysis, combined with the idea that you are an autonomous, freely choosing individual with your own mind, means that it can be morally OK for you to get a tattoo. Miori even goes so far as to maintain that getting a tattoo can be therapeutic for some.

In his chapter, WRITING ON THE BODY, Simon Woods takes a serious look at an idea that most of us – especially tattoo people – would reject without even thinking about it; namely, the connection between getting a tattoo and being a criminal. Believe it or not, however, one hundred years ago most people would have made this connection without hesitation. This connection existed thanks, in large part, to a thinker named Adolf Loos (1870–1933), who claimed in his essay '*Ornament und Verbrechen*' ('Ornament and crime,' 1908): 'Tattooed men who are not behind bars are either latent criminals or degenerate aristocrats. If someone who is tattooed dies in freedom, then he does so a few years before he would have committed murder.' What a claim, huh! 'Can Loos' critique be sustained or regarded with any relevance to contemporary, post-modern, pluralist culture?' asks Woods. What is interesting is that an awful lot of criminals are, in fact, tattooed, as the research of the retired prison doctor and psychiatrist Theodore Dalrymple – among others – has shown.

The final section of the book is made up of three chapters that deal with Eastern and religious perspectives concerning tattoos. There is a long-standing tradition in the Christianity of the West, as well as in the Confucianism of the East, in which not only are tattoos looked upon as signaling a degenerate lifestyle but also there also seems to be some scriptural/textual basis (in both Christianity and Confucianism) for condemning tattoos. In the seventeenth chapter, IS A TATTOO A SIGN OF IMPIETY?, Adam Barkman tells us simply: 'Because neither the non-contextualized Bible verses condemning tattoos nor Confucian philosophical reasoning in respect to tattoos are properly understood, the result is a Christian Confucian confusion over the ethics of tattooing. My goal in this chapter is to dispel this confusion.' What prompted his writing of the chapter in the first place has to do with the fact that many of the 'old folks' at his wedding were uncomfortable with his best man's tattoos. Again, we are left to wonder: Is it possible to detach our perceptions and deeply held preconceptions about tattoos from our 'thinking rationally' about tattoos long enough to realize that having a tattoo doesn't automatically signal that a person is 'a low-life thug,' 'a wild child,' or 'easy'?

In the eighteenth chapter of the book, CONFESSIONS OF A TATTOOED BUDDHIST PHILOSOPHER, Joseph J. Lynch describes the Buddhist principles of impermanence, 'no self,' and suffering (the 'Three Marks of Existence') – which were introduced by the Buddha, also known as Siddhārtha Gautama (c. 563–483 BCE) – and goes on to show how tattoos can reveal these principles. Above, it was noted that Confucians don't take too kindly to tattoos, but the same is true for Buddhists and many other (usually) conservative proponents of Eastern religions and practices. So, it might seem strange to link Buddhism to the tattooing arts. However, in the end you may or may not agree with Lynch that 'while tattoos clearly hurt, they don't have to hurt Buddhist practice at all. In fact, they can be a distinctive kind of expression of the teachings of the Buddha.'

Often times, tattoos contain religious symbols leading one to questions concerning the existence and nature of a god and other issues in the philosophy of religion, a sub-branch of metaphysics. The final chapter of the book, AN ATHEIST AND A THEIST DISCUSS A CROSS TATTOO AND GOD'S EXISTENCE, of which I am the author, is written in a Platonic dialogue style and consists of a conversation that two of my philosophically and religious-minded friends had one time regarding the existence of some god or gods. A matching cross tattoo that they both got on their arms while they were in the high-school Catholic seminary is the springboard for the discussion. Not expecting the meeting at the coffee shop with my old pals to take a turn toward fairly deep philosophical analysis, Bill was right when he noted at the end of the dialogue that 'there's probably been enough philosophical bantering – Rob's eyes are glazing over and my tea is getting cold.' Still, what they had to say is interesting, intriguing, and invigorating. I mean, who *doesn't* like to chat about the existence of god, right?!?

One final note here: I wanted to do a little wordplay in choosing 'I Ink, Therefore I Am' as the subtitle of the book. This was primarily done to catch the eye and entice people to read the book, since almost everyone has not only heard of Descartes' famous dictum but also knows that another name for a tattoo is 'ink.' So, in a sense, the wordplay-ed subtitle has nothing to do with Descartes' original argument, and I admit that freely. However, someone who has chosen to mark her/himself indelibly with a tattoo might be struck by the subtitle and think, 'That's right! I *do* ink, and therefore that ink makes me *who I am* as a unique person with my own thoughts, beliefs, feelings, and experiences.' And that uniqueness found in a tattoo is *at most* something to cherish, celebrate, and cultivate, while being *at the very least* a conversation starter.

ACKNOWLEDGMENTS

Thanks go to Fritz Allhoff, Jeff Dean, Nicole Benevenia, and the folks from Wiley-Blackwell who worked on this project.

THE HISTORY AND NATURE OF TATTOOS

Competition among what society considered the 'degenerates' fueled the need for tattoos. If one sailor was getting an anchor on his forearm, then all of his shipmates were right behind him to receive one as well.

(Charles Taliaferro and Mark Odden, p. 6)

CHAPTER I

TATTOOS AND THE TATTOOING ARTS IN PERSPECTIVE

An Overview and Some Preliminary Observations

Punctured

The historical progression, meaning, and significance of tattoos and the tattooing arts are neither smooth nor unified, and actually can be considered as varied and *punctured* as the skin on which the tattoo is placed. A smooth or unified account is elusive in part because of the wide variety of cultures in which tattooing has been practiced, from Japan and the South Pacific to ancient Greece. Moreover, there is evidence of tattooing that can be traced to the Bronze Age, and our historical grasp of such pre-literate culture is highly speculative. Further, tattooing methods have likewise varied: there have been simple methods of creating skin images by cutting the skin and then rubbing ashes into the wound, and there have been more complex methods associated with inserting ink into the skin. Still, notwithstanding the

Tattoos – Philosophy for Everyone: I Ink, Therefore I Am, First Edition.
Edited by Robert Arp.
© 2012 John Wiley & Sons, Inc. Published 2012 by John Wiley & Sons, Inc.

sprawling territory stretching out ahead of us in this volume, in this chapter we address four areas that may prove useful for philosophizing about tattoos: history, cultural meaning, individual meaning, and self-expression.

History

The English word 'tattoo' is most likely adapted from the Tahitian word *tatau,* meaning 'marking something,' but also has obvious affinity with the Polynesian word *ta,* which means 'striking something.'[1] There are good reasons to believe that tattoos go back at least to the Bronze Age (and possibly even Neolithic times). In the 1990s, between Austria and Italy, a frozen human body was recovered bearing fifty-seven tattoos; it is estimated that the man died somewhere around 3200 BCE. It is possible that the body marks were in some ways medicinal or used in a practice of healing; however, it could also be that tattoos were decorative and bearers of meaning in terms of rank and identity. There is also reason to believe that tattooing took place in ancient Greece, Persia, and among the ancient Britons and Gauls, as well as in Africa, in the Americas, and throughout Asia. Sometimes the skin markings were colored marks, and at other times simple blackened lines. Below is an account of tattooing by a doctor, Aetius, who practiced medicine in Constantinople and Alexandria during the reign of Justinian (527–565). The tattoo is referred to as *stigmata,* and, while there is reason not to associate the tattoo with a stigma or mark of shame, it is interesting that in his medical notes Aetius also offers instructions on the removal of tattoos:

> They call *stigmata* things inscribed on the face or some other part of the body, for example on the hands of soldiers, and they use the following ink. [The recipe follows] Apply by pricking the places with needles, wiping away the blood, and rubbing in first juice of leek, and then the preparation ... In cases where we wish to remove such stigmata, we must use the following preparations ... When applying, first clean the stigmata with niter, smear them with resin of terebinth, and bandage for five days ... The stigmata are removed in twenty days, without great ulceration and without a scar.[2]

Tattooing came to be shunned in Christianized Europe during the Middle Ages, the reason for this stemming partly from the Old Testament teaching in Leviticus: 'You shall not make any cuttings in your flesh on account of the dead, or tattoo any marks upon you' (19:28). Contemporary scholars propose that this was to help distinguish the Jews (and thus their monotheism) from surrounding polytheistic cultures. Also, in the New Testament, there is a line in Revelations that has been interpreted as implying that Christians should not use tattoos. A scarlet women is described as follows: 'On her forehead was written a name of mystery, 'Babylon the Great, mother of harlots and of Earth's abominations" (17:5). While Christians in the Middle Ages and throughout the seventeenth century in Europe did engage in some tattooing – pilgrims to Jerusalem would sometimes get a Jerusalem tattoo, and it was not unusual for Christians to have the names *Jesus*, *Maria*, *Bethlehem*, and others tattooed on their bodies – it was not a major practice. And the rather negative Biblical portrait of body painting accounts for why Christian missionaries discouraged tattooing throughout Asia, including Polynesia, which is probably the site of the longest-standing cultural tradition of tattooing. When Europe emerged from the Christian Medieval Era into an age of voyages of discovery (as well as trade and exploitation), Europeans rediscovered the tattoo. The first modern record of tattoos dates from James Cook's expedition to Tahiti in 1769.

In many of the Polynesian cultures, the tattooing process tested the endurance of the male population. Tattooing became a ceremony. Puberty usually prompted the inauguration of this intensive process, which took from a few weeks to months to complete. The rebirth of tattooing in the Western world also reincarnated this masculinized history. Around the 1930s, the popularity of tattoos surged among the sailor community. Sailors endured the pain of the tattooing process as a contemporary way of asserting their masculinity over their peers. It soon became a competition for dominance, as no sailor could be perceived as weak. Tattooing also became evident during the Victorian era in European armies (though it was not as widespread as in European navies). For example, as men re-entered civilian life in Britain, the tattoo became known as working class jewelry.

Tattooing in America has had a mixed history. Predictably, European Americans saw the elaborate tattooing by Native Americans as a sign of their primitive (namely, uncivilized and barbaric) way of life, but tattooing during the Civil War seemed to be an acceptable expression of loyalty. Thus, tattooing slowly became an American folk art during the late nineteenth century. Tattoos were featured in the context of carnivals and circuses, but they slowly became integral to some elements of popular culture. Common icons in the early 1900s included hearts, women, flowers, animals, ships, birds, serpents, the American flag, the Christian cross, and so on. Toward the middle of twentieth century, up to the 1960s, there were a host of standard tattoo characters: Bugs Bunny, The Road Runner, Betty Boop, Mickey Mouse, Mighty Mouse, Maggie and Jiggs, Mutt and Jeff, and even The Pink Panther.

Some comments are in order in terms of sexuality and tattooing. Tattoos intrigued the famed sex researcher Alfred Kinsey (1894–1956). After befriending a tattoo artist, Kinsey interviewed sailors and patrons at the tattoo parlor to determine the sexual urges behind tattooing. Samuel Steward has noted: 'Kinsey was quite interested in this confirmation of our jointly-developed theories about tattoos and the assertion of masculine status, narcissism, and the sexual aftermath of a first tattoo.'[3] Though Kinsey focused mainly on sexual motivations behind tattooing, he also brought up a unique feature of tattooing around his time – the assertion of masculine status. Competition among what society considered the 'degenerates' fueled the need for tattoos. If one sailor was getting an anchor on his forearm, then all of his shipmates were right behind him to receive one as well.

Interestingly, the art of tattooing seems to have been a predominantly female practice in Ancient Egypt, breaking the stereotype of tattooing as inherently masculine. Female mummies from Egypt with tattoos were often assumed to be prostitutes, but a high priestess named Amunet has been found among other tattooed women, showing that women of all social classes likely were tattooed. The cosmic nature of tattoos – to protect the holder against illness or to ward off bad omens – also applied to the struggles of pregnancy and birth in women's lives. Net-like dot tattoos around the abdomen illustrated the custom of wrapping mummies in bead nets as a way of containment; the tattoo would imbue magic to help carry the baby throughout the pregnancy. Mummies have also been found with the symbol of Bes – a deity believed to protect women during labor and birth – on their upper thighs.[4] The role of the tattoo as a safeguard during pregnancy and birth seems to vouchsafe that in Ancient Egypt tattooing was a custom reserved for women.

Tattoos also played a punitive role in history. Greco-Roman cultures would use tattoos as a way of marking prisoners and slaves, visually symbolizing their inferiority. This tradition continued through to the twentieth century. The Nazis tattooed Jews in Auschwitz and other concentration camps with identifying numbers, usually on their arms. Prisoners today tattoo themselves to take control of their convict and marginalized status in society, which could, in a way, be viewed as a voluntary punishment.

The blend of tattoos received in prison and in the outside world represents a very real juxtaposition of incarceration and freedom.[5] We'll say more about the history of tattoos as we move on to the cultural meaning of the tattoo.

Cultural Meaning

In her brilliant book, *Written on the Body: The Tattoo in European and American History*, Jane Caplan rightly notes that establishing a cultural identity is one common and important role the tattoo has played throughout history:

> The tattoo occupies a kind of boundary status on the skin, and this is paralleled by its cultural use as a maker of differences, an index of inclusion and exclusion ... The tattoo has been taken to mark off entire 'civilizations' from their 'barbarian' or 'savage' neighbors; to declare a convict's criminality, whether by branding him as a punishment or because he has inverted this penal practice by acquiring voluntary tattoos (thereby, ironically, marking himself); and more generally to inscribe various kinds of group membership, often in opposition to a dominant culture.[6]

As noted earlier, we have reason to believe that tribes on virtually all continents have used skin images as a mark of identification, from the Celtic and Germanic peoples of Europe to Japan and Polynesia. These images have also had roles within tribes of identifying particular practices (religious devotion, or warrior or healer status), histories (ancestry, images symbolizing bravery or victory, recovery from illness), positions of leadership (domain of power or allegiance), and availability to mate (symbols of fecundity), and have even served as devices designed to protect the bearer of the tattoo – in this context the tattoo is seen to have magical powers to ward off evil or bad luck, thereby functioning as an amulet. And, as Caplan suggests, paradoxically, tattoos also have been used both to mark criminals to identify them as having been subject to punishment and by criminals or gangs themselves as a sign of their dangerous power over others, including rival gangs.

To see the powerful role of tattoos in establishing cultural meaning, consider seventeenth-century Japan. Around this time, *ukiyo-e prints*, *irezumi*, and the Kabuki Theatre drastically rose in popularity as forms of counter-culture in the Imperial world. *Irezumi*, the name for Japanese tattoo art meaning 'the insertion of ink,' contrasts with *ukiyo-e* ('images of the floating world'), which describe Japanese woodblock prints. The merchant middle class relished this new culture that freed them from the rigid social system. The narratives of all three art forms depict the ordinary life of the time, which began to alter the imperialized ethos of Japan's cultural identity.[7]

This shift shows that art can mirror its audience and simultaneously alter them, though this was not the initial role of Japanese tattooing. *Irezumi* began as a punitive procedure, but, in an attempt to put a positive spin on the tattoo and the tattooing arts, Japanese tattoo artists adopted for themselves the term for woodblock carvers – *horishi*. This shift also separated tattoos from their previously negative connotations and solidified the connection between tattoos and woodblock prints. Soon after, tattooing became an expression of love. Lovers began to exchange tattoos of small dots, representing 'love tokens,' which some claim to be the predecessor to the modern popularity of tattooing names of loved ones.

The important point to stress here is that tattoos have a cultural dimension that is not necessarily subject to private interpretation. Though the cultural sea may ebb and flow, cultural norms can control how society collectively interprets common imagery. The image may be permanent, but, contrastingly, the meaning or interpretation of the image is fluid. Let us consider the example of a young German soldier who, in the early 1940s, decides to get the swastika tattooed on his forearm and views it as a symbol of his national pride. For a brief time, in German-controlled territory, that may well be its meaning. But, after World War II and the exposure of Nazi crimes, the world views the young solider's tattoo as a symbol of genocide (even though he may never have killed anyone). Certain images have such enormous weight (a crucifix, a star of David) that their meaning resists privatized meaning (it would be hard to claim that a crucifix tattoo on one's chest is a symbol of one's passion for fair-trade coffee), but some symbols that are quite trenchant (for example a skull) can shift in meaning if there is a sufficient culture or subculture to support it (a skull tattoo might well identify its bearer as a Deadhead, for example).

Here are another two examples of what we're getting at concerning the cultural meaning and interpretation of tattoos. Ancient Polynesian societies required tattooing as a way to anchor the organizations within their society, regulating everything from politics to religion. To these ends, the tattooing process seems to also have been representative of the

CHARLES TALIAFERRO AND MARK ODDEN

overarching social institutions. The Maori tattooing tradition from New Zealand has recently risen in international popularity, but its roots are very traditional. *Moko* (facial tattoos) and other tattoos depicted pivotal moments in a person's life, as a visual guide to the individual's history.[8]

Correspondingly, the tattoo process can be as utilitarian as the actual resulting image. Samoan *Pe'a* is a very ritualized process. The intricate design of the body tattoo is always expertly symmetrical. The tattooing process involves multiple assistants, each with distinct responsibilities, with prayers being recited or sung throughout the whole session, and it can take several days to complete. The tattoo process is often overlooked in this respect. Achieving a type of revelation during the process is often regarded as more important than the final image. The tattooing process can, thus, vary in importance, depending on what aspect of the process is valued the highest. As stewards of superstition, sailors banded together through tattooing as a way to ward off potential harms. In their early forms, tattoos conjured up a sense of magic, which is still alive today. Some sailors, for example, get 'H-O-L-D F-A-S-T' tattooed on the fingers of their hands to prevent them from falling into the ocean, or get roosters and pigs tattooed on their feet – these hydrophobic animals are known for quickly finding land if thrown overboard.[9]

From the early 1950s to the early 1970s, the bearer of a tattoo tended to be perceived in North American and European societies as existing on the margins of society, whether he (most tattooed people at this time were men) was a sailor, convict, or belonged to a gang. At this time, tattoos seemed to be strong markers for *conformity* and *non-conformity* in some segments of society. They became unifiers to others with tattoos; long hair and beards were initially symbols of hippie culture counter to traditional culture, but these images of defiance became distinguishing characteristics for the collective. Today, tattoos seem to be less of an indication of marginalization or counter-culture and increasingly part of the mainstream, thus allowing for a greater role of the personal meaning of tattoos.

Contemporary redefinition of the iconography and ideology of tattoos creates a new discourse about tattoos, and many would claim that some tattoos are fine art. It seems that the tattoo is no longer steeped in the stigmatized murk, but has higher significance. The role of the tattoo is malleable, as tattoos have never constituted a consistent marker in Western society. Using the foundations of American tattoo design and history as a point of departure, the emerging youth, trained in the fine arts, pump a breadth of creativity and skill into contemporary tattooing.

Individual Meaning

Alongside a tattoo's cultural meaning is its individual meaning. Tattooing can simply entail a customer walking into a shop and choosing an image off a sheet, which is straightforward, yet unoriginal. But it is more commonplace for tattoos to have individual natures and meanings, and these begin with an appreciation of the sheer individuality of the skin markings. It could be argued that, on a basic level, each tattoo is inherently individualistic, even those that are sheet-bought. If we consider tattooing as an art form, the tattoo is an image composed on a cellular level, and each person's individual DNA makes the cellular medium different in each case. Tattoos are beyond reproduction in the sense that the medium is a living body. Consider the generic images: if one hundred people were to pick the same image and all corresponding tattoos were executed identically, there would still be one hundred unique tattoos. The imagery can be replicated but, as DNA is unique, the tattoo is non-reproducible. This is in many respects in line with individualism, which asserts that an individual is beyond reproduction.

In addition to the inherent physical individuality of the tattoo, tattoo artists have defended their art as purely individualistic: a person may be tattooed in a way that reflects their individual dreams, their particular loves, or specific events of fulfillment or loss (one of us has a tattoo commemorating his love for his grandfather), or that involve symbols that are so esoteric that their 'public meaning' is unavailable.

Tattoos might also represent an existential, individual act. While there are temporary tattoos (usually in the form of body stickers, which produce sometimes waterproof but temporary images), tattooing is more typically perceived by society as involving permanent or semi-permanent images. Once a tattoo, and its associated context, is created, it cannot be undone, or it cannot be undone without severe laser treatments. There is, in a sense, an inherently existential, individual nature to getting a tattoo: the decision to be tattooed is one that will mark you as an individual indefinitely.

Self-Expression and Double Skin

Intimately connected to individual meaning is self-expression. We noted above some different means of creating skin images. Consider the fascinating process in which inks are applied to the skin by inserting metallic

CHARLES TALIAFERRO AND MARK ODDEN

chemicals that the body then tries to repel. Through the healing process, the body seals off the pigments because they cannot be rejected and the barrier from the inks allows the tattoo and the body to (as it were) 'adapt' to each other. This underscores Jane Caplan's description of the tattoo as 'something rejected from which one does not part.'[10] In this latter model, the tattoo is, paradoxically, both the visible image itself and the underlying markings beneath the skin.

The tattoo becomes a double skin, in a sense. In its very nature it juxtaposes interiority and exteriority – which might be a factor in the fascination and controversy it creates. It is a physical object – the ink used in the drawing takes up tangible space – but it is also an inferred object, an image. The physical barrier between the ink and the skin draws attention to the exterior of our skin while also sectioning off access to the interior. That being said, a tattoo is still an inferred object. It is a skin image.

Rarely are tattoos thought of as objects separate from skin, but more as a collection of colored cells part of the larger grouping of cells we call our skin. This might be likened to optical illusion drawings in which it is possible to see two images – the rabbit-duck, for example. It is possible to see one or the other, but not both at the same time. One cannot simultaneously see a tattoo as a separate physical object and also part of the skin. The image itself is easily distinguishable, but it is difficult to visually discern whether the tattoo is inked skin or a separate object entirely.

The position of a tattoo underneath the skin but visually on top of the skin also seems to assert its nature as a double skin. Caplan notes the tattoo's position 'as a particular elaboration of the skin's surface, an indelible insertion that is both visible and out of reach.'[11] Paradoxically, the tattoo's permanence seems to be a way of achieving a sort of quasi-immortality. Our bodies cycle through cells every seven years, but the tattoo remains. Thus, as our bodies change, the tattooed image lives on, forever marking its position. The skin as a makeshift canvas changes every seven years, with each iteration essentially a different medium to portray the image. The visual sense is always subject to alterations, but a tattooed visual seems unalterable.

An alternative to the double skin theory is to think of tattooing as a process beyond decorating an exterior, and instead creating the skin as a surface. In this process, one may consider tattooing as a bodily expression of one's inner thoughts – the exteriorization of one's internal ideas without repression. This position can be better understood if it is considered to stem from self-infliction. Adopting the position that regards tattoos as self-mutilation for a moment might allow us some insight. In this line of thought, consciously displaying one's inner psyche through a series of self-inflicted markings involves debasing oneself while having power over the debasement, but through this attaining elevated clarity of consciousness. This concept of the revelation of one's inner self seems to be the means through which the West has adopted tattoos as an art form. The almost ritualized notion of creating the skin as a surface might be seeded in the line of thought that to be oneself one must create the self, and so to be tattooed is to become subjected to one's own self.

Inescapable Seriousness

We conclude with an observation about the serious nature of tattoos. Altering one's skin in ways that are permanent or semi-permanent has a seriousness to it that is inescapable. This is because of the foundational character of skin itself as marking the very boundary of our identity in the world, and also the skin's function as an organ, embodying or instantiating our sense of being in the world. The foundational character of the body, and thus the inescapable seriousness of tattooing, comes out in this puzzle put forward by the sixteenth president of the United States, Abraham Lincoln: How many legs does a dog have if you call the tail a leg? Answer: four. Calling a tail a leg doesn't make it a leg. The point is that there is a reality to the body; its parts are stubborn and resist relabeling.

We hope we have made clear that tattoos can have competing cultural (public) and individual (private) meanings, and that the body resists relabeling through tattooing, according to the double skin theory we talked about. Still, a permanent mark on one's skin has an inescapable seriousness to it such that, even if you had the words 'This is not serious' tattooed on your arm, it would still be very serious indeed. If you actually have a tattoo with these words or are planning on getting one, you should read this book.

NOTES

1   For good introductions to the history of the tattooing arts, see Jane Caplan (ed.), *Written on the Body: The Tattoo in European and American History* (Princeton, NJ: Princeton University Press, 2000); Steve Gilbert, *The Tattoo*

History Sourcebook (New York: Juno Books, 2000); and Maarten Hesselt van Dinter, *The World of Tattoo: An Illustrated History* (The Netherlands: Mundurucu Publishing, 2007).

2 Cited by C.P. Jones, 'Stigma and tattoo,' in Caplan, *Written on the Body*, pp. 4–5.

3 Samuel Steward, *Bad Boys and Tough Tattoos: A Social History of the Tattoo with Gangs, Sailors, and Street-Corner Punks, 1950–1965* (London: Routledge, 1990), pp. 40–43.

4 Cate Lineberry, 'Tattoos: The ancient and mysterious history,' *Smithsonian Magazine* (January 1, 2007, http://www.smithsonianmag.com/history-archaeology/tattoo.html?c=y&page=2).

5 Margo DeMello, *Encyclopedia of Body Adornment* (Westport, CT: Greenwood Press, 2007), p. 266.

6 Caplan, *Written on the Body*, p. xiv.

7 Takahiro Kitamura, *Tattoos of the Floating World: Ukiyo-e motifs in the Japanese Tattoo* (Amsterdam: Hotei Publishing, 2003), pp. 23–24.

8 See Adrienne Kaeppler, *The Pacific Arts of Polynesia and Micronesia* (Oxford: Oxford University Press, 2008), chapter 5.

9 Steward, *Bad Boys and Tough Tattoos*, p. 78.

10 Caplan, *Written on the Body*, p. 64.

11 Ibid., p. xiii.

CHAPTER 2

HOW TO READ A TATTOO, AND OTHER PERILOUS QUESTS

I Tattoo Myself, Therefore I Will Commit Murder

Several late-nineteenth-century and early-twentieth-century thinkers believed it was possible to create tattoo lexicons, predicting a person's character on the basis of her/his skin art. The Austrian design theorist Adolf Loos (1870–1933), for one, was apparently mortally offended by tattoos and the tattooing arts. He declared that any tattooed European man who died without committing murder had simply died before fulfilling his destiny.[1] The pattern forms a sign, pointing toward the future. Read the design, and you read the wearer's unspoken intention, which will later be fulfilled in action. According to this first interpretive scheme, the tattoo wearer declares:

'I tattoo myself, therefore I will commit murder.'

Criminologists, including Alexandre Lacassagne (1843–1924) in France, attempted to devise schematic maps of tattoos and criminality. For Lacassagne, tattoo number and quality corresponded to criminal offenses, and a pattern might indicate a particular convict's crime.[2] Here,

Tattoos – Philosophy for Everyone: I Ink, Therefore I Am, First Edition.
Edited by Robert Arp.
© 2012 John Wiley & Sons, Inc. Published 2012 by John Wiley & Sons, Inc.

the interpretive promise often seems more retrospective. A person who committed an offense could wear (whether with regret or defiance) a testament to the misdeed: a tattooed dagger, indicating that the wearer had stabbed someone; or, in today's tattoo parlance, a teardrop, documenting a human life one has taken. Again, whether inked tears show remorse or triumph is up for grabs. In either case, the tattoo here seems to point backward in time:

'I committed a crime, therefore I now tattoo myself.'

The lure of such approaches is obvious: it seems that tattoos hold out an interpretive promise, gesturing toward future or past. Emblazoned on skin, legible for all who know how to read them, tattoos make visible an individual tattoo wearer's interior state. According to these particular theories, skin art makes visible internal states ranging from mildly felonious to outright murderous. In a city like Baltimore – where I live and work, and where we have too many homicides – such an obvious indicator would surely be welcomed by law enforcement. Of course, any homicide is one too many; so, according to Loos and Lacassagne, perhaps we should round up all tattooed men and women everywhere, as criminals potential or actual. But just how readable is a tattoo?

The Mark of Cain

Consider a case that goes even further back in the annals of cultural history: the Hebrew Bible's first recorded murder. Cain killed his brother Abel and God decreed that he would be banished from the land where he spilled his brother's blood. Cain protests that in his wanderings 'anyone may kill me at sight.' 'Not so!' declared the Lord, and 'put a mark on Cain, lest anyone should kill him at sight' (see Genesis 4:1–16).[3] In other words, the so-called mark of Cain, a tattoo, is as much a sign of God's protection as it is an indication of the wearer's having committed fratricide. The mark of Cain, often mentioned as a synonym for Cain's infamy, also signals his preservation. God both casts him out and gives him life, and the sign that ensures his life continues is most likely a tattoo. To sum it up, Cain too has committed a crime, but might say:

'I wear a tattoo, therefore I live.'

So, tattoos might also be protective. Staying within the Judeo-Christian tradition for a moment longer, that is certainly how Paul saw tattoos. Writing to the Christians at Galatia, he declared, 'I bear the marks of Jesus on my body' (Galatians 6:17).[4] The word here, translated as 'marks,' is *stigmata*, a plural form of *stigma*, or *tattoo*. Paul likely refers to scars he bears as a result of having suffered beatings or stoning for his faith; he transforms such scars into a sign of salvation. The imprint that would testify to denigration or suffering becomes transfigured. Those who created scars might have intended them to cause harm or signify defamation. Instead, they become an emblem of divine favor. In accordance with the previous case, Paul declares, 'I wear marks that indicate divine life.' Now the tattooed man is not a criminal but a saint, and may declare:

'I wear a tattoo, therefore I am saved.'

Maybe tattooed people simply break open any interpretive scheme one might create. Let's consider a few of the most profound.

Tatau: First Signifier

French philosopher Jacques Lacan (1901–1981) proclaims that a tattoo is the first mark that signifies, that points toward a meaning. He declares, 'the subject himself is marked off by a single stroke, and first he marks himself as a tatoo [sic], the first of the signifiers.'[5] The first signifier – first symbol that represents a meaning – is a tattoo. As Lacan tells it, a tattoo is the initial meaningful mark, and making such a mark creates both human subject and signifier. Creating a tattoo, one marks oneself, and then one becomes evident as separate from that mark ('marked off,' to use his phrase). So one becomes a subject: a distinct individual, one who must come to terms with expressive marks.

In Lacan's explanation, the first tattoo (and first sign) is created when a hunter wishes to record his kills. Lacan's hunter is specifically male: he creates a notch, a single stroke that can be read as the number one or, in English, the letter I. The explanation begins to determine what counts, and also suggests that tattoos point specifically toward language, a primary human marker. Meaning accrues: the tattoo becomes a sign of success in the woods, a sign of human awareness. Putting it concisely:

'I tattoo, therefore I am human, not animal.'

Let's turn for a moment to another key interpretive tradition, one that also sees tattoos as inseparable from human existence, and one that sparked much modern tattooing in Europe and the United States. Our English word *tattoo* – like the French *tatouage*, German *Tätowierung*, and Spanish *tatuaje*, among other similar European words – derives from a Tahitian and Samoan word, *tatau*. Captain James Cook imported *tatau* into English in 1769, and so popular were his travel accounts that the word spread like wildfire across Europe and the world. Meanwhile, Cook's sailors copied in their flesh the flourishing practice they witnessed in the Pacific, so tattooing traveled equally rapidly in both print and skin.

In the Pacific, tattooing was traditionally integral to human beings, and was not just a form of art but a way of life. Tattoos allowed one to become a full adult, to own land, to marry, to assume one's place in both community and cosmos. In traditions distinct to each cultural group, patterns might wrap one in images from navel to knees, from chest to knees, or from head to feet. Without tattoos, one lacked social standing and floated free, unregistered in relation to other humans and the gods. Tattoos placed one geographically and spiritually, showing that one was ready for service to one's people. As Samoan writer Albert Wendt puts it, even today *tatau* clothes one for life:

> Clothed not to cover your nakedness but to show you are ready for life, for adulthood and service to your community, that you have triumphed over physical pain and are now ready to face the demands of life, and ultimately to master the most demanding of activities – language/oratory.[6]

Tatau readies one for the world. So, in an independent tradition that long predates Lacan's theories, Pacific thinkers, too, see tattoo as making room for language. A tattoo is a first sign that declares:

> 'I am tattooed, therefore my community speaks through me and I am able to speak in my community.'

Pacific tattooing offers a distinct philosophy. Where criminologists see the practice as cutting an individual off from other humans, and where Lacan's lone hunter stalks through the forest without reference to other human beings and marks himself spontaneously, Pacific tattooing is created ritually in community, by community. In many Oceanic traditions, tattoos also adorn women – and in some Oceanic traditions women are the primary tattoo artists. In any case, wearing such tattoo designs, an individual becomes fully incorporated into a collective. Person and public shape one another mutually, with tattoos signaling their interaction. Designs are more than personal, carrying culture beyond a single individual's life span. A person's patterned skin is mortal, but designs travel onward, connecting future to past, creating a passageway that shows where an individual and a people have been and where they are going. Tattoos, moreover, help propel such a journey.

Name Beyond Face

When Ngāti Toa paramount chief Te Pehi Kupe (c. 1795–1828) traveled from Aotearoa/New Zealand to England in 1826, his facial tattoo, a full Maori *moko* design, sparked great interest. For two weeks straight he was kept busy drawing copies of his unique *moko*. Each pattern was so distinctive it could be used as a signature. (Historically, *moko* patterns were in fact used to sign treaties and deeds.) Te Pehi Kupe's design, he declared, could be considered his name. 'Europee [sic] man write with pen his name,' he explained, 'Tupai's name is here' (pointing to his forehead). The Englishmen who transcribed Te Pehi Kupe's words (and devised their own Maori orthography) recorded how earnest he was in conveying what he meant: 'Still further to illustrate his meaning, he would delineate on paper, with a pen or pencil, the corresponding marks in the *amocos* [tattoo] of his brother and his son, and point out the differences between these and his own.'[7] This is a tattoo understood as a name, as a bearer of a person's identity.

What happens when such designs circulate beyond the person who first wears them? Te Pehi Kupe's tattoos, copied by him, now travel the world, adorning the covers of both the HarperCollins/Basic Books edition of Claude Lévi-Strauss' *Structural Anthropology* and the sesquicentennial Norton Critical Edition of *Moby-Dick*. In a very real sense, mechanical reproduction promulgates copies of Te Pehi Kupe, whose personhood multiplies, replicated first by him and then by presses that imprint on paper designs once etched into his skin. Some Maori activists and scholars say a form of identity theft occurs; some might offer a rejoinder that Te Pehi Kupe is enjoying the last laugh, even though his name is now separated from his face.

Thinkers outside Pacific traditions have not always understood a pattern's meanings or functions, and have ventured to separate designs from faces that bore and shaped them. Immanuel Kant (1724–1804) never ventured more than a hundred miles from his birthplace in Prussia, yet he includes this about Pacific tattooing in his *Critique of Judgment*:

> Much might be added to a building that would immediately please the eye were it not intended for a church. A figure might be beautified with all manner of flourishes and light but regular lines, as is done by the New Zealanders with their tattooing, were we dealing with anything but the figure of a human being.[8]

Kant's criteria for taste and judgment preclude adorning churches and human beings, even though the patterns are otherwise pleasing.

Even anthropologist Claude Lévi-Strauss (1908–2009) did not understand the way a human face shaped such designs – which had to be fitted to a brow's contours, a cheekbone's sweep – and suggested instead that a tattooed face wore an impersonal, imposed mask. 'In native thought,' he declared, 'the design *is* the face, or rather it creates it.'[9] In his view, tattooed faces signal that collective predominates over individual, forcing a person to conform to a pattern's shape. Exterior determines interior. In place of the individual convict marking himself and setting himself off from the larger human community, Lévi-Strauss' explanation proposes that a larger community incorporates the individual into itself by means of a forcible – or at least not quite optional – tattoo.

But Maori tattoo artists suggest quite strongly that there is no battle between interior and exterior. Design makes both visible, and both inform one another seamlessly. Contemporary tattoo artist Henriata Nicholas declares that a design portrays a person's 'genealogy, specific landmarks, historical events, and *Kaitiaki* (spiritual guides).'[10] A tattoo maps physical and spiritual landscapes, and the two are not separate from one another. A pattern is so intimate and specific to an individual that borrowing another's design would be something like borrowing another's skin. Recognizing and honoring harmony and unity within and among people, tattoo patterns signal that our culture is 'based essentially on the connection we have with one another, the environment, all living things, the universe, our ancestor connections, and the creator of all things.'[11] Rather than obscuring an individual's face, in this tradition, patterns enhance it, extending an individual's name beyond finite realms and into the infinite. *Moko* declare:

> 'I am tattooed, therefore I am connected to all.'

In this light, creating a tattoo means encountering vital energies of human existence and creativity, carving patterns where flesh and spirit meet. Artist, wearer, and informed viewers recognize that such designs touch life itself, offering a bridge between mortality and immortality. *Moko* formed using traditional techniques, in which motifs were chiseled into skin, also meant (and continue to mean) that a person receiving a tattoo could venture perilously close to human limits. The chisel technique required incising the patterns once and then going over them again with a second, ink-laden, serrated chisel. In some cases, the designs were so deeply inscribed that a pin could be laid down in them. A full facial design, not to mention a full body design, could take weeks or even months. Pain and blood loss could be severe, with swelling so extreme one was able to eat only through a funnel. Designs could mean life or death for the wearer. Mortal as living skin, and at the same time more than personal, such patterns continue beyond any individual body.

Thus, transcending lines between individual and collective, private and public, and even life and death, a tattoo makes visible a process of creating and proclaiming meaning. As Emmanuel Lévinas has it, 'The face speaks. It speaks, it is in this that it renders possible and begins all discourse.'[12] A tattooed face offers particularly eloquent speech, speech that reverberates beyond known limits, if one is able to listen and understand.

Truth Itself, Unread

Not all Pacific tattoos are facial, and not all Pacific tattoos appear in situations where they can be understood. What the patterns communicate in the latter eventuality might be something else entirely. Consider James F. O'Connell (1808–1854), an 1830s castaway who identified himself as an Irishman and ended up a proud recipient of a Pohnpeian tattoo. In the Pacific, his *pelipel* allowed him to live as an adult member of a family: he married, was adopted by a chief, and participated in a fully human existence. But in New York, where he traveled after leaving the Caroline Islands, women and children reportedly ran screaming through the streets to flee his presence. Ministers, after all, had promised from the pulpit that viewing his designs would transfer tattoo patterns to any woman's unborn child. Immaculate reproduction, indeed!

After Cook and his sailors began portraying designs in print and skin, tattooing proliferated in new populations, but not perhaps as contagiously as screaming women and children feared. What is clear is that O'Connell's patterns sparked wild interest and speculation. Thousands of miles away from anyone who could interpret his patterns, they became a cipher. A viewer was free to assign them any meaning or none.

O'Connell became the first person to exhibit his tattoos professionally in the United States, appearing in P. T. Barnum's American Museum and for twenty years making his living by appearing up and down the eastern seaboard in circuses and melodramas. As 'the tattooed Irishman,' O'Connell presented himself as a text published by Pacific tattoo artists. He declared that a 'squad of these savage printers'[13] created the designs he wore. In his metaphor, women tattoo artists made his body a book. He confessed that he 'never learned to read their marks,'[14] which meant he could not read his own body, the living book he promoted as his profession and identity. He had internalized but was also distanced from the print he wore under his skin.

O'Connell, in other words, represents a historical version of the dilemma Melville gives his Pacific Islands character Queequeg in *Moby-Dick*: an unreadable tattoo. Queequeg, from the fictional island of Kokovoko, bears upon his body a tattoo that offers nothing less than 'a complete theory of the heavens and the earth, and a mystical treatise on the art of attaining truth.' But alas, such 'mysteries not even himself could read, though his own live heart beat against them.'[15] Truth itself – as well as access to mysteries of heavens and earth – appears to be as close as the nearest Pacific tattoo. But here, even a Pacific Islander remains unable to say exactly what such patterns suggest. Melville points generously toward meanings that elude his ability to speak them; oddly, he also deprives Queequeg of access to meaning.

Nonetheless, Queequeg's patterns are so intrinsic to *Moby-Dick* that they quite directly carry Melville's own narrative. Queequeg recovers from a seemingly mortal illness and copies his tattoo patterns onto what would have been his wooden coffin. When the Pequod sinks, along with Queequeg and all others aboard ship, that intricately carved coffin forms a lifebuoy that transports the narrator, Ishmael, to safety: 'And I only am escaped alone to tell thee,' he declares, citing Job.[16] Without the floating life-borne-from-death casket, no Ishmael means no first-person narrative and no novel. A tattoo again stands for meaning-making, here wrested from ocean waves: signification becomes possible insofar as it is delivered atop a tattoo vessel.

Such signification becomes both universalized and unmoored from its Pacific origins. O'Connell's *pelipel* and Queequeg's unnamed patterns show various ways in which tattoo and meaning transit from one cultural landscape to another. The same designs indicate vastly different things, depending upon whether a viewer is ignorant or aware. A tattoo derives from and signals cultural, geographical, and spiritual landscapes; as it moves away from those points of creation and out into the rest of the world, home landscapes and spiritual guardians travel with it, according to contemporary tattoo artists. That is good reason to become informed viewers, rather than unaware ones. Along the lines we saw in discussing contemporary *moko*, these patterns, too, proclaim:

'I am design, and therefore connected to all.'

Tattoo Devotion

A tattoo's profound connection to deeply rooted Pacific ways of life made it a target for missionaries. Not all bringers of the good word objected, of course: in Samoa and throughout the Pacific, tattooing continued in the midst of missions and colonial administrations. In the late twentieth century, contemporary artist Petelo Sulu'ape, who stems from a well-known family of *tufuga ta tatau* or tattoo-priests, declared, 'In the Catholic church even priests can get tattooed; I have executed complete pe'as [traditional tattoo from naval to knees] on several priests. Methodists and Mormons also allow it.'[17] But, despite such current understandings of the way Christianity and tattoos may co-exist, many historical figures who taught about the word made flesh objected mightily to a rival, visible tradition that appeared to be formed of words made flesh. And so tattooing was banned in many places, usually by people who did not understand patterns' specific meanings but recognized that the designs signaled allegiance to Pacific ways of knowing and being.

Of course, banning tattooing consolidated its ability to signal indigenous power. Those who continued to create and wear tattoos, in the face of brutal bans, made it a defiant proclamation of indigenous sovereignty over indigenous bodies – and, by extension, indigenous lands and worlds. The art that is a way of life might have gone underground, and under clothes also introduced and mandated by missionaries, but it continued. Whether seen or unseen, motifs continued to travel across bodies and books.

Ironically or beautifully, depending upon your perspective, many European travelers both praise missionaries and record receiving tattoos. English physician Frederick Bennett, for instance, received illegal tattoos in both the Society Islands and the Marquesas Islands.[18] Such travelers appear not to recognize that missionaries often attempted to stamp out tattooing. In some cases, travelers received designs decades after bans were instituted and after the practice was declared long gone. The sources that most often proclaim and celebrate a tattoo's absence are missionary accounts – which must be considered suspect, given the counter-testimony provided by various newly tattooed Europeans.

In Tahiti, tattooing was banned in written law codes (formulated with missionary advice) and soon became an intensified way to assert native sovereignty. A thriving tattoo business occurred on Sundays, in particular – during church services. In reaction, Christians adopted shockingly brutal countermeasures. One pious church woman, Mrs. Favell L. B. Mortimer, writing anonymously for the American Tract Society in 1836, reports, 'The only way to prevent tattooing was at length found to be, having the parts that were marked, disfigured by the skin being taken off, and foul blotches left where beautiful patterns had been pricked in.'[19]

This account, offered in celebration of forty years of Society Island missions, contradicts its own logic. The Christian corrections to 'beautiful patterns' are 'foul blotches' and 'disfigured' skin. Mrs. Mortimer notes that she writes for children, in a 'manner acceptable to youth';[20] yet she offers an approving description of flaying other people. Of course, she adopts passive phrasing, describing it as 'the skin being taken off.' Reading her accounts today, it is impossible to muster an Amen. By making a time-honored way of life criminal, those who create outrageous penalties also inevitably bring criminality into their own time-honored ways. From one vantage point, it is not Tahitian tattooing but such Christian piety that looks like a crime. From today's perspective, as we saw in St. Paul's case, but now with Christians as perpetrators of disfigurement, it becomes more and more difficult to tell criminals and saints apart, at least in regard to tattoos and the tattooing arts.

Free from such criminalizing Christian piety, but not from devotion to tattoos, Pacific Islanders historically continued to create and wear patterns. Bans and penalties did not work as well as missionaries wanted to believe. Around the turn of the twentieth century, forty years after a ban in Nuku Hiva, a man named Moa-e-tahi boasted a script tattoo. Marquesan letters on his arm declared 'Kahau hee atua Iova! Ii kehu, ahi veu; vave te etua!' In English, the script proclaims, 'You are invited to follow the God Jehovah! [His] anger is ash, the flames are wet! Hurry to the gods!'[21] He uses the same writing taught in mission schools to forge his own testament. (Prior to the missions' arrival, Marquesan was strictly an oral language, complete with its own literatures.) Tattooing takes on a banner of protest, of sovereignty, declaring in prophetic voice that Marquesan gods speak, in land and sea and through people connected to land and sea.

Tattoos can become a keen expression of self-determination. Moa-e-tahi proclaimed on behalf of all that it was possible to write a Marquesan future, one worn on skin. Tattoos became an early text of decolonization, anticipating the correlation Albert Wendt draws between tattoos and newly independent countries and literatures.

The liberating aspect of tattoos may explain why early-nineteenth-century English missionary George Vason was unable to convince a single Tongan to convert to Christianity, but obtained a full-body *tātatau*. According to his own assessment, 'I looked indeed very gay in this new fancy covering.'[22] Later English visitors determined that Vason and his colleagues had so signally failed to communicate their evangelical purpose that Tongans believed the Englishmen lived among them because they enjoyed their warmer weather.

So, communication may certainly fail in more than one direction: missionaries may give up a shepherd's staff and instead don a tattoo, or carry both; Pacific tattoos may circulate wildly free from the names and faces that shaped them; saints and criminals may share both common ground and the same skin pattern. But, no matter what an artist or wearer intends tattoos to say, no matter what a viewer believes designs proclaim, in Pacific and in European traditions tattoos stand as a point of origin: first sign made and interpreted, first threshold of meaning crossed, first declaration of the subject's existence and sovereignty:

'I tattoo, therefore I am.'

or even:

'Tattoo I am.'

Within and beyond the Pacific, a tattoo's proclamation reverberates in both the most secular and sacred realms.

NOTES

1 Adolf Loos, 'Ornament und Verbrechen,' in Franz Glück (ed.), *Sämtliche Schriften* (Vienna: Verlag Herold, 1962), vol. 1, p. 276.

2 Quoted in Jane Caplan, '"National tattooing": Traditions of tattooing in nineteenth-century Europe,' in Jane Caplan (ed.), *Written on the Body: The Tattoo in European and American History* (Princeton, NJ: Princeton UP, 2000), p. 161.

3 Confraternity of Christian Doctrine, *The New American Bible* (Iowa Falls, IA: World Bible Publishers, 1991).

4 Ibid.

5 Jacques Lacan, *The Four Fundamental Concepts of Psycho-analysis*, trans. Alan Sheridan (New York: Norton, 1978), p. 141.

6 Albert Wendt, 'Tatauing the post-colonial body,' *SPAN: Journal of the South Pacific Association for Commonwealth Literature and Language Studies* 42–43 (1996): 16.

7 George Lillie Craik, *The New Zealanders* (London: Charles Knight, 1830), pp. 331–332.

8 Immanuel Kant, *Critique of Judgment*, trans. Werner S. Pluhar (Indianapolis, IN: Hackett), p. 77.

9 Claude Lévi-Strauss, *Structural Anthropology*, trans. Claire Jacobson and Brooke Grundfest Schoepf (New York: Basic Books, 1963), p. 259.

10 Henriata Nicholas, with Ngahuia Te Awekotuku, '*Uhi Ta Moko* – Designs carved in skin,' in John Ruszkiewicz, Daniel Anderson, and Christy Friend (eds.), *Beyond Words: Reading and Writing in a Visual Age* (New York: Person Longman, 2006), p. 158.

11 Ibid.

12 Emmanuel Levinas, *Ethics and Infinity: Conversations with Philippe Nemo*, trans. Richard A. Cohen (Pittsburgh, PA: Duquesne University Press, 1985), p. 87.

13 James F. O'Connell, *A Residence of Eleven Years in New Holland and the Caroline Islands*, ed. Saul H. Risenberg (Honolulu, HI: University Press of Hawai'i, 1972), p. 115.

14 Ibid., p. 153.

15 Herman Melville, *Moby-Dick*, ed. Hershel Parker, Harrison Hayford, and G. Thomas Tanselle (Evanston, IL: Northwestern University Press, 1988), pp. 480, 481.

16 Ibid., p. 573.

17 Petelo Sulu'ape, 'History of Samoan tattooing,' *Tattootime* 5 (1991): 107.

18 Frederick D. Bennett, *Narrative of a Whaling Voyage Round the Globe From the Year 1833–1836* (New York: Da Capo, 1840/1970), vol. 1, pp. 118, 307.

19 Favell Lee Mortimer, *The Night of Toil; or, a Familiar Account of the Labors of the First Missionaries in the South Sea Islands* (New York: American Tract Society, 1838), p. 204.

20 Ibid., p. 5.

21 Karl von den Steinen, *Die Marquesaner und ihre Kunst: Studien über die Entwicklung primitiver Südseeornamentik nach eigenen Reiseergebnissen und dem Material der Museen* (New York: Hacker, 1969), vol. 1, p. 95.

22 George Vason, *An Authentic Narrative of Four Years' Residence in Tongataboo, One of the Friendly Islands, in the South-Sea by —— Who Went Thither in the Duff, under Captain Wilson, in 1796. With an Appendix, by an Eminent Writer [Solomon Pigott]* (London: Longman, Hurst, Rees, and Orme, 1810), p. 179.

TATTOOS AND ART

What makes tattoos special is the choice of surface – a human body. The person is the surface, the canvas. So is there any reason that we should not consider artistically crafted tattoos 'art' just as we would an artistically crafted painting art?

(Nicolas Michaud, p. 29)

CHAPTER 3

ARE TATTOOS ART?

Nice Tattoo

Imagine that you're sitting on a bar stool in your favorite bar enjoying a beer when a large, angry-looking man walks in. The first thing you notice about him is the fact that his arms and neck are covered with tattoos. He sits down on the bar stool next to you, leather squeaking. You glance over, nervously, and say, 'Nice tattoo.' Smiling, your new friend replies, 'Thanks! It's a da Vinci.'

This seems like an improbable turn of events. But, when you think about it, a tattoo is an image presented to us on a surface and a Leonardo da Vinci painting is an image presented to us on a surface. What makes a tattoo all that different, then? What makes tattoos special is the *choice* of surface – a human body. The person *is* the surface, the canvas. So, is there any reason that we should not consider artistically crafted tattoos 'art' just as we would an artistically crafted painting art? In this chapter, we'll explore what it means for something to be art. We'll also figure out whether tattoos should count as art, and, if they should, what kind of art. The examination will also help to illuminate what we mean when we say of something, 'That is art.'

Tattoos – Philosophy for Everyone: I Ink, Therefore I Am, First Edition.
Edited by Robert Arp.
© 2012 John Wiley & Sons, Inc. Published 2012 by John Wiley & Sons, Inc.

What is Art?

Aesthetics is the area of Western philosophy concerned with the nature of art, beauty, and taste. So, as can be imagined, the definition of art is an integral – yet hotly debated – idea in this area.[1] The question of what does, and does not, count as art is one that is heavily contested in the art world; but to most people the question seems to be easy to answer. When I teach philosophy at an art school, the students are very confident. When I ask them how they know something is a work of art, they will confidently tell me, 'I know art when I see it.' When I ask them how they know they are right, well, they 'just know.' But, what is really happening is that my students aren't defining art at all. They are just saying they know what it is without actually saying *how* they know what it is.

If art is defined as 'I know it when I see it,' then I could call anything that I see art. What, then, is to stop me from spitting on the sidewalk, pointing at the spit, and saying, 'That is art'? Given this definition, everyone else would have to agree that it is art to me, and, therefore, that it is art. The definition of art would be up to each individual. What is the point of art museums if what should belong in them is different for each individual? There can be no criticism and no challenge to the claim that something is art if art is just a matter of what we see and feel. If we argue that tattoos can be art, we probably want it to be for a better reason than just because anything we call 'art' is art.

Further, if art has no actual definition, then it sounds like we're talking about nothing. But we talk about art all the time; we point to it, enjoy it, and share it. It is meaningful, and we want it to be meaningful. To some degree, this is because of the tremendous amount of work and talent some art objects exhibit. And this worth probably is a result of the fact that the work of art – whether it be beautiful, terrifying, or evidence of incredible talent – has a special status as an art object. So, it seems that art is not an *anything* or a *nothing*; it is a *something with meaning*.

What some philosophers think is that we can develop a theory of what counts as art and what doesn't. That way, we can say with some degree of accuracy and certainty, 'That is art.' Sometimes this is scary, because if we accept a certain definition and something we love and think of as art doesn't fit into that definition we have to admit it isn't actually art. But I don't think we should worry about that. We should consider the best possible answer for what is art, and, perhaps, tattoos will fit into one or more theories of art.

NICOLAS MICHAUD

Let's first look at three popular theories of art – art world theory, formalism, and expressionism – and consider their application to tattoos. Here, I won't be assuming that any particular theory is right or wrong, but only using them as lenses through which we can view tattoos. As there is no *complete* agreement as to which theory best describes art, we can only survey the possibilities and consider tattoos as possible candidates. And we should not throw out a theory because it doesn't qualify tattoos as art – we should objectively consider each theory and what it tells us about tattoos.

Art World Theory: Art is Participation in the Art World

Art world theorists believe something is art when the art world *itself* – complete with an art history, art tradition, and art experts – claims that something is art.[2] Note that this is different from the 'I know it when I see it' approach, which is *purely* subjective.

Where do tattoos stand as far as art world theory is concerned? When we think about art museums, art history, and art critics, we rarely think of tattoos. Granted, there is a tattoo art museum in San Francisco, but that museum is generally considered to be more a novelty than a full-fledged representative of the art community. So far, tattoos have not been accepted into the tradition of the art world and so, by the art world's standards, tattoos aren't art.

But it is important to note that this position can be challenged. If, upon further reflection, the art world changes its collective mind, then tattoos would be considered art. I think this change is likely. As tattoos continue to become more mainstream, it is difficult for artists – who are as a whole constantly pushing the envelope of art – to continue to relegate tattoos to outside the art world.

Formalism: Art is the Result of Formal Properties Working Together

Conversely, it would seem that a formalist could easily consider a tattoo to be art, depending on the tattoo. Formalists believe that art should only be appreciated for its art qualities – its formal qualities. In other words, a piece of art should be considered art for its own ability to be art, not because of what the art world thinks. The formal qualities are best understood as those qualities that are only about the piece. Formalists consider the intention of the artist, the historical context of the art, as well as the potential meanings and feelings generated by the viewer, all to be *distractions* from the work itself. For example, if I am listening to a particular musical piece and feel profound sadness, I am not really paying attention to the piece; instead, I am paying attention to my own feelings. Formalists think we should pay attention to the work itself; for example, the lines, shading, dimensions, harmony, and organization, and the ways those parts work together to create a whole in an art piece.

For modern formalists, just having the properties we associate with art – such as lines, shading, dimensions, perspective, and so on – is not enough to make something art, though. According to Clive Bell (1881–1964), the parts create a 'significant form,' the quality that an artwork has by virtue of all of its part working together to produce in us a feeling of 'ohhhhh, that's art.'[3] This idea is hard to express, but can be thought of like solving a puzzle. There is a point, right when you realize what the solution is, that you see how all the parts work together. It is the fact that the parts work together to create a whole that makes an object a piece of art to the formalists, and it is the fact that it can produce an aesthetic experience in us that means it has significant form.

So, to a formalist, if a tattoo demonstrates the physical properties – when viewed from an aesthetic perspective – that work together to generate a whole, it is art. Some tattoos therefore would not be art in the same way that a bad painting may not be art. Yes, the painting may have the formal properties of art – such as lines, dimension, shading, and perspective – but these components don't work together effectively to create a whole that can be considered art; they lack significant form.

This theory may miss something essential about tattoos, though. Formalists want to ignore the canvas; they are not concerned about what museum the art is in, or the frame, or the context surrounding it. They would view a tattoo only as a piece of visual art, and the fact that it is placed on a person would be *irrelevant* – likely just a distraction from its formal qualities. Should we really ignore the fact that the tattoo is on a person, though? Doesn't the fact that a tattoo is engraved on a person add to its artistic qualities?

NICOLAS MICHAUD

Expressionism: Art Elicits an Emotional Response from the Viewer

The last theory we'll talk about – expressionism – is about as far from formalism as you can get. Whereas formalists believe that as viewers we should take on a perspective of disinterest, focusing on the art and not the context of the art, expressionism is the position that art should express some kind of emotion. Whereas a formalist thinks our feelings have little or nothing to do with a work's art value, the expressionists think that emotion is essential. To expressionists, a work that can make us feel something deeply is of greater worth than one that does not.

The expressionist, then, probably would consider some tattoos art and others not art. A tattoo that can draw us in and move us deeply is one that would be considered art. On the other hand, a generic butterfly on the ankle would not be considered art – it would simply be a picture on a person.

Leo Tolstoy (1828–1910), famous novelist and aesthetician, argued passionately for expressionism, saying that art should produce *universal* emotion in the viewer.[4] The key component, according to Tolstoy, is that this art is first felt by the artist, then expressed in the work, and then felt by the viewer. In essence, the viewer should be infected with the emotion of the artist. And, the more effectively a piece of work infects the audience with the artist's emotions, the better the work of art is. How exactly this expression of emotion occurs is not made clear by Tolstoy, but many artists today still believe that what they do through their art is share their feelings.

Expressionism can provide a powerful perspective on tattoos as works of art. The fact that the tattoo itself is on a person may add relevance and context to an image that, by itself, has little meaning. For example, a friend of mine has a broken chain tattooed on her shoulder. Considered alone, the image of a broken chain is not particularly meaningful. But she had that image placed over a former bruise left on her by an abusive husband, and had the image tattooed on the one-year anniversary of her freeing herself from the relationship. Knowing this, the canvas brings deep meaning to the work, which may have a deep emotional impact on the viewer.

What Do These Theories Accomplish for Tattoos?

These theories help us to understand what we mean by art and how tattoos fit into the world of art. Art world theory helps us to recognize that tattoos need to participate in the world of art for their aesthetic merit to be recognized and appreciated. Formalism helps to demonstrate that the tattoo itself, regardless of its context, can be appreciated as an art object. The tattooed image itself can be such that the lines, shading, and perspective work together to create an aesthetic whole. The formalist reminds us not to get lost in the fact that the image is on a person and instead to focus on the image as well. And finally, the expressionist encourages us to consider that the fact that the tattoo is on a person is, in some cases, relevant to the aesthetic experience.

What this discussion of theories should also demonstrate to us is that it is not a stretch to view tattoos as art. What we don't know is whether or not the image should be the focus of the tattoo, or whether its placement on a person should be the focus. In other words, is a tattoo art because it's an artfully created image or because of the fact that it is placed on a person? If its context – placed on a person – is the most important, then it almost seems as if tattoos are more *performance art* than visual art.

Tattoos as Performance Art

Performance art, which has gained in popularity over the past couple of decades, emphasizes art in which not only the piece but also the performance matters. For example, traditionally, when a poem is read, the person reading the poem tries to distract from the poem as little as possible. In performance art, by contrast, the poem may be read while the poet also dances, acts, or changes her voice. When we take the person as a canvas in context, it is possible to consider a tattoo as a piece of performance art – a work that constantly moves and changes.

One important reason for describing tattoos as examples of performance art is that, otherwise, few instances of tattoos could be considered to be original art works. Most tattoos are copies of images onto a human canvas. If the only thing of aesthetic merit of a tattoo is the image, then the original rendering of the image is the only true and original artwork – the tattoo is just a copy. Now, it might be reasonably argued that the original drawing is just a draft and not the final product. But, conversely, we must ask ourselves whether each tattoo placed on every person after the first is just a copy? If this is true, the original work is the image tattooed on the first person and, when it is tattooed on another, that person is just presenting us with a copy of original piece.

This way of thinking ignores the fact that every person acts as a unique and different canvas, which will display the work in different places and in different ways. Consider, for example, an exact copy of the *Mona Lisa*: in and of itself, this is unimpressive and just a copy. But if an artist such as Marcel Duchamp (1887–1968) were to create a copy of the *Mona Lisa* and draw a mustache on it, it may well be considered a wholly different artwork.[5] With that one small change, the context of the piece – and thereby the meaning – is radically different.

Perhaps then the canvas can be significant and each tattoo, even if a copy, presents an entirely different meaning when applied to a different person. Granted, we may still want to be tentative about classifying as art common and overly used tattoos that only exist for the purpose of pop culture indulgence, but even a generic ankle butterfly may provide the viewer with significant meaning when the context of the canvas is taken into account.

The Human Canvas

This creation of meaning may require that the person upon whom the tattoo is placed actually *tells us* what the tattoo is, or what it means, which is similar to placing a title on a painting. Without the title plate, a piece of art may have very little meaning to us. For example, when one views the painting *Lee and Jackson Meeting for the Last Time 1864* from afar for the first time (without reading the nameplate), one might think that Lee and Jackson are meeting for the first time, or for the last, or are standing around sharing war stories, or are relaying solemn news to each other, or are preparing to leave on a trip together, or any number of things. The image in itself is not enough to fulfill the full potential of meaning of the painting. It isn't until we see the title that the painting becomes truly powerful. Had the title been instead 'Lee Telling Jackson a Dirty Joke,' we would take away a very different experience of the work.[6]

Of course, a formalist would disagree adamantly with what I've just said. But, whether or not the context of the work is just a distraction does not change the fact that the experience or context can provide a viewer with a powerful aesthetic experience, questions of *legitimacy* aside. Knowing the context of the tattoo – even facts as trivially true as that it's permanent on the person and was painful to have inked – seems very relevant. The fact that the tattoo is ever-changing, ever-moving, and doomed to cease to exist in the short time the body takes to decay upon death can have a profound effect on the viewers of a tattoo. Should we really ignore all of these things?

Tattoos, Mortality, and Deep Meaning

Knowing that some piece is moving toward an end – as with ice sculptures, for example – can heighten our aesthetic experience of the work. This is especially true of tattoos. Unlike music and ice sculptures and other art objects that are expressed through the passage of time, tattoos are directly tied to our mortality. Often deeply meaningful to the person (the canvas), the tattoo is inexorably tied to how the person changes. As the person changes, the tattoo changes; as the person ages, the tattoo begins to show wear, too; and, when a person dies, the tattoo decays with his body.

It is not a stretch, then, to view tattoos as a deeply meaningful kind of performance art. The tattoo is a piece that challenges the notion of 'art,' and this is often sufficient to warrant respect in the art world. Tattoos also often display powerful visual unity and beauty, as a formalist would require. And they can express the emotional content of the artist, the canvas, or both. In all cases, tattoos act as a testament to the inevitable end that the human canvas will suffer, causing us to reflect on our inevitable end.

We can view tattoos as meeting none of the theoretic criteria mentioned above, or all of them; tattoos challenge the art world and so may fail their test. They express meaning and so may fail for the formalist, and they are composed images, which may have no expressionistic content. Ironically, it is those same facts that may qualify them as works of art – they challenge us, often display complex unities, and bring out emotion in us. For this reason, I posit that tattoos may be significant art works. They can cause us to think deeply about the nature of art, the unity of the image, the meaning of the image, the performance inherent in the canvas' life, and the canvas' death. In this way, tattoos provide us with a potential layering of meaning that is essential to what we consider art. It is that layering that unites all of these theories in the experience of tattoos – whether it's layers of potential commentary, forms that create unity of meaning, or combinations of thereof.

What we should realize, then, is that there is little or no reason to assume that a work, because it is a tattoo, shouldn't be considered art. The image alone may well be of great artistic merit. Moreover, the fact that a tattoo is placed on a person adds a significant layer of context and potential meaning that makes tattoos a fertile ground for aesthetic experience. The way tattoos are presented to us likely should not be ignored, but instead treated as a form of performance art of great merit and potency. When we look at a tattoo, we see a work of art that is slowly disintegrating with the person upon whom it is placed. Because of that mortal disintegration, as an art form tattoos are in a special position to make us think deeply about art, performance, and our own mortality.

NOTES

1   Besides Thomas Adajian, 'The definition of art,' in Edward N. Zalta (ed.), *Stanford Encyclopedia of Philosophy* (Fall 2009, http://plato.stanford.edu/entries/art-definition), good introductions to aesthetics include Matthew Kieran (ed.), *Contemporary Debates in Aesthetics and the Philosophy of Art* (Oxford: Blackwell, 2005) and Stephen Davies, *The Philosophy of Art* (Oxford: Blackwell, 2006).
2   See Arthur Danto, 'The Artworld,' *Journal of Philosophy* 61 (1964): 571–584.
3   Clive Bell, *Art* (London: Chatto and Windus, 1914); see also Cynthia Freeland, *But Is It Art? An Introduction to Art Theory* (Oxford: Oxford University Press, 2002) and Cynthia Freeland, *Art Theory: A Very Short Introduction* (Oxford: Oxford University Press, 2007).
4   Leo Tolstoy, *What is Art?* trans. Alymer Maude (Indianapolis, IN: Hackett Publishing, 1960).
5   Which is something Duchamp did do. The work is entitled *L.H.O.O.Q*, the first version of which was created in 1918.
6   This example is developed by Mark Twain in his autobiography, which has been recently released. See Michael B. Frank, Victor Fischer, Harriet E. Smith, Sharon Goetz, Robert Hirst, and Benjamin Griffin (eds.), *Autobiography of Mark Twain*, 3 vols. (Berkeley, CA: University of California Press, 2010).

KIMBERLY BALTZER-JARAY
AND TANYA RODRIGUEZ

CHAPTER 4

FLESHY CANVAS

The Aesthetics of Tattoos from Feminist
and Hermeneutical Perspectives

Mobile Art Gallery

In a joke from the late 1970s, George Carlin once referred to a heavily tattooed person as a 'mobile art gallery,' and further added that when 'a guy like that dies, you don't bury him, you stick him in a museum somewhere.'[1] Carlin's comedy never fails to get a laugh, whether about tattoos, dirty words, politics, or religion, but we have to ask: what are we laughing at here exactly? Tattoo artistry and social acceptance of tattooed people has evolved so much since the 1970s, when Carlin originally cracked this joke. Tattoos are no longer only worn by society's degenerates (e.g., prisoners, gangs, sailors) – they are for everyone and anyone. On TV, we see people from all walks of life getting tattooed by a member of the *LA*

Tattoos – Philosophy for Everyone: I Ink, Therefore I Am, First Edition.
Edited by Robert Arp.
© 2012 John Wiley & Sons, Inc. Published 2012 by John Wiley & Sons, Inc.

Ink or *Miami Ink* crews, and we see celebrities such as Megan Fox, Susan Sarandon, and Angelina Jolie showing off some ink on the red carpet. And of course we see many an inked musician, such as Lady Gaga, Pink, and Henry Rollins. But if all this is true, if tattoos have become so mainstream and acceptable as a significant art form, why is Carlin's joke still funny? Maybe it's the mental image of a dead person covered in colorful tattoos hanging in an art gallery next to the *Mona Lisa* or *Starry Night*. Or maybe it's the idea of a person, scantily clad, walking about being appreciated by the public as if they were an installment at the Louvre. Whatever the silly imagining, one cannot deny that part of the humor here lies in the fact that many people don't see tattoos as legitimate art or tattoo artists as 'real' artists like Dali, Van Gogh, or Rodin. But why is that? It seems that the only thing that distinguishes tattooing from other fine arts is the fleshy canvas its content appears on. Aye, there's the rub.

'Aesthetics' is the branch of philosophy that concerns the definition and nature of art, beauty, and taste.[2] In this paper, we first investigate a bit of feminist and hermeneutical aesthetics. Building upon these theories, we expand the discussion of art to include the fleshy canvas. We argue that a feminist philosophy of art suggests a sound theoretical framework by which one can maintain that skin art is just that – *art*. In its contemporary practice, tattooing has become a new form of art, and feminist theory provides context for interpretation. The tattooed body may agitate conventional conceptions of fine art – but art evolves, and history makes this much clear. Definitions of art tend to develop, as does artistic practice. Artistic innovations subvert what is old and stale within the institutional art world, while art theory empowers that subversion and provides a context for the appreciation of art. There is usually some initial resistance, of course, to this evolution – impressionism, cubism, and photography, for example, were initially met with criticism and even damnation by mainstream artists and art theorists of the time.[3] Similarly, feminist aesthetics might seem subversive to some; yet, in our view, it serves the same end for tattoos, teaching us to see the skin painter's art.

Of course, aesthetics concerns much more than definitions of art and beauty. One of the ways we value art is for its meaning and for the various interpretations of its message. This is where the second approach, hermeneutical aesthetics, can help. By picking up on the meaning of art, hermeneutical aesthetics takes us from a definition that includes the fleshy canvas to one that reveals its significance.

The State of Aesthetic Theory

What is art, you ask? There are a few standard views we can look at here; among the most influential are formalist, expressionist, and institutional definitions of art. These theories emphasize totally different values in aesthetics: formalism attends to the form of the artwork, expressionism considers what is expressed by the artist and what emotions are elicited by those who experience the art, while the institutional theory includes audience appreciation, the approval of the art world, and art history and expertise as necessary parts of determining what art is. In spite of dramatic differences in how they estimate value, however, each of these theories insists upon distinguishing between fine art and craft; that is, ranking 'high' and 'low' art.

Formalism in aesthetics is the view that what matters in art is *form*: color, composition, texture, size – all (and only) what can be seen or heard in the work itself: 'The properties in virtue of which it is an artwork and in virtue of which it is a good or bad one – are formal merely, where formal properties are typically regarded as properties graspable by sight or by hearing merely.'[4] Evaluating visual art, then, involves *looking* at it without reference to 'external' considerations. Clement Greenberg and Clive Bell are the most famous of its proponents. As art critics, they redirected audiences to appreciate line, color, pigment, and shape when people protested the lack of 'realism' in modern art.[5] According to the formalist definition, art appreciation requires detachment – even from the notion that art should look like something recognizable. In one sense, formalist detachment acknowledges 'artistic license' and sets art free from the conventional task of representing (copying) things in the world.

Unfortunately, formalism also severely restricts the experience of art, since it does not attach aesthetic value to artistic intention, historical context, or social setting. More specifically, formalism excludes consideration of gender (it shouldn't matter to the work who the artist is), artistic process (it isn't relevant how the artwork was made, and why, where, or when), and utility (if it is supposed to have a function beyond being art, then it isn't art). When artistic merit is limited to form or beauty, art undervalues objects with any practical use.[6] As Carolyn Korsmeyer points out, feminists have scrutinized the category of fine art 'because its attendant values screened out much of women's creative efforts or actively dissuaded their attempts to practice certain genres.'[7] In other words, historically, women put their creativity into making useful things (quilts, for example); as a result, their work was considered craft, not high art.

While formalists emphasize formal beauty in art, *expressionist* theories advocate the view that art is an expression of genius. Korsmeyer describes it as 'a kind of personal expression that externalizes the vision of the individual artist in a work of autonomous value.'[8] For philosophers Maurice Merleau-Ponty (1908–1961) and Jean-Paul Sartre (1905–1980) and other expressionists, art communicates the significance of human existence.[9] Thus, expression is not merely subjective – it communicates universally, not only expressing the artist's thoughts, intentions, beliefs, feelings, and so on but also eliciting thoughtful and emotive responses from those who experience the art.

A discussion of extensive scholarship on what exactly is expressed by expressionist art is not possible here, but one theme stands out that is relevant for our work in this chapter. Thalia Gouma-Peterson makes the interesting observation that there is a 'confrontation between the submissive female nude and the sexual-artistic will of the male artist.'[10] If you have any doubts about this particular expressive theme, consider female nudes by Delacroix, Ingres, Munch, Miro, Picasso, and de Kooning; not to mention Degas, Manet, and Renoir. Unfortunately, we often mistake 'masculine' values for universal ones: 'Men act and women appear. Men look at women. Women watch themselves being looked at.'[11]

Unlike expressionist aesthetics, which prescribe what art *should* be, *institutional theory* aims to describe art as it is. According to the institutional aesthetic theorist George Dickie, a work of art, in the purely descriptive sense, is anything 'upon which some society or some sub-group of a society has conferred the status of candidate for appreciation.'[12] A thing is art (though not necessarily good art) simply because people label it as such. Arthur Danto, famous art critic, philosopher, and institutional theorist, offers a slightly more demanding version: theory makes the difference between art and non-art. He writes, 'To see something as art requires something the eye cannot decry – an atmosphere of artistic theory, a knowledge of the history of art: an artworld.'[13] The institutional theory explains why we want to call Andy Warhol's 'Brillo Boxes' art but not the package of Brillo boxes sitting on the grocery shelf. It also acknowledges the cycle of art history, which goes something like this:

1 Art puzzles us, so we come up with a definition.
2 Art bends the rules, and so we tweak them.
3 Art defies the rules, and we redefine.

4   Art bends, we tweak; art scoffs, we condemn.
5   Repeat.

This cycle and the people involved make up the art world. Of course, the art world that institutional theorists describe happens to be male-dominated, upper-class, educated, and set primarily in the context of industrialized nations.

Formalism, expressionism, and the institutional theory each offer definitions of art; unfortunately, as we have just noted, these definitions interpret art in ways that have been particularly damaging. Interestingly enough, for the most part these theoretical positions exclude tattoos as art for the same reasons they excluded art as practiced historically by women. Since the art world exists in public, it excludes non-public art. Historically, women's lives were in the domestic – *private* – realm. Embroidery and quilting, for example, would have been inappropriate activities for social gatherings.[14] Similarly, the body occupies a private sphere; and, as a result, public displays of tattoos become acts of vulgarity.

So, while formalistic, expressionistic, and institutional aesthetic theories enrich our understanding of canonical art, they also can be a source of class divisions, patriarchy, and ethnocentrism. Such effects demonstrate more than practical flaws of an ideal system. Symptoms on this scale indicate a theory in need of revision.

The Female Fleshy Canvas: Body Art from a Feminist Perspective

The tattoo artist produces a beautiful work on someone's body using a stencil, ink, and needles, instead of brushes and paint on a canvas. Consider a tattoo of some natural thing. With this kind of tattoo we are aware of nature in a twofold way: not only can the subject matter of tattoos be found in the natural world – for example tattoos of roses or koi fish – but the flesh these tattoos are inked into is also itself a living, breathing, feeling thing of nature. Beautiful art can happen on a variety of living things, of course; one can decorate a tree or paint a face, but these kinds of art are applied to the surface, not injected into the living nature itself like a tattoo is. Once the tattoo is executed, it moves with the skin, becomes a part of the flesh, and can even change shape, expression, or color with movement or over time. In this way, the art becomes one with nature. This very fact comes into account when we judge the beauty of a tattoo since it must not only resemble its original object but must be properly placed on the body, sized for the wearer, and not be distorted badly with movement. Here, it seems size and technique matter.

According to Carolyn Korsmeyer, one of the significant ways in which feminist artists defy expectation is 'the presentation of the body as a component of art.'[15] This trend is more than mere defiance, however. By using her own body within the work, the artist takes control of the relationships found between artist, artwork, and audience. Consider the fact that in the Modern Arts section at the Metropolitan Museum of Art in New York City some eighty five percent or so of the nude pieces feature females while around five percent of the artists are women.[16] Looking at a woman's body depicted in an artwork, the audience attends to the formal properties such as color, light, and balance. Formal properties exist on only on the surface and formalist aesthetics privileges surface over all else. Beauty, according to formalist definitions, also exists on surfaces. Art that depicts mere surface renders the body passive and subservient, and the tendency, then, is for viewers to 'objectify' a woman by focusing on her body as a mere object. Conversely, when the artist uses her own body within the work, she compels the audience to confront her agency. The artist's intention imparts subjectivity to the body; we become aware of the person revealed by the surface.

What is the standard of taste for tattoos? The dominant tradition insists that the significance of art comes from its universal value, not its individual value. Judgments of taste are supposed to be detached from individual concerns without objective significance. Tattoos, however, are often thick with personal meaning and private symbolism. Social stigma insinuates a contradiction and sees a 'will to vulgarity' in body art.[17] The illustrated female body is even more subversive since tattoos have often been predominantly a male body art. And, consider Iris Marion Young's insightful claim that a 'woman's social existence' can be summed up as the 'object of the gaze of another, which is a major source of her bodily self-reference.'[18] A tattooed woman redefines beauty on her own terms, according to her individual taste. Sadly, individual taste holds little merit in traditional philosophy; universal taste holds all the stock. Deference to convention has dominated aesthetic theory and disregarded our personal experience with art. By contrast, Anita Silvers points out that feminism 'addresses this connection with such intensity that it famously elides the personal with the political.'[19] Women with ink make an artistic statement unavailable to men. The female fleshy canvas participates in a distinct category of art, creating its own feminist aesthetic. The tattooed woman says, 'You want to look at my body? I'll give you something to look at!' Like other feminist artists, she asserts agency, directing the gaze according to her will.

Gadamer's Hermeneutics and Tattoos: Play, Festival, and Symbol

'Hermeneutics' is the study of interpretation theory (either as 'art of' or 'theory and practice of' interpretation), and 'hermeneutical aesthetics' focuses on human experience and interpretation of art. As the *Stanford Encyclopedia of Philosophy* so eloquently puts it:

> Hermeneutical aesthetics regards aesthetic appearance not as a distraction from the real, but as the vehicle through which real subject matters reveal themselves. It over-turns the notion that art works are at one remove from reality. Hermeneutical aesthetics is dialogical in character. It recognizes that practitioner and theoretician share in bringing a subject matter to light and plays down any theory/practice division in the arts. Interpretation is a means to a work's realization.[20]

We think that hermeneutical and feminist aesthetics share a common goal in that both seek to account for modern forms of art that traditional aesthetics leaves behind, for example the body art of tattoos. However, hermeneutical aesthetics can account for value beyond the scope of feminist aesthetics altogether because it explains why tattoos are valuable and outlines the significant role tattoos have in advancing the art-historical narrative.

Hans-Georg Gadamer (1900–2002) put forward one of the most developed hermeneutical philosophical methods in Western philosophy, and his aesthetics offers a deconstruction of the traditional philosophy of art and beauty, as well as the construction of a theory that wishes to focus on the cognitive ways in which we experience art and the meanings we come away with when encountering art.[21] For Gadamer, something worthy of being deemed 'art' has the power to say something directly to us: art addresses us and makes a claim. This claim can be shock, surprise, anger, excitement, or joy – any emotion we are capable of feeling. The experience of art is an experience of meaning, one that can only come about through and with understanding, and the relationship we have with art is ongoing and deep. One is never a disinterested onlooker when approached by art; instead, one is deeply affected and has a dialogue with the work in which understanding is constantly renegotiated. The deeply invested involvement we have with art is demonstrated by three analogies in Gadamer's work: play, festival, and symbol.

Art as play

Art puts something into play: a witness to art (e.g., an audience member at a drama play) shares a similarity with sport spectators in that they are both immersed, drawn into something bigger than what is simply presented to consciousness. To be immersed in something is to surrender to it, to be caught up in it. Comparing art to a game also serves to show that:

1 Traditional views that ground the interpretation of art in the artist's own subjectivity are inappropriate and do not reveal what goes on in the subjectivity of the viewer;
2 Art is not understood with sole reference to the equipment, tools, methods, or medium – it is more than that; and
3 Like a game, art requires an appreciation of the rules or conventions, but its lifeblood is not solely in those rules or conventions.

In short, art cannot be reduced to intention, materials, or conventions.

Now, taking this into consideration, we think Gadamer would agree that tattoos are properly works of art for the following two reasons. First, a tattoo's beauty cannot be reduced to intention, materials, or conventions. A tattoo is more than the ink, more than the needle, and more than the intentions of the artist or the wearer. As much as a well-placed, well-sized, well-executed tattoo can make the skin on which it appears more enticing, the tattoo's beauty cannot be *purely reduced* to the skin it is within or the fact it appears within skin at all.

Second, tattoos do make a claim on the person who witnesses them, and this claim can be any range of emotions, from shock or outrage to joy or erotic stimulation. The experience of a tattoo is one of meaning, and often there are various meanings discovered that relate to one's own experiences, cultural background, or taste. The quality of the meaning you walk away with after experiencing a tattoo has as much to do with what you bring to the table. When one sees a tattoo, the first moment is often taken up by figuring out what it is of and the second moment by trying to figure out what it means (i.e., what it says in itself and of the person it is on); then one feels a judgment of quality or taste. Another moment of deep investment is felt when you find the tattoo makes you want to know more about the person wearing it: What does it mean to them? Did they create it or find it? How was their experience of being tattooed? And so on. From this, we see the dialogical nature of tattoos, and in fact this can go from an inner dialogue (and the work of art) to an outer dialogue with the other person (i.e., we see a sense of community and connection with others).

Art as festival

As much as art has a very intimate, individuating aspect, it is also a way in which the witness to art participates in something beyond themselves, something communal. The individual comes to stand in a relationship with others, united in a shared interest in what the work has to say. People forget the everyday trials and tribulations of their individual lives to come together in the experience of art, and this once again speaks to its power. The analogy of festival also reveals a horizon of meanings: Art's communicative capacity brings about the realization that, in as much as I understand art making its claim on me personally, I must acknowledge that I already belong to something larger than myself – I am indebted to past and to future communities of meaning. The meanings present have been there before me, and new ones will eventually come about after me. This is what Gadamer calls the 'hermeneutic collective.'

There are a few ways in which tattoos exhibit the festival. First, tattooed people and tattoo artists often form a community among themselves, to share in the experience and the significance of tattoos and celebrate all things tattooed. Once you get a tattoo, you join that community and running across someone else who is tattooed becomes a moment of shared experience: You share in the feelings about getting tattooed, you share in the appreciation of the image and the craft, and you share the meanings involved for you both personally. Sometimes we even see portions of society gathering to dislike or shun tattooed people – a darker sense of community but a community nonetheless, coming together to respond to the claim made by art.

Second, in getting a tattoo you realize that you are part of something larger than yourself. In one sense, this is in the fact that tattoo is an art form that has been around for a long time, in different cultures and for different purposes – there are many different reasons for getting tattooed. Tattoo has a history. In another sense, you recognize that the meanings bound up in tattoo images are horizontal: you know that each image had some meaning before, that it has a meaning now, and that a new meaning will evolve. A tattooed person also knows that their tattoo can change meanings as they travel into different nations, cultures, age groups, or races. A great example concerns Russian prison tattoos, which have a specific meaning and status in Russia and yet in the West are exotic and culturally different. Traveling around Canada with Russian prison tattoos would be a completely different experience than traveling around Russia or Ukraine. In recognizing these things about tattoos, you realize that you are a part of a collective, sometimes even more than one.

Art as symbol

On this subject Gadamer begins with some Greek, speaking to the origins of the word 'symbol' (σύμβολον, *sýmbolon*) as a token of remembrance. A 'symbol' was an object broken into two pieces, with one piece given to the house guest in the hopes that later the two pieces could be re-joined in an act of recognition – recognition of something known to the people involved. It is a fragmentary promise of completeness (wholeness) at a future moment, which has an abundance of meaning. Symbols are speculative in this way. The symbol also does not refer to something outside itself; rather, it presents its own meaning, and an indeterminate one at that. This is another side to its connection with speculation – any statement pertaining to the meaning of a symbol brings forth more than is actually spoken. As Nicholas Davey puts it in the *Stanford Philosophical Encyclopedia*:

> The 'speculative' capacity of an image or word concerns its ability to sound out or insinuate the unstated nexus of meanings which sustain a given expression but which are not directly given in it. The speculative power of an image or phrase has something in common with the sublime: it illuminates in the spoken or visual image a penumbra of unstated meanings whose presence can be sensed but never fully grasped or conceptualized.[22]

Hence, a work of art is never fully exhausted by the symbols that carry it, but does not exist apart from those who or that which sustain it. The symbol resonates with suggestions of meanings, and at the same time we are also presented with the notion that not all is given to us. There is an excess of meaning in an artwork, and simultaneously there is the promise of more meaning, and the promise of there being other meanings.

An artwork is not reducible to its history, or to its situation within a movement or genre. Its meaning is not immediately apparent to us and is impossible to fully interpret, and yet we turn to art in search of significance, something that completes the puzzle of our lives or existence. The point to be gained here is that, while art is symbolic, it does not stand for something else, or for some hidden impersonal meaning that needs to be explained. Art as symbol involves an act of self-recognition, in which we approach it seeking to understand ourselves.

Tattoos are symbols in this very sense, and like art tattoos are excessively filled with meaning and bring the promise of more to come. The promise of completeness or full understanding is felt when you have the urge to ask the person what the tattoo means to them, and even after you get the answer the meaning for yourself is never exhausted. Tattoos are also sublime in that their meanings are never fully fixed or determined, and this is true whether the tattoo is an image or script. When we gaze upon a tattoo, we do so in self-reflection – whether in admiration, inspiration, shock, or disgust – but all roads lead to self-reflection. Some people admire the art and dream of similar things for themselves, while others realize or reaffirm that tattoos are not for them. Either way, self-reflection is involved and what is sought is a better understanding of ourselves through the work of art on the skin before us.

Art Cannot Change the World, but it Can Influence Those Who Will

As these wise words painted on the wall of a tattoo shop[23] suggest, tattoos themselves may not change the world but the 'mobile art gallery' sitting beside you on the bus just might. We can laugh at Carlin's humor because it uses irony to reveal a social and aesthetic injustice, one that continues today (albeit to a lesser degree): Tattoo body art, as much as it should be considered beautiful art for reasons we have argued here, remains unaccepted by traditional and mainstream aesthetics. However, tattoos and the artists who create them have the power to change the art world and the conventions that surround it. They can also reveal to us new levels of meaning and experience, and novel ways in which we can come together as a community. So, we can laugh with Carlin and celebrate tattoos as artwork, but let's keep the beautiful tattooed dead bodies out of the museum.

KIMBERLY BALTZER-JARAY AND TANYA RODRIGUEZ

NOTES

1 George Carlin, 'Tattoos,' *The Little David Years Volume 7, 1971–1977* (New York: Atlantic Records, 1999), disc 7, no. 2.

2 Besides Thomas Adajian, 'The definition of art,' in Edward N. Zalta (ed.), *Stanford Encyclopedia of Philosophy* (Fall 2009, http://plato.stanford.edu/entries/art-definition), good introductions to aesthetics include Cynthia Freeland, *But Is It Art? An Introduction to Art Theory* (Oxford: Oxford University Press, 2002); Matthew Kieran (ed.), *Contemporary Debates in Aesthetics and the Philosophy of Art* (Oxford: Blackwell, 2005); Stephen Davies, *The Philosophy of Art* (Oxford: Blackwell, 2006); and Cynthia Freeland, *Art Theory: A Very Short Introduction* (Oxford: Oxford University Press, 2007).

3 See, for example, the accounts and analyses put forward in Grant Pooke and Diana Newall, *Art History: The Basics* (New York: Routledge, 2008). Also, scholars such as Clement Greenberg have helped the world to understand and appreciate artwork that at first blush has struck people as bizarre or distasteful; see Clement Greenberg, 'Modernist painting,' in Francis Frascina and Charles Harrison (eds.), *Modern Art and Modernism: A Critical Anthology* (London: Harper & Row, 1982), pp. 5–10.

4 James Shelley, 'The concept of the aesthetic,' in Edward N. Zalta (ed.), *Stanford Encyclopedia of Philosophy* (Fall 2009, http://plato.stanford.edu/archives/fall2009/entries/aesthetic-concept).

5 Ibid. Key works include Clive Bell, *Art* (New York: Capricorn Books, 1958) and Greenberg, 'Modernist painting.'

6 Carolyn Korsmeyer, 'Feminist aesthetics,' in Edward N. Zalta (ed.), *Stanford Encyclopedia of Philosophy* (Fall 2009, http://plato.stanford.edu/archives/fall2008/entries/feminism-aesthetics).

7 Ibid.

8 Most notably, Maurice Merleau-Ponty. For an overview, see Jean-Philippe Deranty, 'Existentialist aesthetics,' in Edward N. Zalta (ed.), *Stanford Encyclopedia of Philosophy* (Fall 2009, http://plato.stanford.edu/archives/fall2009/entries/aesthetics-existentialist).

9 Ibid.

10 Thalia Gouma-Peterson and Patricia Mathews, 'The feminist critique of art history,' *The Art Bulletin* 69, 3 (1987): 340.

11 Ibid.

12 George Dickie, 'The institutional theory of art,' in Noel Carroll (ed.), *Theories of Art Today* (Madison, WI: University of Wisconsin Press, 2000), p. 93.

13 Arthur Danto, 'The artworld,' *The Journal of Philosophy* 61, 19 (October, 1964): 580. For more on the institutional theory/art world approach, see ARE TATTOOS ART?(Chapter 3).

14 'No matter how feminists may try to harness women's craft production into an arena of significance, the very vocabulary of modernism is exclusive of

the conditions of production, reception, and distribution and the incumbent meanings of the majority of women's made images/objects in the past' (Tamar Garb, 'Engaging embroidery': A review of Parker, *The Subversive Stitch in Art History*, *The Art Bulletin* 69, 3 (September, 1987): 131).

15 Carolyn Korsmeyer, *Gender and Aesthetics: An Introduction* (New York: Routledge, 2004), p. 119.

16 See *The Guerrilla Girls' Bedside Companion to the History of Western Art* (New York: Penguin Books, 1998). The Guerrilla Girls explain, 'Asked to design a billboard for the Public Art Fund in New York, we welcomed the chance to do something that would appeal to a general audience. One Sunday morning we conducted a "weenie count" at the Metropolitan Museum of Art in New York, comparing the number of nude males to nude females in the artworks on display.' The result? 'Less than 5% of the artists hanging in the Modern and Contemporary Sections of New York's Metropolitan Museum of Art were women, but 85% of the nudes were female.' And things are not getting better: see http://www.guerrillagirls.com/posters/venicewallf.shtml.

17 William Ian Miller, 'Upward contempt.' *Political Theory* 23, 3 (1995): 476–499.

18 Iris Marion Young, *On Female Body Experience: 'Throwing Like a Girl' and Other Essays* (Malden, MA: Oxford University Press, 2005), p. 39.

19 Anita Silvers, 'Feminism: An overview,' in Michael Kelly (ed.), *Encyclopedia of Aesthetics*, vol. 2 (Oxford: Oxford University Press, 2007), pp. 161–167.

20 Nicholas Davey, 'Gadamer's aesthetics,' in Edward N. Zalta (ed.), *Stanford Encyclopedia of Philosophy* (Fall 2009, http://plato.stanford.edu/entries/gadamer-aesthetics).

21 Hans-Georg Gadamer, *Truth and Method*, 2nd ed., trans. Joel Weinsheimer and Donald G. Marshall (New York: Continuum, 2003).

22 Davey, 'Gadamer's aesthetics.'

23 This phrase is painted on the wall of Nighthawk Tattoo & Gallery in Guelph, Ontario, Canada.

THE TATTOOED WOMAN

'Both tattooing and feminism elicit powerful emotional responses, often in the forms of hasty judgments about a person's moral character ... for the uninitiated or simply ignorant, it is far easier to deny the tattooed person or feminist (as well as the tattooed feminist!) human complexity than to actually excavate the contradictory cultural circumstances that make tattooed women possible, especially given the stigmas they faced a century or even half a century ago'

(Nancy Kang, p. 66)

CHAPTER 5

FEMALE TATTOOS AND GRAFFITI

A New Tattoo Space

Tattoos are no longer just for bikers, sailors, and criminals; they have become acceptable for the educated and professional middle class. In the past, tattoo spheres could be located within the margins of society, and, once an identity had been assumed through the adoption of a tattoo, the person could be assigned a particular geographical position within an urban sphere. In this chapter, I argue that contemporary female tattoos no longer have this one-dimensional identifying function. Interestingly, in 1991 women made up almost half of those persons who got tattooed.[1] To support my argument regarding female tattoos, in this chapter I also show there is a new 'tattoo space' in which the skin need not necessarily bear the stigmatic mark, nor need it function as a screen of male desire. In fact, the tattooed skin becomes a wall on which multiple thoughts and desires are projected; in this sense, tattoos have become graffiti.

The Savage and Civilization

First, it is necessary to disentangle two notions that have been used in order to characterize tattoos in society – those of the 'savage' and the

Tattoos – Philosophy for Everyone: I Ink, Therefore I Am, First Edition.
Edited by Robert Arp.
© 2012 John Wiley & Sons, Inc. Published 2012 by John Wiley & Sons, Inc.

'civilized.' Historically, in many cultures tattoos have been read through a paradoxical scheme that opposes the 'primitive' to civilization, and simultaneously – but for reverse reasons – nature to culture. Very often, the tattooed body has been called primitive because it has been held to be incompatible with intrinsic standards of civilization. When this is done, curiously, these standards are defended by reference to nature. Christine Braunberger summarizes the situation with regard to female tattoos as they are seen in contemporary industrialized countries: 'When a woman's body is nature, a tattooed woman's body is primitive.'[2]

If something is primitive, it usually means that it is against civilization. This then begs the question as to whether the primitive – being removed from civilization – is not actually *closer* to nature, instead of being against it. Mark Taylor interprets the primitivism that is supposed to be responsible for tattooed bodies as the 'infantile state of humanity.'[3] So, almost by definition, this infantile state is closer to nature. Braunberger's claim in the above paragraph remains paradoxical to the core. However often we turn it around, the opposition of nature – which is presented here as compatible with civilization – to the primitive remains puzzling. The non-tattooed body is praised for its naturalness, held to be highly compatible with civilization, while tattoos are said to refer to a non-natural sort of primitive pre-civilization.

Why does a civilization consider tattoos to be apart from itself, declaring them to be inappropriate on the grounds of their unnaturalness? And why would a civilization put forward arguments regarding *nature* as the main reasons why tattoos should be rejected?

Taylor correctly states that 'for those who believe in the rationality and morality of modernity, history represents a steady march from uncivilized barbarism to cultivated refinement.'[4] Still, this does not explain why those who believe in rationality and morality cannot accept tattoos as signifiers of cultivated refinement. There are many reasons to interpret a tattoo – in and of itself – as being part of a civilizing process. Tattoos alter nature and resist time as they create lasting marks on the body that defy aging. Tattoos also signify commitment. In contemporary civilization, the body is more and more 'caught in the expectation that it should constantly be modified and reformed through diets, aerobics, plastic surgery and fashion.'[5] Here tattoos can re-establish the body as a concrete, stable, and reassuring human condition and provide authenticity where identities become increasingly disposable. Tattoos fulfill many functions that *could* make them eligible as catalysts of civilization. Still, tattoos are said to be 'against civilization,' paradoxically *because* they alter nature.

In a somewhat convoluted way, their search for permanence and commitment is interpreted as a 'lack of discipline and self-control, of an inability to consider the future.'[6]

In reality, the rejection of tattoos is not caused by a fear of pre-civilized primitivism. The primitive represents rather the mystifying substitute for a fear that is typical of upward-striving classes. For these classes, the tattooed body is not necessarily primitive but is intrinsically linked to the culture of the lower classes. Historically, in Western (but also most Asian) societies, tattoos were associated with the culture of the working class and to that of bikers, sailors, and the underworld.[7] Originally, having a tattoo meant to be stigmatized, and in most East Asian societies a certain degree of stigmatization is still present.[8]

Nothing Ladylike About Being Tattooed?

Unfortunately, all this remains unconsidered when it comes to contemporary evaluations of the tattooed body. The ensuing vagueness leads to a considerable amount of confusion that has become particularly palpable since the recent tattoo wave beginning in the early 1990s, which has turned tattoos into fashion items. What adds to the complexity is the fact that this new fashion has made tattoos more acceptable for women. Were this fashion to concern men only, it could easily be explained as a renewed search for masculine 'coolness.' As mentioned, in most of the world's cultures, tattoos have had a bad reputation. However, in the case of men, the aesthetic play either with stigmas or the voluntary forfeit of a large amount of social approval is much more acceptable. Tattoos have always been dominated by masculine aesthetics and the concept of male coolness has most often included the playful refusal of social recognition, while for women there is 'nothing ladylike about being tattooed.'[9] Female tattooed bodies could even be read as 'criminal trespasses into the masculine, their inky digressions a secret language stolen from men.'[10] However, in reality, female tattoos are much more than an imitation of male tattoos; they, in fact, create a new aesthetic category.

In the case of women, the ideology that superposes the scheme 'civilization versus nature' with the scheme 'civilization versus the primitive' brings forth a very specific claim concerning the meaning of the natural: in a modern, bourgeois context, naturalness equates to 'purity.' The advantage of purity as a concept is that it can function as an attribute of both nature and civilization, which becomes clear in De Mello's statement that the female body is 'inviolate, too pure to be disfigured.'[11] A concept of purity intrinsic to non-civilized nature is here silently transferred to the realm of the *civilized* female body, thus turning purity into an attribute of civilization. This is how smoothness, for example, became a feminine privilege – a smoothness that Jean Baudrillard suggests is on par with castration! Baudrillard points out that the male body 'can never really become a smooth, closed and perfect object since it is stamped with the "true" mark.'[12]

The 'standards of acceptable beauty for women still dictate unblemished skin.'[13] Both the natural male and the natural female body have been idealized, but male shifts toward the 'non-natural' as well as toward the 'primitive' do not have to face charges of purity. Though women have been using makeup and jewelry for centuries, for a long time only men had the right to decorate themselves with tattoos. While women have been allowed to undergo aesthetic surgery and receive silicone implants with relatively little public outcry, the only sanctioned way for men to transform their bodies was through the application of tattoos.

Purity is a central notion because tattoos are all about the skin. Diets and plastic surgery might destabilize the metaphorical power of the body more than tattoos, but they do not interfere with the body's purity. In the first place, female tattoos are not a matter of decoration or body transformation, but instead they concern the symbolic purity that is important for the economy of male desire. Baudrillard states that there is 'something incredibly powerful about the blank, perfectly made-up face of the living doll. She is the void we rush to fill with our own dreams and desires.'[14] This means that the female body-screen is supposed to *reflect* male desire; that is, to desire *because* she (or her skin) is desired. The woman is the recipient of male desire and her sexual pleasure is constructed around her objectification by a male.

Here, the subject of tattoos becomes clearly distinct from that of modern primitivism as a parallel subcultural movement that employs other means of body modifications such as piercing and flesh hanging. These movements refer to 'indigenous practices as alternatives to Western culture, which is perceived as alienated from the body's spiritual, sexual, and communal potential.'[15] Ironically, the less extreme forms of such body modifications have been found much more acceptable by mainstream society than female tattoos. I would argue that the reason is that piercing does not corrupt the imperative of purity and the symbolizing

THORSTEN BOTZ-BORNSTEIN

quality of female skin. Most piercings resemble a sort of jewelry affixed to the skin. Tattoos, on the other hand, are similar to writings and their inscribing power can be conceived as much more polluting.

Ornaments, Crimes, and the Creation of a Feminine Tattoo Space

Consider the proverbial war cry issued by the Austrian architect, Adolf Loos (1870–1933), at the beginning of the twentieth century against pre-modern ornamentalists. It was based on the assumption that cultural evolution is synonymous with removing decoration from utilitarian objects, as well as persons: 'if someone who is tattooed dies in freedom, then he does so a few years before he would have committed murder.'[16] The tendency to identify crimes with ornament was common during Loos' times and cultivated in 'natural history, medicine, criminal anthropology and architectural and aesthetic theory.'[17] The 'ornament and crime' theme went hand in hand with Darwin's theory of the savage's passion for tattoos[18] leading to the generally accepted conclusion that ornaments would most probably follow evolutionary patterns of development. Loos' concept that 'one can measure the culture of a country by the degree to which its lavatory walls are daubed'[19] is not original, but was almost commonplace at the peak of modernity. More original is Loos' inference from the primitive state of tattoos to the particularly vicious connotation of *female* tattoos. He states that 'in the final analysis women's ornament goes back to the savage, it has erotic significance.'[20]

It is interesting to note that Loos' ideas are still influential for people nowadays who automatically and inappropriately jump to the conclusion that tattoos and the morally challenged go hand in hand. Despite what Loos has claimed, the contemporary tattoo renaissance implies that women empower themselves, which in return implies that women have the right to decide *themselves* what is erotic and what is not. Women who choose to have tattoos don't reject the male gaze (they might even encourage it), but they refuse to receive an erotic mark from the hands of male fantasy. These women draw the mark in their own fashion, thus potentially alienating male desire. The result of such post-feminist behavior is the paradoxical combination of 'both radical and conservative, real and unreal, feminist and feminine' values that can let the woman appear as 'slave and master, victim and perpetrator.'[21]

The current fashion for feminine tattoos has changed the idea of the tattoo itself. For centuries, tattoos have served 'to make the amorphous self into something certain, strong, unchanging'[22] and even today they are often erroneously presented as marks of commitment. According to Donald Richie, 'tattoos are able to reduce the world to a firmly opposed series of rights and wrongs'[23] and 'a man who is fully tattooed is stable, unchanging. He has solidified his own skin and become that solid object, that permanent identity that all men in fear of the amorphous become.'[24] The post-modern female tattoo does not establish identities, but destroys conventional female identities such as 'neatness, diligence, appliance, femininity, [and] passivity'[25] without replacing them with something more precise than 'more feminine, sexual' ideologies.

Feminine tattoos allow for the emergence of an alternative space in which not only right and wrong but also purity, desire, and the self adopt a new, ambiguous status. In other words, what is in question is no longer the provocative or demarcating affirmation of a position *within* a given social space but the *creation of a space* dependent on more female priorities. Some analysts have recognized this spatial function. Margo DeMello claims that the task of tattoos is 'to revitalize modern North American society – to change the world by changing its body.'[26] Tattoos reclaim a feminist, but also a more erotic, space in a world where sexuality is rationalized and commercialized. According to Florence Boodiakian, 'eroticism is close to and almost extinct in certain Western cultures, and especially in the United States of America. The current political and social climate can't sustain it.'[27] The new erotic space cannot be established through the re-establishment of a resisting, pure, and modernist nude, but instead depends on complicated spatial devices, which, in turn, seem to depend on tattoos.

From Tattoos to Graffiti

Tattoos have become a spatial project in the largest sense. In the past, (predominantly male) tattoo spheres could be located within the margins of society. Once an identity had been assumed through the adoption of a tattoo, the person could be assigned a particular geographical position within an urban sphere. When women received tattoos from men, they would usually be *identified* as belonging to the same space. Contemporary female tattoos no longer have this one-dimensional identifying function,

THORSTEN BOTZ-BORNSTEIN

which influences the way in which these tattoos create space. Within the new tattoo space, the skin does not wear the stigmatic *mark*, nor does it function as a screen of male desire, but it becomes a wall on which multiple desires are projected. In this sense, tattoos have become graffiti.

According to Mindy Frenske, tattoos have not simply shifted 'from the practice of desecration to one of decoration'[28] but have evolved from an interesting mark into a body decoration that remains 'indifferent' in the sense that it does not establish a clearly demarcated symbolic space. This does not mean that post-modern tattooing does not include the use of strong symbols; on the contrary, the symbols are even stronger than before. However, these tattoos are no longer perceived by society as a spectacle or a show disclosing a vertically determined symbolic meaning. They are simply *looked at* in passing, establishing a half-abstract and half-concrete space. Because the symbolizing power and the expression of desire of these tattoos are complex, their spatial economy has shifted to a horizontal level. While conventional (predominantly male) tattoos tended to create a social sect or a caste, female body-graffiti creates an environment.

Like tattoos, graffiti inscriptions are narratives of the self, but they are inscribed in a spatial dimension, which makes their identity more abstract. Both tattoos and graffiti are 'savage' writings that establish identity in a world of anonymity, but in the case of graffiti a partial conservation of anonymity is part of the concept. While the conventional tattoos tend to establish a ghetto-space providing feelings of community and belonging, graffiti tends to be expansive, as it screams 'I don't respect your boundaries – textual or spatial.'[29] Graffiti is a form of communication that permits communication through specific use of jargon and symbols not only between members of a community but also within urban space in general. According to Victoria Carrington, all graffiti poses the 'interesting philosophical question, where private property begins and where it ends and where the public area begins.'[30] This means that graffiti is not merely tattoos drawn on walls attempting to draw attention to the materiality of the body they occupy. It is, instead, more that the being of graffiti is involved with the spatiality of the city.

Most of the time, graffiti is put where it is not supposed to be. The wall does not change its being *because* it has received graffiti but it has to 'cope' with it. This is what signifies the shift from tattoo to graffiti. Instead of identifying its bearer through the tattoo (postulating that all tattoo bearers are criminals, savages, and so on), the post-modern tattoo involves the bearer in a more complex social game through which she has to define her identity within a social space. This is why both graffiti and post-modern female tattoos 'can be read as an important textual practice that ties individual and communities in a complex dance around identity, power and belonging.'[31]

Most analyses of tattoos still cling to the symbolic order of the tattoo, just like classical psychoanalytical interpretations of dreams used to insist that dreams must be seen as a consecution of symbolic expressions. For these analysts, the space of the tattoo is represented by a tattoo-covered skin area whose symbolic power needs to be traced. The tattoo 'invests the incised region in tactile and sensory terms, marking it as a special, significant bodily site, eroticizing the region,' writes Elizabeth Grosz.[32] What is lacking in these interpretations is the depiction of a 'tattooscape' (just like psychoanalysis rarely talks about a dreamscape) that sees tattoos as aesthetic expressions able to create space. The mere decoding of symbols has been useful for conventional tattoos; however, the shift to the spatial dimension brought about by the new type of graffiti-like tattoos implies that any commitment found in tattoos needs to be seen through perspective. In space, perspectives are constantly changing; there is no absolute signifying message. Grosz believes that tattoos 'create not a map of the body but the body precisely as a map.'[33] The body is not an object used by individual consciousness but is always actively involved in the world. The tattooed body (just like any body) creates human space because it is able to resume both space and time in itself. When the body wears tattoos that are more complex than simple symbols, it becomes a historical phenomenon, linked to the history of the place by creating it.

Skinscape

For this reason, a word such as 'skinscape' could become more prominent. De Mello insists that, for tattooed women, the body is 'a temple to be decorated.'[34] Architectural metaphors like this are telling because they demonstrate how the skin has adopted the spatial function of a wall. Compared to skin, walls are indifferent and disperse symbolizing meanings in a spatial fashion. The effect of graffiti is very different from that of branding. Tattoos corrupt the smoothness of the skin while graffiti leaves the walls as smooth as ever. Skin desires, while walls don't desire anything. Contrary to the *tattooed* body, the

THORSTEN BOTZ-BORNSTEIN

graffiti-invested body is neither a material object nor a center of perception, but becomes, in a very Bergsonian sense, a spatial 'center of action.'[35] Everything works toward spatial dispersion rather than toward symbolic concentration.

What also disappears in body graffiti is the binary opposition of the civilized non-tattooed subject to the tattooed savage. It becomes untenable to assume that a non-tattooed subject whose cultural value is too complex, significant, and intimate to be announced on the skin is superior to the subject wearing all relevant information about her person on her skin in the form of a mark.

Tattoos become spatial, which means that they become more playful and less serious. Walls containing graffiti are neither decorated nor branded. They instead undergo a process of spatial reanimation through inscriptions. Graffiti involves walls in an urbanistic game where persisting architectural symbolisms are destroyed by creating new spatial environments. Baudrillard says that 'by tattooing walls, SUPERSEX and SUPERCOOL free [those walls] from architecture and turn them once again into living, social matter, into the moving body of the city before it has been branded with functions and institutions.'[36] The city shifts from official geography to the organically urban. Likewise, the body shifts from a merely biological function to that of a historical being.

Recuperating the Political Body

The skinscaping of the body through tattoos has unexpected consequences. Like graffiti, the contemporary tattooed body 'challenges notions of consumption-driven public space'[37] and forms a 'counterpoint to commercialization of the city and its public space via the use of particular forms of text.'[38] Like graffiti, the tattooed body is 'shouting to be recognized against the dehumanizing forces of modern city life.'[39] While all forms of body transformation position 'the body as a site of exploration as well as a space needing to be reclaimed from culture,'[40] body graffiti does not merely attempt to 'rescue the body and the self from the problems of the modern world,'[41] but also attempts to modify urban space.

Interestingly, through this mechanism the female body becomes again a political body. The female tattooed body doesn't accept the moral imperatives derived from the sphere of advertisements and athletics, which increasingly transforms bodies into non-political, self-sufficient egos. It becomes political in the way in which bodies have been political in the past. Examples include the naked body of the 1920s, which had been submitted to an ideology of modernism; the totalitarian athletic body of the Nazis, which was submitted to racial politics; and the absolutely clothed body, which was once submitted to the imperatives of the Christian Church.

The female tattooed body sticks out in the post-modern body landscape, which almost exclusively employs neutral and post-political bodies. The realms in which both the male and the female body are featured most of the time are those of advertisements and of athletics. Here the body is post-political because it is predominantly commercial and its politically symbolic meaning has been reduced to almost nothing. This goes hand in hand with the general tendency of commercials and athletics, which have reduced the world to *images* that deprive the body of its spatial dimension by reducing it to an object whose aesthetic aspect can be freely fashioned. The tattooed female body, conversely, creates its own space that depends neither on universal laws nor on rules valid only within a presumed tattoo ghetto. The tattooed female body escapes the post-political replacement of the body with the symbolizing ego (or the projection of another symbolizing ego) by rethinking the body as a spatial phenomenon.

In the contemporary world, all of this concerns female tattoos much more than male ones. Female tattoos are prone to creating their own 'tattoo sphere' because they have an incorporated spatial function dependent on an interesting circular pattern. Generally speaking, while male tattoos are macho, female tattoos don't refer to a firm signifying substance but simply to *themselves*. As a consequence, the symbolizing process of the female tattoo works in the service of women's own economy of thought, will, and/or desire.

NOTES

1 Myrna Armstrong, 'Career-oriented women with tattoos,' *Image: Journal of Nursing Scholarship* 23 (1991): 215–220.
2 Christine Braunberger, 'Revolting bodies: The monster beauty of tattooed women,' *The National Women's Studies Journal* 12 (2000): 2.
3 Mark Taylor, 'Skinscapes,' in Richard Serra (ed.), *Pierced Hearts and True Love: A Century of Drawings for Tattoos* (New York: Hardy Marks Publications, 1995), p. 31.

4   Ibid.

5   Paul James and Freya Carkeek, 'This abstract body: From embodied symbolism to techno-disembodiment,' in David Holmes (ed.), *Virtual Politics. Identity and Community in Cyberspace* (Thousand Oaks, CA: Sage, 1997), p. 117.

6   Margo DeMello, *Bodies of Inscription: A Cultural History of the Modern Tattoo Community* (Durham, NC: Duke University Press, 2000), p. 140.

7   See Steve Gilbert, *The Tattoo History Source Book* (New York: Juno Books, 2000).

8   For more on this topic, see IS A TATTOO A SIGN OF IMPIETY? (Chapter 17).

9   Silja Talvi, 'Marked for life: Tattoos and the redefinition of self,' in Ophire Edut (ed.), *Body Outlaws: Young Women Write About Body Image and Identity* (Seattle, WA: Seal Press, 2000), p. 212.

10 Braunberger, 'Revolting bodies,' p. 4.

11 DeMello, *Bodies of Inscription*, p. 140.

12 Jean Baudrillard, *Symbolic Exchange and Death* (Thousand Oaks, CA: Sage, 1993), p. 104.

13 Talvi, 'Marked for life,' p. 212.

14 Jean Baudrillard, *De la Séduction* (Paris: Gallilée, 1979), p. 81.

15 Victoria Pitts, *In the Flesh: The Cultural Politics of Body Modification* (Gordonsville, VA: Palgrave Macmillian, 2003), p. 8.

16 Ibid.

17 Jimena Canales and Andrew Herscher, 'Criminal skins: Tattoos and modern architecture in the work of Adolf Loos,' *Architectural History* 48 (2005): 235–256, 251.

18 Charles Darwin, *The Descent of Man* (Amherst, NY: Prometheus Books, 2007 [1871]), p. 606.

19 Adolf Loos, 'Ornament und Verbrechen,' in *Sämtliche Schriften* (Vienna: Herold, 1924), pp. 276–288.

20 Adolf Loos, 'Ornament und Erziehung,' in *Wohnungskultur* (Vienna: Herold), pp. 2–3, 81.

21 Susan Hopkins, *Girl Heroes: The New Force in Popular Culture* (Annandale, Australia: Pluto Press, 2002), pp. 6, 44.

22 Donald Richie, *The Japanese Tattoo* (New York, Tokyo: Weatherhill, 1980), p. 65.

23 Ibid.

24 Ibid., p. 68.

25 DeMello, *Bodies of Inscription*, p. 173.

26 Ibid., p. 3.

27 Florence Dee Boodiakian, *Resisting Nudities: Study in the Aesthetics of Eroticism* (New York: Peter Lang, 2008), p. 49.

28 Mindy Frenske, *Tattoos in American Visual Culture* (New York: Palgrave Macmillian, 2007), p. 56.

29 Victoria Carrington, 'I write, therefore I am: Texts in the city,' *Visual Communication* 8, 4 (2009): 409–425, 418.

30 Ibid., p. 417.

31 Ibid., p. 419.

32 Elisabeth Grosz, *Volatile Bodies: Towards a Corporeal Feminism* (Bloomington, IN: Indiana University Press, 1994), p. 218, note 9.

33 Ibid., p. 139.

34 DeMello, *Bodies of Inscription*, p. 93.

35 Henri Bergson (1859–1941) called a living being a 'center of action.' See the first chapter of his *Time and Free Will: An Essay on the Immediate Data of Consciousness* (London: George Allen and Co., Ltd., 1913).

36 Baudrillard, *Symbolic Exchange and Death*, p. 82.

37 Carrington, 'I write, therefore I am,' p. 420.

38 Ibid., p. 417.

39 Ibid.

40 Pitts, *In the Flesh*, p. 7.

41 Ibid.

NANCY KANG

CHAPTER 6

PAINTED FETTERS

Tattooing as Feminist Liberation

Getting Under Her Skin

Popular portrayals of feminism often use simple, sensational terms such as 'man-haters,' 'penis-enviers,' or 'closet lesbians' to depict proponents of this 'f-word.' These misogynistic stereotypes and attitudes fundamentally overlook the diversity and complexity of feminist history and philosophy. Feminism in the West may be characterized as a series of intertwined roots that connect women as well as men across class, racial, and gender lines. They also traverse sexual, regional, national, and generational identities, complicating political allegiances all around. The ground in which these roots are embedded is probably best described as *oppression*; that is, the economic and social suffering that results from the assumption that women are inferior and don't deserve equal treatment as men. Justifications are many; the most common tend to be by reason of lack (*not enough* physical, intellectual, spiritual, or metaphysical power) or surplus (*too much* emotion, sexual passion, fertility, willfulness, or confidence, among others). As a result, most feminists will agree that women don't enjoy equal treatment with men on a global scale.

Tattoos – Philosophy for Everyone: I Ink, Therefore I Am, First Edition.
Edited by Robert Arp.
© 2012 John Wiley & Sons, Inc. Published 2012 by John Wiley & Sons, Inc.

This inequality, both individual and collective, has a long intellectual history. Aristotle (384–322 BCE), for instance, was dismissive of women's moral capacities, declaring that a 'rational soul' did not function in them, leaving them challenged by any issue that required either ethical sense or self-control. His discussion in *Politics* placed women in the intellectual company of slaves and children, clearly below men.[1] Alternatively, as one of the earliest liberal feminist philosophers in the Western tradition, John Stuart Mill (1806–1873) advocated for both slaves' and women's rights. *The Subjection of Women* (1869) underscored the necessity of men's participation in the dismantling of glaringly hierarchical power structures, particularly those that sanctioned the denial of equal access to education and necessitated women's submission in marriage. Such strictures kept women socially disenfranchised, economically dependent, and sequestered in largely domestic roles.[2] Being called the 'weaker' or 'inferior' sex may have been countered by poetic descriptions such as 'angels in the house,' 'terrestrial goddesses,' or the 'fairer sex,' but the outcome was the same: men still held the power to define women. This is a form of cultural *hegemony*, or what Marxist philosopher Antonio Gramsci (1891–1937) defined as the way those in power create and reiterate an image of society that is supposed to be natural or universal but ends up benefiting themselves, the ruling class. Certain tactics may be violent and directly coercive, while others are subtle and conveyed through clever, if specious, rhetoric; for instance, 'you must cover up your body art not for us but for *yourself*, for your own protection and feminine integrity.'

Both tattooing and feminism elicit powerful emotional responses, often in the forms of hasty judgments about a person's moral character. Many tend to associate each of these with extremes – extreme lifestyles, extreme communities, extreme ideologies – and for the uninitiated or simply ignorant it is far easier to deny the tattooed person or feminist (as well as the tattooed feminist!) human complexity than to actually excavate the contradictory cultural circumstances that make tattooed women possible, especially given the stigmas they faced a century or even half a century ago. Tattoos, as any history of the art form will relate, were popularized in Europe and later North America after colonization in the South Pacific, while three waves of (still-evolving) Western feminism have worked to erode the long-standing pillars of exclusionary social privilege: sexism, racism, classism, and homophobia. Fans of tattoos have not had an equal fight in terms of gaining acceptance for the medium as a widely legitimized form of personal and collective expression. While sailors and servicemen may have acquired tattoos as unique decorations and as badges of pride during the eighteenth and nineteenth centuries, tattooing has long suggested the gritty carnival exhibit, the uncouth working class, and the odd rituals of the criminally deviant. Later, when tattooing was embraced by the post-1970s middle class, this apparent democratization neutralized many of these stigmas, but negative connotations remain, particularly for women.[3]

What this chapter illuminates is the tattoo's place in a liberatory (that is, freedom-seeking) feminist ideology. Instead of diminishing femininity, tattoos can actually *accentuate* and *amplify* it by pointing out the differential treatment between tattooed men and women. This impasse makes room for negotiating various feminist concerns about tattooed women's hypervisibility (hence vulnerability to criticism) and the overall body consciousness issues that strike feminists as detrimental to women's self-esteem. Tattoos on women create a *hermeneutic* (meaning-producing) impasse whereby the viewer has to not only question the identity of the tattooed person (asking 'Why that tattoo?' 'What kind of person is that?' or 'What story lies behind that image?') but also confront her/his own reading practice based on gender norms and stereotypes. As Mindy Fenske points out, tattoos make the body an 'aesthetic and visual event,' acting as a 'productive metaphor' for the practice of visual analysis itself.[4] By forcing interpreters to be aware of gender and sexual difference, tattoos are richly compatible with contemporary feminist philosophy, particularly the branch of radical feminism called 'corporealism,' which places the utmost value and analytical emphasis on women being able to make choices about their own bodies.

Revolutionary Politics and Feminist Body Consciousness

Feminism has numerous theoretical schools, and not every feminist can claim the same degree of adherence to any given philosophical or social principle.[5] For instance, a straight white feminist may have a different view of inclusive marriage than a black lesbian separatist. Let's briefly discuss radical feminism, Marxist feminism, liberal feminism, and corporeal feminism within the context of tattoos.

One of *radical feminism*'s common premises is a commitment to revolutionary practice, usually dependent on grassroots activism rather than top-down, hierarchal administration.[6] As Charlotte Bunch explains, radical feminism needs to be accessible, and, as such, espouses that any activist philosophy is problematic if it enables complacency and the status quo as a result of people not understanding its tenets.[7] Vitally important is individual *agency*, or the understanding that every woman can be – or become – capable of action, despite her differences from a majority (here, the male majority). The woman as agent is someone with revolutionary potential both on her own and as part of the larger group. Granted, not every woman is empowered in the same way, and oppression is not a monolithic, trans-historically unchanging phenomenon. What exactly does a revolution imply? Could participating in a march on Washington to protest abortion legislation, the publication of a feminist autobiography by a small publishing house, or deciding to get a visible tattoo when (or where) 'nice' girls wouldn't count as examples of revolution? Possibly.

Radical feminism focuses upon and even elevates the physical selfhood as a tool for critical analysis and personal enjoyment. A body-centered consciousness facilitates active contestation against sexist forces that seek to dictate how women should behave, look, and feel. The strongest of these is *patriarchy*, or a belief in the dominance and supremacy of men. Radical feminists view self-love, acceptance, trust, and confidence as imperative values because women's bodies have rarely been their sole jurisdiction; even today, contentious debates arise when addressing reproduction and reproductive technology (birth control, fertility treatments, abortion, same-sex couples adopting, and surrogate motherhood); sexuality (choices about marriage or civil union, legal parameters for partnerships, types of partners, abstinence and celibacy, public disclosure or displays of sexuality, and the traumas of rape, incest, and sexual abuse); media representations of women's bodies (usually the dichotomy between ideal and real women, and how discrepancies should be remedied, often through rigorous campaigns and lobbying); and varieties of body consciousness (artistic, religious, spiritual, and political orientations that emerge through miscellaneous physical acts such as performance art, dance, fasting, self-mutilation, plastic surgery, and personal hygiene).

Marxist feminists are most invested in tracing, and eventually overturning, the economic bases of oppression that keep working women exploited in the labor market, while *liberal feminists* seek to include women in traditionally male occupations as proof of similar if not equal capacities. Both of these cases are activisms writ large. *Corporeal feminists* tend to view revolution as the accumulation of small-scale acts of resistance, with the female body as something to be appreciated, differentiated, and

NANCY KANG

celebrated, often without the approval or even presence of men.[8] Tattooing can be one such action because it acknowledges the body as a place not only for others to exert control but also where self-control emerges. To exercise one's own will over the body, especially in light of risks to health, professional reputation, or personal relationships, is a revolutionary act precisely because it *is* risky. Overall, then, corporeal feminism espouses a specific understanding that the body is integral if not sacred to women and ideally to the men in their lives as well. Every body, in other words, is somebody.

Homosociality Skinship Bonding, and Corporeal Feminism

One aspect of tattooing's migration to the West has been its use as a signifier of social class, professional ties, and community affiliation. Most often, sailors, soldiers, working-class people, prison inmates, and gang members (usually street or biker) have been the poster boys for tattooing culture. 'Poster boys' is the operative term here because so many of these groups have been or remain *homosocial*, meaning that they comprise people of the same sex (here, male), which creates and facilitates particular types of gender-inclusive bonding and communication. The solidarity is often cemented by homogenizing rituals, among them familiar expressions and in-group references, gestures, costumes or uniforms, ideologies (including sexism and misogyny), and material status symbols.

Another manifestation of homosociality is what I call 'skinship,' or particular individualized visual expressions on the body, such as tattoos. A pun on 'skin,' 'kin,' and 'friendship,' skinship can be exclusionary of women by reiterating their outsider status. Females have been traditionally barred from participation in many professionally determined homosocial groups, or they have been subordinated or treated differently if included. Homosocial groups, while not always consciously sexist, often work to the exclusion of sexual and gender outsiders.[9]

Now, corporeal feminists will contend that it is up to women to create their own skinship bonds. Many traditionally male institutions and occupations, for instance, have become more inclusive after the civil rights movements of the late 1960s, but the road to access has not been smooth and continues to be contentious for feminists of all kinds.

Cultural anthropologist Maria DeMello points out that, before the popularization of tattoos in the late twentieth century, women were more often the *subject* of tattoos than the bearers. Emblazoned on men's arms, backs, thighs, and chests were names of girlfriends and mothers as well as images of toothsome hula dancers, cowgirls, bikini pin-up models, ethnic stereotypes (such as Native princesses and geishas), or simply voluptuous naked ladies.[10] A corporeal feminist would notice the irony of 'in-corporation' here (with *corps* the Latin term for 'body'): through the engraving of the image in the skin, the woman literally becomes part of the body. She is commissioned, designed, overseen, and literally 'made flesh' by him and by his contact/contract with the tattooist. It is the exercise of an almost Adamic power, recalling the biblical story where the first woman, Eve, can only be divinely created through the body and desires of the prototypical human, Adam. In many ways, this kind of objectifying tattooing may be argued away as a tribute or celebration of women, yet their role in empowering men may not be mutually satisfying.

Meeting Narrative Needs

Historically, tattoos have not always been incompatible with femininity, nor have women been excluded from the cultural history of mandatory or recreational body modification. Polynesian cultures, which catalyzed the rise of tattooing through European imperialism and other geopolitical migrations, did not prohibit women from participation in the practice, especially because they were integral to the family systems associated with these kinds of bodily inscriptions.[11] It is precisely a *supplementary gender bias* that has made Western women more prone to being criticized for having tattoos, which is why feminism and tattooing elicit dialogue about differences *within* difference. Women, like gay or working-class men, often feel the need to narrate their stories of tattooing in concert with their experiences of marginalization. Being affiliated through tattoos with homosocial, male-dominated professions may be a point of pride for some women, yet tattooed individuals of both sexes still find themselves engaged in justifications about why they have tattoos in the first place.

Media such as Paul Haggis' film *Crash* (2004) have often served as platforms for evaluating the social hermeneutics of tattoos, or how their function as symbols changes through the mediation of popular culture in diverse environments. In this Oscar-winning film, a middle-class white woman (played by Sandra Bullock) expresses suspicions about her Latino maintenance worker's integrity after seeing his arm and neck tattoos; in actuality, rather than a gangbanger or ex-con, he is a loving and hardworking family man.[12] This revelation reminds us of the 'appearance versus reality' binary so prevalent in ontological discussions about difference. It also recalls the tendency by many to use tattoos as a premise for *ad hominem* attacks against the wearer, underscoring how tattoos elicit misconceptions as if they were a kind of 'second skin.' In a movie intimately attuned to the problem of prejudice against skin color, Haggis skillfully intertwines racism and classism into the stigma of visible bodywork.

Similarly, Darren Aronofsky's psychological dance thriller *Black Swan* (2010), very much a commentary on the archetype of the doubled self, presents the sensuous black swan character as a tattooed person, someone diametrically opposed to the straight-laced, perfectionist lead.[13] The black swan may be named Lily (evoking delicacy and whiteness) but her raciness, heightened by associations with recreational drugs, alcohol, casual sex, West Coast liberalism, and possible lesbianism, finds renewed expression in her large back tattoo. It is a stark contrast to the hysterical reserve of the main character, the non-tattooed – but still deeply scarred – white swan, Nina. As her name implies (*niña* in Spanish means 'child'), the main character remains very much an immature and un-self-certain subject, whereas her other self, Lily, is an adult who ends up surviving a *danse macabre*, perhaps justifying her massive tattoo and all of its connotations of toughness, permanence, and transcendence.

Pricks as Needles

While a tattooed man may evoke a range of excitingly ambiguous associations – social menace, seductive criminality, sexual risk, proximity to danger, adventurous worldliness, raw narcissism, and hyper-masculinity – the meanings are different for women. Females are still supposed to be 'everything nice,' as we recall the Mother Goose nursery rhyme that asks and answers the question 'What are little girls made of?' Radical feminism would argue that the resistance to tattooed women comes from the patriarchal assumption that the environments and experiences associated with tattooing are not an appropriate domain for women. In the nineteenth century, this paradigm was called the 'ideology of separate spheres': women belonged in the home, men outside of it. The 'bad girl' archetype in *Black Swan* highlights how popular culture has targeted and maintained the tattooed female as a suspicious person, a marked (wo)man morally as well as epidermally. Visible ink is a new kind of scarlet letter, or, in this case, a painted fetter.

The idea of tattooed women as sexually promiscuous or deviant remains an enduring misogynist stereotype. Certainly, some women appreciate the connotations of kinkiness, self-confidence, and verve that their tattoos may evoke, and from a feminist perspective that welcomes sexual diversity this can definitely be empowering. At the same time, critics of tattooing have historically ascribed sexual meanings to tattooing that are skewed against women. With the ink gun as a kind of trans-dermal phallic substitute, the actual act of being inked has become synonymous with illicit sex. As Albert Perry postulates in *Tattoo: Secrets of a Strange Art Practiced by the Natives of the United States* (1933), 'There are the long, sharp needles. There is the liquid poured into the pricked skin. There are the two participants of the act, one active, the other passive. There is curious marriage of pleasure and pain.'[14] Clearly, by this logic, a tattoo enthusiast must be a 'strange' person, a fan of sex or a crude masochist. Perry attempts to mitigate the illicit nature of the transaction by mentioning the subduing, balancing effect of 'marriage.'

The irony here is that Perry equates the tattooed person with being passive and feminine, while the tattooer is active and masculine. This is a fallacious model in the literal sense because the woman, as customer, may actually be the more active participant; she dictates the terms of her aesthetic transformation and initiates the contact as a paying customer. This exchange is physical and even deeply intimate, but it is a business exchange, not a sexual one. Similarly, why would it not be feminine to wield the tattoo gun? Could the recipient of the 'curious … pleasure and pain' not also be male? Granted, not all tattooists *are* male (although during the early to mid-twentieth century, most were), nor are all recipients female. By placing the woman in the passive recipient role, essentially the vessel for male artistic and sexual prowess, Perry's analogy acutely captures the relationship of proprietorship and surveillance that characterized women seeking tattoos from the 1950s to the 1970s.[15]

NANCY KANG

Odd Girls Out

A radical feminist would criticize Perry's reading as both sexist and highly *heteronormative*; it assumes that heterosexuality is the normal and necessary way of partnering two people, either sexually or in marriage. By catering to this image, the author acts to quell the anxieties aroused by the pleasure/pain paradox and the dangerous sexuality evoked by the tattoo encounter. The union of male and female forces in tattooed 'marriage' is historically limited and exclusionary. Tattooing has had a long history in the LGBT community, particularly with lesbians in the 1950s. Often, they were not subject to the same degree of patronizing infantilization, surveillance, discipline, and overall coercive control of their bodies that straight, middle-class, and usually white women faced. Given Perry's portrayal of the passive tattooed female, conservatives believed that any straight woman interested in tattoos must have been led astray by some wild impulse or negative influence such as a corrupting boyfriend or immoral friends. Lesbianism and abnormality were, at the time, more or less synonymous (given the former's criminalization in many states), so tattoos and lesbians were quite the logical pairing. What these critics did not grasp was that tattoos were becoming a sign of pride – indeed, a ticket to legitimacy within those excluded and stigmatized communities.

Lesbians embracing tattoos as self-expression did not have the same accountability to parents, boyfriends, and husbands that straight women did; as Samuel Steward reflects, during the 1940s and 1950s, the procedure prior to tattooing a woman might have been to ascertain that she was at least twenty-one years old (with documentation), married (again with written proof), or accompanied by her spouse to the actual appointment. Lesbians, as 'lost cases,' didn't require a male to hover around them as moral or epidermal gatekeepers.[16] Also, while they might be seen today as anti-establishment, many male tattoo artists of post-war America found themselves acting *in loco parentis*, deterring a woman from being tattooed even if it meant losing business.[17] The profit motive was displaced by an ethics of sexual guardianship. Such supposedly professional measures on the part of these tattooists/tabooists reflected an ironic reality for women at the time: even the personal choice of a tattoo required male permission. Lesbians, whose difference frustrated that McCarthy era's desire for manageable, acceptable, sexually contained womanhood, were trespassers into the predominantly male sphere of the early tattooing underground. They were doubly marginalized as 'odd women out' who evoked fear and derision from the society at large as well as the tattooing vanguard. Many tattoo enthusiasts today forget that the genealogy of tattooing as homosexual expression has a much longer history than a red AIDS ribbon or Keith Haring figure across a chest during a mid-summer Pride parade.

'By the Father's Hand': The Tattoo Taboo, Public Anxiety, and India(n) Ink

Given that people satisfied with one tattoo may acquire more over time, each moment of acquisition is accompanied by a set of motivations and circumstances that the wearer often wishes to *narrativize* (that is, weave into a story that can be shared with others). Tattoo narratives are also platforms where gender difference emerges. Women's stories, whether or not they have anything to do with tattoos, have traditionally not received the same critical attention as those by and about males.[18] The dispersal of tattoos on individual bodies – and then more widely throughout the body politic – mirrors the spread of public anxieties about the moral corruption caused by this 'deviant' art. The later twentieth century ushered in fears of AIDS and hepatitis from dirty needles and other unsanitary body modification tools, but biological contagion is just one concern that has affected how some detractors portray tattoos as a cultural threat.

One example was the often-racist narratives adopted by early tattoo celebrities in the United States, among them the famous Prince Constantine and other carnival and circus regulars. These personalities described being forcibly tattooed by indigenous peoples, usually after unlawful capture by these 'heathens' and 'cannibals.' Assumed to be alien in looks, intelligence, and sensibilities to the Euro-American majority, these Native peoples were portrayed as wholly un-American. As such, they wielded the needle and ink as readily as other weapons of murder and mayhem. Furthering the association of tattooing with savagery, the Native peoples' artistic assaults against defenseless white men and women were portrayed as nothing short of rape or amputation. The moral panic that ensued from forced tattooing seemed to justify large nationalistic projects such as colonization, enslavement, or even genocide.[19]

We see here how the body represents a territory to be fought over and claimed; forced tattooing foreshadowed the Natives' threat of (re)claiming their lands and livelihoods. Yet these strategic narratives persisted; by contrasting themselves with these ill-favored groups, the tattooed individuals appeared quite civilized, thereby bringing themselves back into the fold of acceptability while maintaining their uniqueness as heroes and survivors. The sheen of adventure attached to the tattooed person if his or her narrative was memorable, and many of these were certainly crowd pleasers. We might even allege that the fear of contamination by ink also allegorized the threat of racial mixing, which often arose with the popularization of a literary genre called Indian captivity tales. This phobia of being 'marked,' 'stained,' and symbolically 'indigenized' became heightened when women were the prisoners. They were thus exposed to the pricks and needles of all sorts of dangerous and unfamiliar men.

The exotic narratives reached a crescendo when tattooed women such as Irene Woodward, Nora Hildebrandt, Artoria Gibbons, and later Betty Broadbent started entering the scene through expeditions and carnivals in the late nineteenth and early twentieth centuries.[20] Here, men were the veteran survivors, but women posed strong competition. Not only were they sensational for showing skin on their legs and thighs (infrequent in the tight-laced Victorian era) but they also were very popular because of the novelty attached to seeing females who had survived the outrageous assaults. With women entering (sometimes against their will) into the predominantly male arena of imperial conquest, the forced tattoo narratives were fraught with sexual undertones, a strong selling point for those who fetishized white women's then-untouchable status vis-à-vis non-white men. The paradox here was that, although these tattooed females were arguably 'tainted' or even emasculated (rendered masculine) through their body art, they profited from making money from their bodies while maintaining an image of carefully constructed respectability.

Vivacious Betty Broadbent was apotheosized as the 'Tattooed Venus,' while Irene Woodward's narrative stressed: 'The lady ... is not offensive to any one, no matter how sensitive they may be. Her tattooing is of itself a beautiful dress.'[21] Many such women had tattoos that displayed 'honorable' subjects such as love of nation, fidelity to family, nature, popular sayings and proverbs, moral themes (liberty, safety, mercy, love), or religious faith. Woodward was described by the *Sunday Mercury* as being 'a marvel of punctured pictures,' as her body art did not detract from, but rather enhanced, 'delicate features and perfect form.'[22] *Truth* magazine called its article on her 'Tattooed Femininity' and praised her 'fair white skin'; the narrative itself, *Facts Relating to Irene Woodward, the Tattooed Lady*, repeatedly evokes her skin color and even gushes about the contrast of dark ink against the 'heaven of white skin.'[23]

Woodward's is an intriguing case for feminist critique: her 1886 promotional pamphlet describes her as her father's child, raised in a single-parent household with a brother, no mother, and a covered wagon as a home. Much of the text revolves around the unnamed father, a former sailor. Feminist readers will smirk at the logic of how it is because he is 'a most loving one' that he marks his child's flesh from the ages of six to twelve. His motivation? Self-interest, as the narrative explains: 'In constant dread that she would be stolen from him, he commenced at an early age to tattoo her. His own flesh was punctured by the aid of the needle.'[24] Clearly, he claims her body as his property, not unlike a contract signed in ink, an extension of his own flesh and something that must not be stolen *from him*. There are other ways for a parent to show love; as a child of 'early age,' she probably did not have any choice in the matter, although we learn later that, allegedly, 'In spite of the pain, the girl was delighted, and coaxed her father to continue.'[25] *Truth* magazine surmises, 'The girl must have gone through a terrible ordeal.'[26] Not only does her father forbid her from questioning him about his past, but she also remains ignorant about her own particulars, including her place of birth and mother's name.[27] He also 'implant[s]' his own interests into her skin as if she were a blank canvas, adding stars and flowers, an American eagle, angels, sailor's scenes, and robust mottos such as 'Never Despair' and 'Nothing without labor.'[28] The narrative stresses that only after her father and brother died did Woodward pursue profit through self-display; evidently, a self-respecting woman should not do so without the permission of her male keepers.

The Skin She's In: Keeping Tattooing Personal and Political

Tattooed women who traveled the show circuit profited from their exposed yet covered bodies, many surpassing their male counterparts through the sale of handbills, cards, photos, and stories.[29] Even today, women's motivations for getting tattoos may differ remarkably from men's, although not always irreconcilably. Generally, women's tattoos commemorate a healing journey, offer tangible reminders after extremely positive or negative events, signify bonding and community affiliation, or simply convey personal truths.[30] Broadbent, Woodward, and their inked sisters were anomalies in their time, but were acceptable to the extent that they remained in the minority and could be corralled into comprehensible spaces without unduly 'offending' public opinion. Tattooed women today still face prejudice to degrees different from most men, but not necessarily in relation to sexual morality; some just find tattoos too permanent a commitment in an age of fast-shifting trends and prescriptions for physical attractiveness.

In 2010, American audiences were captivated by the juxtaposition of the heavily tattooed model Michelle 'Bombshell' McGee and the aforementioned actress Sandra Bullock, wife of the philandering celebrity mechanic Jesse James.[31] McGee's prodigious tattoos, coupled with her penchant for skimpy outfits, ostentatious makeup, and unapologetic self-promotion, created a public relations package that was the antithesis of the professional and likeable persona projected by Bullock. Put bluntly, McGee was the 'trashy' to the wronged wife's 'classy.' Later, when James – himself much-tattooed and photographed delighting in Nazi paraphernalia and narcissistic posturing – became engaged to tattoo celebrity Kat Von D a short time after his divorce, the public perceptions of the male adulterer were displaced and re-placed onto these two tattooed women. Because McGee and Von D shared a penchant for ink, these tattoos became synonymous with all the negative associations attached to 'other women,' 'rebounds,' and 'home wreckers.' Being tattooed meant subscribing to a *carpe diem*-type hedonism; ignorance of social graces such as restraint, conscientiousness, and modesty; a gleeful indifference to public perception; and a danger to stable couples everywhere. Their tattoos became emblematic of their lack of shame, and, indeed, were literal *marks* of shame that deepened alongside the public's disapproval.

This anecdote reminds us that it is a feminist imperative to question, deconstruct, and critique any bias against women based on physical appearance. Ien Ang declares that gender identity today is 'multiple and partial, ambiguous and incoherent, permanently in process of being articulated, disarticulated and rearticulated.'[32] Her fluid model underscores how women *and* men find themselves in a matrix of changing representational demands, primarily from popular media. Whether to opt for a highly conspicuous image and where to place it are no longer the sole questions that arise when a woman contemplates being tattooed; any major visual statement is a subversion of social expectations and a way of shifting the power from the outside lens to the inside perspective. We might recall the case of Midwestern professor Natalie Kusz's choice to pierce her nose at thirty despite being one-eyed, overweight, and already out of place in her conservative college town. Having been ridiculed for her appearance all her life, the Alaska native declares, 'I have now, after all, deliberately chosen a "facial flaw," a remarkable aspect of appearance. Somehow now, the glances of strangers seem less invasive, nothing to incite me to nunhood.' She explains how, like any artificial addition to the body that is noticeable and risky, she has 'invited it … made room for it, [such that] it is no longer inflicted upon [her] against [her] will.'[33] Women who choose tattooing, whether for self-love or to make a social statement, are deploying the same homeopathic strategy: they are etching, coloring, healing, and revealing themselves to a more vivid and potentially revolutionary existence.

NOTES

1 Aristotle, *Politics*, trans. T. Sinclair (London: Penguin, 1972), p. 52.
2 John Stuart Mill, *The Subjection of Women* (Boston, MA: MIT Press, 1970).
3 See Maria DeMello, *Bodies of Inscription: A Cultural History of the Modern Tattoo Community* (Durham, NC: Duke University Press, 2000).
4 Mindy Fenske, 'Introduction,' in *Picturing Tattoos* (New York: Palgrave Macmillan, 2007), p. 3.
5 To learn more about first-, second-, and third-wave feminist movements, see the articles on feminism in the *Stanford Encyclopedia of Philosophy*, including the entry by Sally Haslanger, Nancy Tuana, and Peg O'Connor entitled 'Topics in feminism' (http://plato.stanford.edu/entries/feminism-topics). See also Miranda Fricker and Jennifer Hornsby (eds.), *The Cambridge Companion to Feminism in Philosophy* (Cambridge: Cambridge University Press, 2000); Miriam Schneir (ed.), *Feminism: The Essential Historical Writings* (New York: Vintage, 2004); Miriam Schneir (ed.), *Feminism in Our Time: The Essential Writings, World War II to the Present* (New York: Vintage, 2004); Margaret Walters, *Feminism: A Very Short Introduction* (Oxford: Oxford University Press, 2006).
6 Chris Beasley, *What is Feminism? An Introduction to Feminist Theory* (London: Sage, 1999), p. 56.
7 Charlotte Bunch, 'Not by degrees: Feminist theory and education,' in Maggie Humm (ed.), *Modern Feminisms: Political, Literary, Cultural* (New York: Columbia University Press, 1992), pp. 171–174.
8 Ibid., p. 58.
9 See, for instance, Eve Kosofsky Sedgwick, *Between Men: English Literature and Male Homosocial Desire* (New York: Columbia University Press, 1985). I use 'sex' here to denote a biologically determined identity, while 'gender' is more fluid and socially constructed.

10 DeMello, *Bodies of Inscription*, p. 51.

11 See Adrienne Kaeppler, 'Hawaiian tattoo: A conjunction of genealogy and aesthetics' in Arnold Rubin (ed.), *Marks of Civilization* (Los Angeles, CA: Museum of Cultural History, University of California Press, 1988), pp. 157–170.

12 Paul Haggis and Bobby Moresco, *Crash*. Film. Directed by Paul Haggis (Los Angeles, CA: Lions Gate Films, 2004).

13 Mark Heyman, Andres Heinz, and John McLaughlin. *Black Swan*. Film. Directed by Darren Aronofsky (Los Angeles, CA: Fox Searchlight Pictures, 2010).

14 Albert Parry, *Tattoo: Secrets of a Strange Art Practiced by the Natives of the United States* (New York: Collier, 1971 [1933]), p. 71.

15 See Samuel Steward, *Bad Boys and Tough Tattoos: A Social History of the Tattoo with Gangs, Sailors, and Street-Corner Punks, 1950–1965* (New York: Harrington Park Press, 1990).

16 Ibid., p. 127.

17 DeMello, *Bodies of Inscription*, p. 61.

18 For an example of reading tattoos and the collision of masculine and feminine signifiers, see Mindy Fenske's discussion of feminist icon Rosie the Riveter in *Tattoos in American Visual Culture* (New York: Palgrave Macmillan, 2007). Feminist writers have illuminated gender bias in literary texts in such foundational works as Virginia Woolf's 1929 treatise *A Room of One's Own; and, Three Guineas*, ed. Morag Shiach (Oxford: Oxford University Press, 2008).

19 DeMello, *Bodies of Inscription*, p. 56. See also Robert Bogdan, *Freak Show* (Chicago, IL: University of Chicago Press, 1988). Some, like Nora Hildebrandt and John Rutherford, described Native American assault-by-tattoo; Irene Woodward, conversely, explains how her pre-existing tattoos protected her from Natives because of their fear and distaste of them.

20 See Judy Aurre, 'Meet Betty Broadbent.' *Tattoo Historian* 1 (1982): 21–23. See also Chris Wroblewski (ed.), *Tattooed Women* (New York: Carol Publishing, 1992).

21 Irene Woodward, *Facts Relating to Irene Woodward, the Tattooed Lady* (New York: Popular Publishing, 1942), p. 3. This description of the tattoos as 'a beautiful dress' may have been repeated in interviews because it appears in the pamphlet's central narrative as well as in venues such as *Sunday Mercury*, which are compiled in short form at the end of the publication.

22 Ibid., p. 11.

23 Ibid., pp. 2, 4, 6.

24 Ibid., p. 2.

25 Ibid.

26 Ibid., p. 8.

27 Ibid., p. 1.

28 Ibid., p. 4.

29 DeMello, *Bodies of Inscription*, pp. 58–59.

30 Tattoo meanings may be categorized as being *affiliative* (based on collective interests and group activities) or *isolative/individuating* (meant to convey individuality or serve simply as a personal decoration that brings pleasure to a person and her intimates). See Clinton R. Sanders and D. Angus Vail, *Customizing the Body – The Art and Culture of Tattooing* (Philadelphia, PA: Temple University Press, 2008), p. 59.

31 Michelle 'Bombshell' McGee actually endorsed this book. See the back cover.

32 Ien Ang, *Living Room Wars: Rethinking Media Audiences for a Postmodern World* (London: Routledge, 1996), p. 125. For more on reading female bodies from a post-structural perspective, see Stephanie Genz, *Postfemininities in Popular Culture* (New York: Palgrave, 2009).

33 Natalie Kusz, 'Ring leader,' in Quentin Miller (ed.), *The Generation of Ideas: A Thematic Reader* (Boston, MA: Thomson Wadsworth, 2005), pp. 328–331.

PERSONAL IDENTITY

'Just as the tattoo is integrated into the person's body, so too is the bearer a part of the work – if you take the person away, there is no tattoo. In a sense, the tattooed person gives life to the work, and just where the person ends and the tattoo begins is hard to determine'

(Rachel Falkenstern, p. 98)

CHAPTER 7

TATTOO YOU

Personal Identity in Ink

Questions of Identity[1]

Each of us has a birthday, and each of us will one day die: these truths obscure pressing questions about what and who we are. Are you the same person as that crying baby whose entry into the world you celebrate every year? Having suffered serious brain trauma in a car accident and now lying in a hospital bed hooked up to a ventilator, is it really the same you who stepped into the car this morning? When do you come into existence, and when do you cease to exist? Even if we can properly position the bookends of life and death, we still face problems in the middle: what is it to be someone, to have and to keep an identity?

Philosophical issues of personal identity are, well, personal.[2] They touch us all. Tattoos can also be extremely personal, and are frequently intimately associated with personal identity.[3] People regularly use tattoos to externalize some aspect of their inner lives, or as a way of marking or remembering significant events in their life histories. Crucially, tattoos – whether obtained voluntarily or not – persist with their bearers through time: permanent tattoos can endure until the end.

Tattoos – Philosophy for Everyone: I Ink, Therefore I Am, First Edition.
Edited by Robert Arp.
© 2012 John Wiley & Sons, Inc. Published 2012 by John Wiley & Sons, Inc.

In this chapter, we'll focus on two philosophical questions regarding personal identity, and explore the role that tattoos can play in responding to them. The first two sections of our chapter deal with the question 'What does it take for a person to maintain their identity over time?' Here we will argue that tattoos provide evidence for an account of personal identity based on bodily identity. The last two sections of our chapter deal with the question 'Who am I?' Here we will argue that tattoos can play a unique role in constructing identity-constituting narratives. We'll seek to show that the act of getting a tattoo – *and* the act of keeping it or removing it – has important implications for personal identity.

Personal Identity Across Time

The grandfather of the philosophical problems surrounding personal identity is the seventeenth-century British philosopher John Locke (1632–1704), who not only framed the debate itself but also the range of answers to it. As Harold Noonan writes: 'It has been said that all subsequent philosophy consists merely of footnotes to Plato. On this topic, at least, it can be truly said that all subsequent writing has consisted merely of footnotes to Locke.'[4] Locke's motivation for considering the problems of personal identity arose at least in part from ethical concerns.[5] Consider the following problems: Should a senile soldier be imprisoned for war crimes that he no longer remembers? Should a cat be punished for stealing food? Should Dr. Jekyll be held accountable for the murders committed by his alter ego, Mr. Hyde, and should Mr. Hyde be rewarded for the good deeds of Dr. Jekyll? By giving an account of personal identity, Locke hoped to untangle some of these ethical issues.

Before tackling what it is for a person to persist over time, Locke first asked 'What is a person?' For Locke, a person is 'a thinking intelligent being, that has reason and reflection, and can consider itself as itself, the same thinking thing, in different times and places.'[6] This immediately distinguishes being a person from being a member of the species *Homo sapiens*. The Lockean conception of personhood allows for human beings who are not persons, such as zygotes or brain-dead patients. Further, it allows for non-human persons such as Martians or disembodied ghosts (or, if you prefer, rational talking parrots).[7]

KYLE FRUH AND EMILY THOMAS

Bearing this conception of a person in mind, we will formulate the problem of personal identity over time. Imagine being presented with two photographs, each of which shows a mountain. In one of the photographs snow is falling, while in the other the sun is shining. One might ask, 'Are these two pictures of the *same* mountain, or are these two pictures of two different mountains?' If the photographs were of the same mountain at different times then the mountains would be *numerically identical* in the sense that there would be numerically one mountain. In contrast, if the photographs showed different mountains, then there would be numerically two mountains, regardless of whether they appeared to be *qualitatively identical* in the sense that they had indistinguishable contours.

This example can be modified to apply to people. Imagine being presented with two photographs, one showing a young brunette and the other showing an elderly, grey-haired lady. Despite the fact that people undergo more obvious changes than mountains – our bodies grow older and change in appearance, we acquire new memories and forget old ones, and we may suffer permanent injuries and scars – we still accept that the young lady and the elderly lady *may* be numerically identical. In other words, it is an open question as to whether the two photographs depict the same woman or whether they depict two different women.

Now imagine comparing the photograph of a young brunette to the reality of a brain-dead lady in an intensive care ward: is it possible that *these* two women are the same person? If so, then we must accept that a person at one time (i.e., the young brunette) can be numerically identical to a non-person (i.e., the brain-dead patient) at another time. We must be careful to leave this latter possibility open by not asking 'What makes one person numerically identical to another person?' but rather by formulating the problem of personal identity over time as follows: under what conditions is a person existing at one time numerically identical to some *thing* existing at another time?

Somatic and Psychological Accounts

Answers to the problem of personal identity over time fall roughly into one of two camps. *Somatic accounts* claim that a person is numerically identical to something else existing at a different time if and only if some material bodily relation holds between them, such as being the same body, biological organism, or animal. A tree changes over time – it grows larger, sheds its leaves and grows new ones, and wends its roots deeper into the ground – but we accept that a young sapling is numerically identical to an old oak tree because it is the same biological organism. Similarly, we accept that a puppy is numerically identical to a later dog because they are the same animal. On the somatic view, the persistence conditions for living organisms such as trees and dogs are akin to the persistence conditions for human beings. For example, Eric Olson argues that a person at one time is numerically identical to something else at another time if they are the same animal.[8]

Psychological accounts, conversely, claim that two people are numerically identical if and only if certain psychological relations hold between them, such as memories, desires, or beliefs. For example, Locke advocated a psychological account based on memory:

> Since consciousness always accompanies thinking, and it is that which makes every one to be what he calls self, and thereby distinguishes himself from all other thinking things, in this alone consists personal identity, i.e., the sameness of a rational being: and as far as this consciousness can be extended backwards to any past action or thought, so far reaches the identity of that person.[9]

Psychological accounts presuppose that a person cannot be identical with a non-person, because a non-person would not enjoy a psyche. One might think that this is an advantage of these accounts, as it entails that a person cannot be numerically identical to a zygote or a brain-dead patient. Nonetheless, these accounts allow for some other equally odd scenarios. For example, a severe case of multiple personality disorder – wherein a single human being develops distinct personalities, complete with distinct mentalities and memories – could be described as a literal case of multiple people inhabiting the same body. This might mean that Dr. Jekyll and Mr. Hyde are literally different people (which might lead one to think that Dr. Jekyll is genuinely innocent of the crimes committed by Mr. Hyde). Perhaps surprisingly, the number of contemporary philosophers advocating psychological accounts far outstrips the number of their somatic counterparts.[10]

Psychological accounts of personal identity enjoy popularity primarily because they appear to be supported by a number of thought experiments. For example, Locke claims that, although we ordinarily hold that a person's consciousness and his body go together, it is conceivable that they could come apart, such that the consciousness of a prince could enter the body of a cobbler. Locke argues that if the consciousness of the prince carried with it the memory of the prince's past life then everybody would see that the 'cobbler' was really the same person as the prince.[11] Contemporary versions of this 'body swapping' thought experiment consider the consequences of brain transplants, teletransportation, or uploading one's consciousness to a computer. The implication is always that, were someone's consciousness and memories transferred to a medium other than their original human bodies, we would still hold that we were confronted by the same person. This conclusion acts as a straightforward denial of the somatic account, which holds that one person is only the same as another if they share some relation involving sameness of body.

Tattoos and the Somatic Account

Despite the current unpopularity of somatic accounts, there are good reasons to endorse them. When identifying people in everyday life, we do so on the basis of their bodies. Common sense regularly supposes that I am identical to my body and, despite thought experiments to the contrary, it is unlikely that common sense will ever be directly proved wrong on this score. Further, we are generally very attached to our bodies. Not only do we feed them and exercise them and keep them healthy but we also allow them to represent our inner selves through demeanor and dress. Our bodies also represent clear causal links to our past. If a girl fell off her bicycle when she was a child, she might have not just the memory of the event but also the scarred knee to prove it. Tattoos are a peculiar phenomenon: they are, literally, scars filled with ink. Unlike the way we usually come by scars, most tattoos are acquired deliberately and voluntarily. The practice of tattooing stretches back thousands of years, occurs all over the world, and can be seen to add weight to the somatic account of personal identity.[12]

The fact that so many people feel so strongly about their tattoos is the first indication that we should take the somatic account more seriously. As an introduction to her argument in favor of the somatic account, Judith Thomson writes:

> I feel inclined to think that this fleshy object (my body is what I refer to) isn't something I currently inhabit: I feel inclined to think that it *is* me. This

bony object (my left hand is what I refer to) – isn't it literally a part of me? Certainly we all, at least at times, feel inclined to think that we are not merely embodied, but that we just, all simply, *are* our bodies.[13]

The intuition here is that, when you conceive of yourself as an 'I,' you identify yourself with your body. Your hands are not merely a part of your body that is somehow attached to your I – they *are* a part of *you*. Similarly, it seems that many people feel that their tattoos are not merely incidental attachments to themselves – unlike, for example, the way we feel about clothing or makeup – but are instead a literal part of their personal selves. For many, tattoos are not just a part of their body; they are a part of themselves.

This is supported by the way that, for many people, tattoos are strongly connected to personal identity. A lot of anthropological research has been conducted concerning the motivations behind acquiring tattoos, and two motivations are of particular interest here; these have been summed up neatly by Enid Schildkrout: 'body art creates identity for the individual and determines boundaries between groups.'[14] For example, Daniel Rosenblatt has studied the increasingly widespread practice of tattooing in contemporary American culture, and discusses how tattoos can be used as tools to indicate either individuality or subcultural membership.[15] Research into the first motivation (creating identity) tells us that many people acquire tattoos in an effort to distinguish their personal identity from that of others. Broadly speaking, all humans are born with very similar bodies – as members of the same species we all have roughly the same humanoid shape and physiological structure – and tattoos provide a way of straightforwardly bucking this similarity. People who acquire tattoos as a way of individuating themselves from the people around them are clearly associating their bodies with their personal identity.

The second motivation is the converse of the first, but the research into it is equally telling: many people acquire tattoos as a way of sublimating their individuality, to further integrate their identity into a bounded social group. The research shows that acquiring a tattoo can indicate one's membership of a community or subculture, such that a person willingly gives up some of their individuality to become an element of a larger whole. The fact that this second motivation is also very common is further evidence that many people associate their bodies with their sense of self.

The global popularity of tattooing, and the motivations behind it, indicate that we should not be so quick to dismiss the somatic account of

KYLE FRUH AND EMILY THOMAS

personal identity. The fact that so many people link their tattoos to their personal identity shows that Thomson is onto something when she claims that our bodies really are ourselves, not just something that is attached to ourselves. Despite the thought experiments that are supposed to rouse our intuitions against the claim that our personal identity is linked to our bodies, tattooing implies that, on the contrary, perhaps we *are* identical to our bodies. This means that a thirty-year-old tattooed woman could be numerically identical to a baby who existed twenty-nine years ago, and to the body of a brain-dead patient bearing the same tattoos some years hence. The practice of tattooing adds weight to an already intuitive account of personal identity.

Narrative Identity

Regardless of how one answers the question of personal identity over time, there is another question looming. How do we account for what it is that makes all the various moments of a life *feel like* a single life lived by a single, continuing subject? In other words, we turn now to the familiar and unsettling question, 'Who am I?'

The sense of identity at issue here is different from the sense of identity at stake in determining what it is to exist as the same person or organism over time. But change over time is still a relevant threat to our sense of identity at any given moment, since one thing you might be struggling with in asking who you are is reconciling seemingly incompatible aspects of your personal history. Are you the idealistic young person dedicated to service and equality, or are you the ambitious professional with the staggering bonus and accumulated piles of luxury goods? Who is the *real* you? The somatic and psychological views of numerical identity allow that you may change quite dramatically, even if only gradually, and as such hold that there is no puzzle about who you are in this case – there is no question of sameness between you now and the idealistic young person. What there is, undeniably, is qualitative change. The same numerical person has experienced changes in some of the characteristics she exhibits. But of course the problem of personal identity over time does not exhaust what we wonder about when we talk about personal identity. When your partner looks at you in horror and proclaims, 'I don't even know who you are anymore,' they are not expressing confusion about numerical identity over time.

What we have now entered is the different but related field of *narrative* identity. Just how theories and questions of narrative identity intersect and interact with questions and theories of numerical identity is a controversial matter. For our purposes, we'll take narrative identity to be a kind of supplement to numerical identity, a way of putting flesh on the bare bones of metaphysical persistence.

We undergo an astonishing amount of change: one can be at various times hairless or hirsute, self-absorbed or empathic, dexterous or uncoordinated, impassioned or apathetic, engaging or withdrawn. Even if we are assured that it is we who are changing (if we're sure that *we* don't cease and give way to someone merely similar), it can be hard to feel like that is so. It can also happen that, because you so strongly identify with your past, you can wake up as a person you don't identify with in the present, as we can imagine might happen to the young idealist mentioned above – can this be me? Have I really become this person?

Narrative identity is more or less the idea that we craft our own personal identities by understanding our histories in narrative form, as stories, certain elements of which we mark as especially significant aspects of who we are. We get to tell our own stories, but we aren't exactly authors – we don't just make up our lives unconstrained by the external world. Constructing our own narratives is thus an uneasy balance between having a say in determining who we are and how events in our lives ultimately inform the person we become, on the one hand, and the constraints on how we construct a narrative so that it is not sheer fantasy on the other. If our narratives feature us exercising utterly fictional superpowers then they will not be informative about, or constitutive of, our actual personal identities (except insofar as they demonstrate that we're charmingly delusional). There is also an uneasy tension between the limitations of self-understanding and first-person authority. In some cases, we may not be the best judges of what effect a given event has had on us – we may never admit to ourselves or even see how much of our life has been lived in reaction to particular events. Others may well be able to see it, and so our own narratives require checking against the stories others would compose of us. Further questions along this road concern the reach of narrative, and the conditions under which it is capable of grounding or comprising identity, and the reader is invited to pursue them.[16] But here we will instead pursue how tattoos can make a contribution to an identity-constituting narrative.

Tattoos of Anchors … and Anything Else as Anchors

Consider writing an autobiography intended to illuminate the person you are at the time of writing. You might pencil a lot of it in the first time around, and some of it might stay forever in pencil – such is the provisional nature of some of our features. But there are bits you would probably write in pen, or in permanent marker, even. Rather than pencil them in, you might well ink in some features that are or reflect an important piece of yourself, and that without which you simply could not be who you are. The nearly unique contribution tattoos can make to narrative identity follows this metaphor rather closely. Tattoos are a chance to ink in some feature of your identity, fixing a point through past, present, and future.

Even if it is conceptually possible for you to outlive your body – and it may not be, as we saw above – so far there's no compelling reason to think this ever happens. Generally speaking, your body will be around (at least) as long as you are, and so will the tattoos you've placed on it. Very little else is co-extensive with you in this way. Despite the myriad changes your tattoos undergo from inking to death, there is a durability about them that it is hard to find an analogue for in mental life. While it would be foolhardy to try to say anything true of all tattoos, here are two relevant functions they might have that seem relatively common.

First, they might prominently memorialize something from the past in a person's self-narrative, marking something, whether an event, a relationship, a characteristic, or whatever, as significant. Second, they are commonly aspirational – they might exert, through their prominence and permanence, an influence on how later events in the narrative can be interpreted and how the narrative should unfold, by expressing a strongly felt commitment. Many tattoos probably have both of these functions, in addition to others.[17] By playing these roles tattoos become capable of unifying disparate strands of a long life that includes many changes. What this suggests is that tattoos can have an *anchoring effect*. As years and miles add up, it becomes easy to feel adrift in your own life. A couple of anchors can keep you in touch with where you have been, commit you to being somewhere you want to be, and provide fixed points by reference to which to chart new voyages. This is the chief contribution tattoos can make to narrative personal identity, and one way of explaining how inking it can make you feel at home in your own skin.

It is true that some tattoos are frivolous, and some are regretted and removed. This is why we speak in terms of what tattoos *can* mean for narrative identity, and not of what they, as a matter of course, *do* or *must* mean. But, especially in the contemporary context, where more and more tattoo art is custom designed (which, perhaps ironically, renders copious flash of tattoo anchors less and less relevant), personal meaning is a commonplace attachment to ink, so it would not be unreasonable to surmise that the anchoring effect is something many actual tattoos do accomplish. And, while tattoo regret is not uncommon, some mistakes – or some choices we come to see as mistakes – may well be just as indispensable in our narratives as our successes. Some tattoos you might regret, in the sense that you would not choose to get them again, yet you might not remove them, because although they were mistakes they're the kind of mistake that becomes a non-eliminable part of your identity.[18] We should certainly concede that it is possible to get a tattoo that does none of this. But, for the most part, tattoos that are autonomously chosen, that carry a personal significance and that are not regretted, perform something that little else could: they at once carry something of the past into the present and project it into the future, both exerting an influence over the current interpretation of the narrative of the wearer's life and also affecting how that narrative unfolds and how its later events are to fit into the narrative and gain their meaning. They are mooring points in the formation of an answer to the question of who I am.

Consider forced tattoos, a practice inflicted, for example, on Jewish (and other) prisoners in Auschwitz. The prisoners were tattooed on their chests or forearms with identifying numbers.[19] The practice was deliberately dehumanizing. Acknowledging the anchoring effect is one way to articulate some (but clearly not all) of the horror: being tattooed against your will is like someone else forcing their pen onto the paper of your story, to replace you as the author of your own life. In this example, this is done even with the purpose of establishing something about what you are – a number, a resource. Of course, it's not possible to radically modify someone else's narrative self-understanding by fiat. The prisoners still had the power to see themselves as human beings, and to see themselves as the particular human beings they knew themselves as. But we are not invulnerable to outside influences, and one's own sense of oneself, both as a particular person and as a person at all, can be made fragile or broken.

The anchoring effect is largely achieved through a tattoo's permanence. Temporary tattoos clearly fail to accomplish anything similar as a result of their ephemerality, which prevents them from unifying temporally distant strands of narrative by anchoring the story in something fixed. Recently, a new kind of ink has become available that is permanent

KYLE FRUH AND EMILY THOMAS

in the sense that it will stay in your skin as long as you have that skin, but that is designed to be readily removable by laser treatment.[20] While traditional tattoos are sometimes removable by laser as well, the results are both more complete and much faster (and therefore less expensive and less painful) with this new kind of ink. This is a more subtle contrast to traditional permanent tattoos, which are permanent both in the sense that if left alone they'll last you a lifetime and also in the sense that you may not be able to get rid of them even if you want to. Traditional tattoos are both permanent and (relatively) irremovable. The new category of ink makes possible tattoos that are permanent but (more readily) removable.

So is it just the permanence of tattoos that makes them capable of anchoring narrative unity, or is it also their irremovability? Here we have uncovered a way of articulating some of the backlash against this innovation in ink. The traditional tattoo is a commitment, and the way it marks and shapes a narrative into the future is by being a very strong sort of commitment. To borrow a phrase famous from another philosophical context, it is a commitment 'come what may.'[21] This is the mark of the anchoring effect – no matter what happens, there is some particular feature of who I am that I won't lose track of. Come what may, I will always be this person. The commitment, in virtue of being permanent and irremovable, is also unconditional. The same cannot be said for removable tattoos. The commitment marked by removable tattoos is conditional, precisely on whether you later feel like getting it removed.

Now, it is true that tattoo regret has a traditional remedy short of removal, namely covering. But this is different from removal in an important way. Modifying a commitment to change its significance without removing or erasing it is rather more like most processes of learning and growth. Revisiting a tattoo and deciding to alter or cover it may change the way in which it anchors a sense of narrative unity, but not that it is an anchor. Removability – the prospect of pulling up anchor – implies the possibility of becoming adrift. The anchoring effect tattoos can have for personal narrative identity is diminished if they are removable.

When You Get a Tattoo, You Tattoo You

We've seen that the practice of tattooing has important implications for two of the most urgent questions about personal identity. Tattoos suggest that, contrary to the general philosophical consensus, we should account for our persistence over time via our bodies. Tattoos are also singularly well positioned to perform an anchoring effect in identity-constituting narratives. Getting a tattoo can express something about the role your body plays in determining how you persist over time and can act as an important step in the process of self-creation. When you get a tattoo, you tattoo you.

NOTES

1 The pictured tattoo belongs to Susan Ruether, friend to the authors.
2 Philosophical questions, issues, ideas, and arguments concerning the essential nature of persons and things, as well as the identity of persons and things through time, are found in the Western philosophical areas known as 'philosophy of identity' and 'philosophy of personhood,' which are disciplines under the umbrella of 'metaphysics.' See, for example, the relevant articles in Michael Loux and Dean Zimmerman (eds.), *The Oxford Handbook of Metaphysics* (Oxford: Oxford University Press, 2003). See also Harold Noonan, 'Identity,' in Edward N. Zalta (ed.), *Stanford Encyclopedia of Philosophy* (Fall 2009, http://plato.stanford.edu/entries/identity) and Eric T. Olson, 'Personal identity,' in Edward N. Zalta (ed.), *Stanford Encyclopedia of Philosophy* (Fall 2009, http://plato.stanford.edu/entries/identity-personal).
3 See the introduction to this book, where Rob Arp makes a similar point.
4 Harold Noonan, *Personal Identity* (London: Routledge, 1989), p. 30.
5 John Locke, *An Essay Concerning Human Understanding*, ed. John Yolton (Cambridge: Cambridge University Press, 1984). In this vein, Locke writes: 'how far the consciousness of past actions is annexed to any individual agent, so that another cannot possibly have it, will be hard for us to determine, till we know what kind of action it is that cannot be done without a reflex act of perception accompanying it' (Book II, 27:12).
6 Locke, *An Essay Concerning Human Understanding*, Book II, 27:9.
7 Locke was persuaded as to the existence of at least one 'very intelligent rational parrot' that lived in Brazil and could speak a number of languages. See Locke, *An Essay Concerning Human Understanding*, Book II, 27:8.
8 For further reading on the somatic account, see Eric Olson, *The Human Animal* (New York: Oxford University Press, 1997). See also Bernard Williams, *Problems of the Self* (Cambridge: Cambridge University Press, 1985) and Judith Thomson, 'People and their bodies,' in Jonathan Dancy (ed.), *Reading Parfit* (London: Blackwell, 1997), pp. 202–229.
9 Locke, *An Essay Concerning Human Understanding*, Book II, 27:9.
10 For further reading on the psychological account, see Derek Parfit, 'Personal identity,' *Philosophical Review* 80 (1971): 3–27; Noonan, *Personal Identity*; and Hud Hudson, *A Materialist Metaphysics of the Human Person* (Ithaca, NY: Cornell University Press, 2001).

11 Locke, *An Essay Concerning Human Understanding*, Book II, 27:15.

12 For an excellent overview of the global history of tattooing, see Enid Schildkrout, 'Inscribing the body,' *Annual Review of Anthropology* 33 (2004): 319–344.

13 Thomson, 'People and their bodies,' p. 202.

14 Schildkrout, 'Inscribing the body,' p. 328. For a good overview, see Silke Wohlrab, Jutta Stahl, and Peter Kappeler, 'Modifying the body: Motivations for getting tattooed and pierced,' *Body Image* 4 (2007): 87–95.

15 Daniel Rosenblatt, 'The antisocial skin: Structure, resistance, and 'modern primitive' – Adornment in the United States,' *Cultural Anthropology* 12 (1997): 287–334. For a study of the widespread practice of tattooing among convicts, examining how 'jailhouse' tattoos can help an inmate to feel both individual and part of a group, see Margo DeMello, 'The convict body,' *Anthropology Today* 9 (1993): 10–13. For an examination of the 'straight edge' movement in America – a youth movement that encourages clean living by, for example, abstaining from drugs and alcohol – and comments on the way in which many of the people involved obtain tattoos as a way of maintaining group identity, see Ross Haenfler, 'Collective identity in the Straight Edge movement: How diffuse movements foster commitment, encourage individualized participation, and promote cultural change,' *The Sociological Quarterly* 45 (2004): 785–805.

16 A good place to start is Marya Schechtman, *The Constitution of Selves* (Ithaca, NY: Cornell University Press, 1996). See also Bernard Williams, *Philosophy as a Humanistic Discipline* (Princeton, NJ: Princeton University Press, 2006), pp. 57–64.

17 In addition to the above references, see Jeff Johnson, *Tattoo Machine* (New York, NY: Spiegel and Grau, 2009).

18 Editor's note: This is how I (Rob Arp) feel about my tattoos, at times.

19 For example, see the United States Holocaust Memorial Museum at http://www.ushmm.org.

20 See http://www.infinitink.com for details, contact, and availability information. In the text, we assume that the ink is as advertised; this may not be true (it may be inferior to traditional tattoo ink in any number of ways, some of which would bear on durability). If that is the case, we can be understood to be addressing the eventual development of an ink with the mentioned characteristics.

21 See W. V. O. Quine, 'Two dogmas of empiricism,' *Philosophical Review* 60 (1951): 20–43.

CHAPTER 8

ILLUSIONS OF PERMANENCE

Tattoos and the Temporary Self

A Permanent Collection?

Tattoos are forever. That's why people are attracted to them, and that's also why people avoid them. While the reasons people get tattoos vary from individual to individual and across cultures – as rites of passage, memorials, markers of inclusion in gangs or subcultures, evidence of faith to one's lover or favorite band – their immutability is the unifying factor among the incredibly wide range of tattoo styles, practices, subject matter, and meanings. As an art form in the West, tattooing is distinct from other arts in that the work is a permanent part of the collector's body. And, unlike almost all other types of permanent marks on a person's body, tattoos are (usually) freely chosen by that person. At the same time, their permanence is why the majority of the population balks at getting one (at least, where visible while fully clothed). Indeed, in my teens and twenties I was often asked about my tattoos: 'What do your parents think?' and 'What if you change your mind, or want to get a real job?' These sorts of concerns prevent many people from imbedding into their skin a constant reminder of what may end up being a bad breakup or an otherwise lost weekend in Vegas.

Tattoos – Philosophy for Everyone: I Ink, Therefore I Am, First Edition.
Edited by Robert Arp.
© 2012 John Wiley & Sons, Inc. Published 2012 by John Wiley & Sons, Inc.

Yet, tattoos are *not* forever. They only last as long as we do. Now, in my thirties, the question I most often get about them is 'What happens as you get older?' In this chapter, I address that very question as one that concerns subjectivity and freedom, highlighting connections between the concepts of a tattoo as permanent and of the embodied self as changing and finite.[1] This is underscored by the importance of a tattoo's uniqueness and temporality, evolving concurrently with its bearer, and of the active and reciprocal relationship the individual bearer has with it. My examination is informed by various perspectives, especially those of the French philosopher Maurice Merleau-Ponty (1908–1961), the aesthetic theories of early German Romanticism and German Idealism (late eighteenth to early nineteenth century), and the Pragmatism of American philosopher John Dewey (1859–1952) as continued today by Richard Shusterman (b. 1949). While these perspectives are diverse indeed (and I don't have space here to give more than a brief outline of each), my intention is not to argue for their connections or similarities, but rather to acknowledge my debt to their influence by pointing out key ideas from each that have contributed to my philosophical development. In this light, I offer my own view, connecting three aspects of a tattoo's multifaceted philosophical significance: a constant reminder of the inextricable link between body and mind, and of the impossibility of dividing subjective experience into either exclusively bodily or mental aspects; an artwork whose meaning is never exhausted, but instead is continually being reinterpreted; and a symbol and a part of the continuous process of self-understanding and self-production.

The Phenomenology of Determining a Changing Object in a Moving Subject

In the context of the arts, a tattoo is singular in that its medium is a person's skin. This has ramifications in a few areas, one of which is the tattoo's temporality. The length of time a tattoo exists falls somewhere between the plastic arts and performance arts – less than most paintings and sculptures but (hopefully) longer than a play. While, like dance and theater, tattooing utilizes the body, a tattoo is relatively permanent; performances tend to last much less than a lifetime (though sitting through a bad show can feel like one!). Yet, one might say, tattoos are no different than paintings or sculptures in that they also eventually fade, deteriorate, and disappear. However, because a tattoo is a permanent part of a person's body, it lasts exactly as long as the skin it's in. In this way, a second implication of the fact that a person's skin is the tattoo's medium is that its very existence depends on a person, and on someone who is neither simply artist nor audience. With ink embedded within his or her skin, the bearer of the tattoo is an integral part of the work, and yet, at the same time, he or she is not the artwork itself. The bearer and the work are in a unique relationship with each other: just as the tattoo is integrated into the person's body, so too is the bearer a part of the work – if you take the person away, there is no tattoo. In a sense, the tattooed person gives life to the work, and just where the person ends and the tattoo begins is hard to determine. This difficulty, however, turns out to be part of the tattoo's philosophical significance, the first of three such significances that I explore in this chapter.

The question of where the subject (the tattooed person) and object (the tattoo) begin and end is part of a larger issue that is not unique to tattooed people, but one that applies to all humans. This issue concerns the nature of mind and body and their relationship, and it involves related questions of the mental and physical, of self and world. I think that examining the relationship between a tattoo and its bearer can be useful in bringing to light two ideas that are common to us all but commonly overlooked (although common issues within academic philosophy): first, that neither one's self nor one's body are fixed, but are ongoing processes; and, second, that it's difficult to demarcate clear boundaries between one's self and one's body. While in everyday speech we speak of 'having a body,' or of 'myself' and 'my body' as distinct from each other, upon closer inspection these ideas are not simply separate. The question 'Where does my body end and my tattoo begin?' is akin to 'Where do I end and my body begin?' And neither question is so easily answered, in my opinion, because there is no clear boundary.

What we think of as our self and our body are both part of the same continually changing process, inextricably linked and in a reciprocal relationship with one another. For example, how you feel physically and emotionally are interrelated, and often indistinguishable. If *your body* is healthy, *you* feel good – they are different aspects of the same moment in experience. Likewise, if you are sad because someone has been unkind, they weren't cruel to either your mind or your body but to you as an embodied being, and you as a whole person feel the negative effects. The physical and mental aspects of a person are in constant transactions with each other, and these relationships help to constitute who we are.

RACHEL C. FALKENSTERN

In a similar vein, the existential phenomenology of Merleau-Ponty explains that our embodied subjective experience is not reducible to either body or mind. While he covered many topics and developed his views during the course of his career, a few general points shed some light on how we view the relationships between ourselves, our bodies, and the world – and thus our tattoos. In contrast to substance dualism, such as that of René Descartes (1596–1650), Merleau-Ponty describes the relationship between mind and body not as between two different substances that are somehow mysteriously connected but as a given fact that we are our bodies.[2] The body and self aren't two distinct things casually working on one another but are integrated with each other within one system. When the body does exist without the mind, it is no longer you, but only an inanimate body; the body and mind are no longer the thing they were when they were interconnected.[3] Likewise, in his view, the 'external world' is not given to us through perception, as we commonly think of it, but, really, we are in the world and the world is in us (think about seeing, breathing, eating). We come into being, develop, and interact with our environments as embodied beings; the world shapes us and we shape the world.

This view helps to explain how my tattoo can be considered both an object distinct from my body and at the same time a part of me. It is not some thing on me, separable from me like clothing, but integrated; we co-exist, as part of a unified system. The tattoo, as part of my body, is not an object that can exist separately from me; if it were apart from me, it would be a different thing – perhaps just ink in a bottle, or an artist's drawing, or someone else's similar-looking but different tattoo. Thus, another implication of the fact that a tattoo's medium is a person's skin is that, like the individual people that bear them, each and every tattoo is unique. If two people get the same exact tattoo, by virtue of the fact that they are part of two different people, the tattoos cannot be identical. Even if they are identical twins, they are not the same person, and their matching tattoos are not going to be exactly the same. Further, the tattoo is ever changing, along with the body. As the sun warms me and tans my skin, it fades my tattoos; as I wrinkle, so do my tattoos.

In keeping with the perspective of Merleau-Ponty's phenomenology, more becomes apparent than just how changes in our environment and in our bodies are related to changes in our tattoos. Changes to ourselves can work 'from outside in' and our experiences – what we see or how we look, for example – affect how we feel, how we *are*. Not only does the body express, and is expressive of, emotions, attitudes, and ideas, but also our emotions, attitudes, and ideas are affected by the body. Being tattooed has changed not only how the world views me but also, inter-relatedly, my perspective of the world and my perspective of my self. I may be confident when my tattoos are visible to my students while teaching an aesthetics class, but insecure when being introduced to my boyfriend's parents for the first time. Having tattoos affects how we act and how people treat us; I may choose to wear long sleeves to meet my boyfriend's parents (or refrain from going out to eat in order to save my money for a new tattoo). And, though my tattoos can be removed (albeit with more money and pain than getting the tattoos originally entailed), they are a permanent part of me; the past cannot be erased. Even if removed, the empty space is a reminder of what was. Even if no one else can see them, I'm aware of them. As reminders of certain moments and of the movement of time, they can make me feel nostalgic, depressed, or comforted.

We have limited control over how our bodies change (though at the time of writing the costs and risks of surgeries and other procedures are rapidly declining), and we watch our tattoos change along with the rest of ourselves. Yet, changes also work 'from the inside out,' and a tattoo is not an accident or a natural mark on one's body but a result of a choice made at a certain point in time. My tattoos are mementos of past experi-ences, including the experience of getting tattooed and the surrounding circumstances, and they also remind me of how I have changed since then. Thus, their permanence acts as a marker of the passage of time; they seem unchanging relative to how things around me change. Further, as an art form in the West, the tattooed individual is not merely an object, a canvas, for the tattoo artist, but is part of the creative process, not only in the initial choice to a get a tattoo but also often working closely with the artist on the design. Here, we begin to see the second aspect of the tattoo's philosophical significance emerge: the link between tattoos and subjective freedom.

Visible Freedom: Nineteenth-Century German Aesthetic Theories and Legacies

Like the first aspect of a tattoo's philosophical significance explored in this chapter, the second is also relevant to all tattoos. Regardless of how or why someone gets tattooed, all tattooed individuals share the facts

RACHEL C. FALKENSTERN

that their tattoos and bodies are interconnected and that tattoos are not accidental or natural, but are the result of an intentional act. This kind of act could have *not been chosen* were it possible to reverse time and go back to the moment the choice was made, and the possibility of the choice to do otherwise is primarily what grounds the act as free.[4] However, I concentrate on tattoos in a scope more narrow than what is implied by the broader definition as design, mark, or symbol made by intentionally imbedding pigment permanently under the skin: namely, when considered as works of art. This chapter focuses on tattoos only within the realm of art, independent from any other use, meaning, or value they may have, both for reasons of brevity and in order to highlight the specific aspect of the relationship between art and freedom that I am interested in. This leaves out of my discussion tattoos given to the bearer without his or her complete consent, as in some cases of tribal or gang rituals or in the horrific and extreme case of Nazi concentration camps (one would be hard pressed to find these tattoos, used as identification on unwilling people, works of art). While all bearers of tattoos share similar phenomenological experiences, and these types of tattoos are indeed the result of an intentional act, they are imposed on a person and, in my opinion, thus better left to other areas of philosophy, such as ethics. Certainly philosophical study of tattoos such as these and tattooing in general could prove very interesting and rewarding (as well as for other fields such as anthropology), but, by examining tattoos that are viewed only as artworks, the metaphysical significance of such tattoos as a manifestation of the bearer's freedom comes to the fore.

My view of art as a symbol, reflection, or manifestation of freedom is influenced by a line of aesthetic theories that started in Germany around the turn of the nineteenth century, beginning with Immanuel Kant (1724–1804), continuing with G. W. F. Hegel (1770–1831) and various forms of Romanticism, and carried through by those such as Friedrich Nietzsche (1844–1900) and Theodor Adorno (1903–1969), as well as others in Western philosophy.[5] While their theories are indeed quite varied, what they and related theories that followed in their wake have in common that is central to this chapter is the strong connection between art and freedom. Briefly put, Kant tried to explain how the pleasurable experience of making judgments of beauty sensuously (that is, using the five senses) mirrors the freedom used in the rational exercise of moral judgments. In reaction to Kant, Hegel postulates that beauty is not *like* freedom but is an *appearance* or manifestation of freedom.[6] Hegel's aesthetics offers an objective view of beauty, in that the artwork itself, as an object created by a rational and free being, sensuously presents the idea of freedom – in a sense, then, it *is* freedom. Thus, an artwork is a way for humanity to contemplate its reason and free will, giving art a metaphysical and cognitive status. Viewing tattooing through this lens highlights a tattoo's significance as a sensuous expression of an individual's freedom. As an artwork, a tattoo can show what unadorned bodies cannot – we are able to reflect upon our freedom through its physical appearance in our skin.

Although their stances are related, in contrast to Hegel, the early German Romantics see art as necessary because the world is not completely rational – not everything can be rationally explained, and there are important non-rational dimensions to human existence, as in nature and art. While there are differences among these Romantics, overall it can be said that they combine Hegel's objective and Kant's subjective aspects in their own brand of aesthetics, in which they prioritize art as a way to escape the overly rational and instrumental aspects of modern society. Thus, in general, much like their counterparts in the rest of Europe and in America, those such as Friedrich Schlegel explain that we turn to art to say what we can't say in everyday discursive language, or to express or understand something about ourselves or the world that we couldn't in any other way.[7] Further, an artwork is connected to something larger than itself, in that it points to the infinite and is open to an infinite amount of interpretations. In this light, rather than mere decoration and more than a mark of identification, a tattoo is tied to something larger than it is – its metaphysical burden as it were. Something our tattoos can offer us is a sort of existential comfort: although our tattoos are a result of a free choice, they change in a way that is out of our control, and we are reminded of the passage of time and of the inevitability of change. But, while they cause us to be constantly aware of our own transience and thus the transience of all existence, they point to something more. Their relative permanence links passing moments together, and, as some of those moments involve the choice to get tattooed, they are also connected to possibilities of further action. Tattoos are in this way also open to new interpretations and meanings, and these possibilities can lead to new understandings of ourselves and of the world, even if ultimately we cannot completely articulate them.

Further, a central notion of the early German Romantics' philosophy and ethos is *Bildung*, which (though it has no direct translation in English) can be understood as the cultural education and self-development of an individual in relation to his or her wider social context. In general, this

RACHEL C. FALKENSTERN

view is that the highest purpose of life is self-determined self-realization, and it stresses individuality and freedom, in that each person should freely chose to make his or her life into a beautiful whole, as both nature and an artwork are. This is epitomized in the *Bildungsroman*, a novel in which the plot is essentially the formation of a character, for example Goethe's *Wilhelm Meister's Apprenticeship*.[8] Thus, freedom, self-understanding, and aesthetic experience are interconnected. An artwork and one's life are similar in that they exhibit freedom and balance of content and form, of inner and outer. I offer the tattooed person as an example of this notion. In the act of choosing to get tattooed, we are taking the first step in a creative process, one that is creative in the myriad implications of the word: artistic, original, and productive. Further, we are actively creating ourselves, not just in deciding on or designing the artwork, not just in physically transforming our skin, but also in the other direction, from 'the outside in.' Keeping in mind the perspective of Merleau-Ponty's phenomenology discussed in the previous section, one can see tattoos as simultaneously both self-expression and self-formation. For, tattoos are not only a symbol and a result of a freely chosen act but also a reminder of it, and, as such, can have as much effect on the bearer as anything else in his or her environment in creating the self – a reciprocal process that lasts as long as we do and one that, in a sense, *is* who we are.

Transformation

I may be the first to connect tattooing directly to the Romantic notion of *Bildung*, but the notion has been influential throughout Western culture, especially in philosophy and the arts. While many philosophers acknowledge their debt to this tradition, few directly link it to embodied experience – the first notable exception that comes to mind is Michel Foucault (1926–1984). Although he spent much of his career uncovering the way in which societal forces construct the individual, Foucault's later work searched for ways to escape or resist these powers, one of which is through aesthetic transformation of the self. He does not discuss tattoos, but I think he is worth mentioning here because his view is influential and related to mine. In his attempt to find an area in which an individual can not only freely express himself or herself but also effect changes in the self and thus the wider world, Foucault connects aesthetic bodily practices, subjective freedom, and knowledge.

In his essay 'What is enlightenment?' Foucault hangs on to the Enlightenment notion that we do have free will, however limited, and looks to Romantics who live an aesthetic life, such as Baudelaire, as examples of those who can display and thus know this freedom.[9] We *choose* to be free, and that choice is our first act of freedom. This is connected to the idea in Foucault's later life and works that subversive sexual and drug practices can be ways of living outside power structures, and that these transformative practices change how we think, thus how we are, and can in that way be seen as changing the world. As Foucault says: 'This transformation of one's self by one's own knowledge is, I think, something close to the aesthetic experience. Why should a painter work if he is not transformed by his own painting?'[10]

Another contemporary philosopher for whom aesthetic bodily practices are central is Richard Shusterman. He calls his own view 'somaesthetics,' which he describes as a critical and meliorative study of embodied experience, which views the human body as a locus of aesthetic appreciation and creative self-fashioning.[11] This means that he uses both critical philosophy and physical practices (such as the Alexander Technique and the Feldenkrais Method) to complement each other, in the reciprocal processes of studying and improving the self and of philosophizing. This is to some extent a version of the art of living, in the Socratic tradition.[12] While Shusterman is influenced by a wide range of philosophers and other practitioners, both East and West, he also sees himself as fitting comfortably into the continuing tradition of Deweyan Pragmatism, which emphasizes the importance of aesthetic experience (among other things). In contrast to the legacy in philosophical aesthetics stemming from Kant that is passive or subjective, Dewey's is inclusive and stresses active transaction between audience and artwork – and, indeed, one can have an aesthetic experience of things other than artworks, such as watching a fire burn or gardening.[13] Dewey's theory is rich and complex, and there is not space here to go into it in detail, but it is important to note his influence on Shusterman and this discussion. While Dewey, like most philosophers (especially during his lifetime), does not discuss tattoos, the important connections he makes between art and democracy I think merit further study in relation to tattoos: not only is his democratization of art an attempt to do away with the distinction between high and low art – taking art out of the museum and instead to, by, and for the people – but it is also a way of showing that we can and should bring art and aesthetic experience into the everyday, and that we already do. The rising popularity of incorporating permanent works of art into our bodies attests to that.

Both Shusterman and Foucault acknowledge their debt to the Romantics, and both have points that are relevant to my own view. Thus, I mention them also in hopes that their perspectives in relation to tattoos may be explored further elsewhere. However, in Shusterman's and Foucault's theories, the aesthetic 'object' is the body and the self – or, better, the embodied self – and the person is thus not an object but is instead both subject and object. In this chapter, as it is for them, the phenomenological experience of being a tattooed person in not simply a fashioning of the self through aestheticization of the body, but is tied to something more. In contrast, however, here, the aesthetic object is an artwork that is inextricably linked to the subject's body, not the body itself. Through experiencing an artwork that is a part of one's embodied self, one is simultaneously aware of one's freedom *and* of one's power-lessness. The tattooed person is not just the subject affected by the object and who, in turn, affects the object over time; rather, the tattoo and the person are part of a whole system that affect each other.

A Lasting Impression

For me, then, it is not the one-time experience of getting a tattoo that is significant, but the wider experience of the processes surrounding the choice to get and then bear a tattoo, and the resulting relationship between subject and object – that is, between the bearer and the artwork. Thus, a tattoo's significance is a combination of its relative permanence and its existence as a result of being freely chosen by its bearer. As an artwork that will last only as long as the bearer's skin, it is unique among the arts. Our tattoos are a visual manifestation of our creativity and free-dom, and as such are a part of the reciprocal process of self-expression and self-creation. Thus, perhaps, in a sense, people tattooed in the Western tradition have the opportunity to reflect upon their embodied subjectivity in a way that the unadorned do not. Tattoos have meanings that are symbolic and, at the same time, are more than what they represent or than we originally intended – meanings that include their history, our relationship to them, and our relationship to other things in the world. As time passes, these meanings change. The tattoo that once represented true love now stands for a broken heart; after overcoming the heartbreak, it will be a symbol of strength, and perhaps eventually it will be a remembrance of youthful folly. It's a point of reference – a visible, physical connection between the past and the present. In this way, tattoos can be thought of as an attempt to hang on to this world or to the past, and perhaps as a way of holding on to the present or of trying to control the future. As grandiose as this may sound, it's nonetheless common. For example, memorial tattoos carry such a significance for their individual bearers; a memorial tattoo is a material representation of a memory. If I'm constantly reminded of a person or an event by my tattoo, this reminder is a way of ensuring that I don't forget in the future.

Yet, while one is reminded of his/her act of free will by the tattoo's existence, one is also reminded of the limits of freedom, as we are powerless to control change or to stop the clock. As we age, tattoos remind us not only of the past but also of the constantly changing present and an uncertain future, of things that are out of our control. Not only are we shapers of ourselves and of our environments but, just as much, we also are products of and are affected by them. Human beings are finite, and we are constantly aware of the passage of time and our fleeting place on earth. Our tattoos' evolving meanings and changing appearance are such reminders. This knowledge, though, is part of who we are. One of the effects of this knowledge is the reaction to one's finitude by striving to overcome it in the Romantics' sense; by incorporating an artwork into one's self, one seeks a link to the absolute, the eternal. Ironically, thus, what we typically think of as permanent reminds us of our impermanence. The tattoo is as permanent as its bearer, the self as temporary as the tattoo. And, although we are never completely free from the constraints of our finitude, the tattoo, as a work of art, allows us a momentary glimpse of infinity. We see our freedom in this temporary beauty.

NOTES

1 Philosophical questions, issues, ideas, and arguments concerning the essential nature of persons and things, as well as the identity of persons and things through time, are found in the Western philosophical areas known as 'philosophy of identity' and 'philosophy of personhood,' which are disciplines under the umbrella of 'metaphysics.' See, for example, the relevant articles in Michael Loux and Dean Zimmerman (eds.), *The Oxford Handbook of Metaphysics* (Oxford: Oxford University Press, 2003). See also Harold Noonan, 'Identity,' in Edward N. Zalta (ed.), *Stanford Encyclopedia of Philosophy* (Fall 2009, http://plato.stanford.edu/entries/identity) and Eric T. Olson, 'Personal identity,' in Edward N. Zalta (ed.), *Stanford Encyclopedia of Philosophy* (Fall 2009, http://plato.stanford.edu/entries/identity-personal). Another study relevant to this

chapter is Charles Taylor, *Sources of the Self: The Making of the Modern Identity* (Cambridge, MA: Harvard University Press, 1989).

2   See Maurice Merleau-Ponty, *Phenomenology of Perception*, trans. Colin Smith (New York: Humanities Press, 1962). See also the introduction to this book.

3   See Maurice Merleau-Ponty, *The Structure of Behavior*, trans. A.L. Fisher (Boston, MA: Beacon Press, 1963).

4   Philosophical questions, issues, ideas, and arguments concerning whether things in the universe – including humans – are free or determined are found in the Western philosophical area known as 'philosophy of freedom,' which is a discipline under the umbrella of 'metaphysics.' See, for example, the relevant articles in Michael Loux and Dean Zimmerman (eds.), *The Oxford Handbook of Metaphysics* (Oxford: Oxford University Press, 2003); also Alfred Mele, *Motivation and Agency* (New York: Oxford University Press, 2003); Randolph Clarke, 'Incompatibilist (nondeterministic) theories of free will,' in Edward N. Zalta (ed.), *Stanford Encyclopedia of Philosophy* (Fall 2009, http://plato.stanford.edu/entries/incompatibilism-theories); and Carl Hoefer, 'Causal determinism,' in Edward N. Zalta (ed.), *Stanford Encyclopedia of Philosophy* (Fall 2009, http://plato.stanford.edu/entries/determinism-causal).

5   Certainly there are many more philosophers than mentioned here who are part of this conversation, and even more who hold aesthetic theories other than those included in this tradition; however, it is these particular views that contribute to my own. For a general introduction to Western aesthetic theories, see Jerrold Levinson (ed.), *The Oxford Handbook of Aesthetics* (Oxford: Oxford University Press, 2003) and Steven M. Cahn and Aaron Meskin (eds.), *Aesthetics: A Comprehensive Anthology* (Malden, MA: Blackwell Publishing, 2008).

6   Immanuel Kant, *Critique of Judgment*, trans. Werner Pluhar (Indianapolis, IN: Hackett, 1987); Immanuel Kant, *Critique of the Power of Judgment*, trans. Paul Guyer and Eric Matthews (Cambridge: Cambridge University Press, 2000); and G. W. F. Hegel, *Aesthetics: Lectures on Fine Art*, 2 vols., trans. T. M. Knox (Oxford: Clarendon Press, 1975). See also Karl Ameriks (ed.), *The Cambridge Companion to German Idealism* (Cambridge: Cambridge University Press, 2000); Terry Pinkard, *German Philosophy 1760–1860: The Legacy of Idealism* (Cambridge: Cambridge University Press, 2002); and Andrew Bowie, *Aesthetics and Subjectivity from Kant to Nietzsche* (Manchester: Manchester University Press, 2003). A wealth of secondary sources exist on Kant's Third Critique; a good place to start is Hannah Ginsborg, 'Kant's aesthetics and teleology,' in Edward N. Zalta (ed.), *Stanford Encyclopedia of Philosophy* (Fall 2009, http://plato.stanford.edu/entries/kant-aesthetics), which has an excellent bibliography. Likewise, for Hegel, see Stephen Houlgate, 'Hegel's aesthetics,' in Edward N. Zalta (ed.), *Stanford Encyclopedia of Philosophy* (Fall 2009, http://plato.stanford.edu/entries/hegel-aesthetics).

7   Friedrich Schlegel, *Lucinde and the Fragments*, trans. Peter Firchow (Minneapolis, MN: University of Minnesota Press, 1971); *On the Study of Greek Poetry*, trans. S. Barnett (Albany, NY: State University of New York Press, 2001); *Philosophical Fragments*, trans. Peter Firchow (Minneapolis, MN: University of Minnesota Press, 1991). Selections can be found in Frederick Beiser (ed.), *The Early Political Writings of the German Romantics* (Cambridge: Cambridge University Press, 1996) and Jay Bernstein (ed.), *Classic and Romantic German Aesthetics* (Cambridge: Cambridge University Press, 2003). See also Andrew Bowie, *From Romanticism to Critical Theory* (London: Routledge, 1997); Richard Eldridge, *The Persistence of Romanticism: Essays in Philosophy and Literature* (Cambridge: Cambridge University Press, 2001); Elizabeth Millán-Zaibert, *Friedrich Schlegel and the Emergence of Romantic Philosophy* (Albany: SUNY Press, 2001)Frederick Beiser, *German Idealism: The Struggle against Subjectivism, 1781–1801* (Cambridge, MA: Harvard University Press, 2002); Frederick Beiser, *The Romantic Imperative: The Concept of Early German Romanticism* (Cambridge, MA: Harvard University Press, 2003); Manfred Frank, *The Philosophical Foundations of Early German Romanticism*, trans. Elizabeth Millán-Zaibert (Albany, NY: SUNY Press, 2004); and Nikolas Kompridis (ed.), *Philosophical Romanticism* (London: Routledge, 2006).

8   Johann Wolfgang von Goethe, *Wilhelm Meister's Apprenticeship*, ed. and trans. Eric Blackall, *Goethe: The Collected Works, Volume 9* (Princeton, NJ: Princeton University Press, 1989).

9   Michel Foucault, 'What is enlightenment?' in Paul Rabinow (ed.), *The Foucault Reader* (New York: Pantheon, 1984).

10   Michel Foucault, *Foucault Live: Interviews, 1961–84*, trans. Lysa Hochroth and John Johnston (New York: Semiotext(e), 1989), p. 379. Richard Shusterman points out this quotation in his 'Profiles of the philosophical life: Dewey, Wittgenstein, Foucault,' which was extremely helpful for this chapter, found in his *Practicing Philosophy: Pragmatism and the Philosophical Life* (New York: Routledge, 1997).

11   Richard Shusterman, *Performing Live: Aesthetic Alternatives for the Ends of Art* (Ithaca, NY: Cornell University Press, 2000), p. 138. See also his *Pragmatist Aesthetics: Living Beauty, Rethinking Art*, 2nd ed. (Lanham, MD: Rowman & Littlefield, 2000) and *Body Consciousness: A Philosophy of Mindfulness and Somaesthetics* (New York: Cambridge University Press, 2008).

12   Richard Shusterman, 'Creating something artful: Interview with Richard Shusterman,' interviewed by Tully Rector and John Bova, *Naked Punch* (October 25, 2009; updated September 19, 2010; http://www.nakedpunch. com/articles/41).

13   John Dewey, *Art as Experience* (New York: Perigee Book, 1980 [1934]). See also Tom Leddy, 'Dewey's aesthetics,' in Edward N. Zalta (ed.), *Stanford Encyclopedia of Philosophy* (Fall 2009, http://plato.stanford.edu/entries/dewey-aesthetics).

CHAPTER 9

MY TATTOO MAY BE PERMANENT, BUT MY MEMORY OF IT ISN'T

Not Fade Away

A series of intricate black marks are etched permanently into my skin, some commemorating the memories of lost friends, others standing as testimonies to the importance of those still with me. It seems no difficult task to look upon any one of my tattoos and conjure a memory of those friends and the profound moments that conditioned those relationships. However, as soon as I begin to reflect on the static, unchanging nature of the ink, I realize that my memories have nothing of the immutable nature of the tattoos themselves. My memories seem to shift like quicksand beneath me, sometimes diminishing to near obscurity, sometimes refocusing toward different points of interest in successive attempts to recapture the past through an act of recollection.

Upon my left arm I have the words 'Not Fade Away,' a tattoo infused with a multiplicity of meanings for me but primarily designed to reflect, word for word, the epitaph of one of my dearest friends. Every time I reflect on it, the images that come to mind are different: sometimes it is the tombstone itself I see, other times events from my friendship, and often something more abstract and less distinct – reflections on mortality or the brevity of life. No two successive reflections are ever quite identical,

Tattoos – Philosophy for Everyone: I Ink, Therefore I Am, First Edition.
Edited by Robert Arp.
© 2012 John Wiley & Sons, Inc. Published 2012 by John Wiley & Sons, Inc.

even when I recall a specific event, or even the contours of my friend's face. Minute details shift and refocus as some things become clearer while others recede into relative obscurity. Not fade away ... Indeed, the ink itself never truly *will* fade away, and so I wonder why it is that the meaning and emotion, even the images themselves, constantly change upon subsequent reflections upon the same *unchanging* tattoo.

The problem is two-fold. On the one hand, we have the problem that the past in itself – precisely because it is *past* and not *present* – can no longer be said to exist at all. Recapturing the non-existent is an impossibility bordering on the absurd. On the other hand, we have the problem of memory; namely, that the very composition and defining characteristic of the act of recollection is that it is inherently protean: constantly changing as we ourselves change. As William James (1842–1910) noted in his *Principles of Psychology*, no two successive brain states can ever be entirely identical, no two thoughts or recollections ever exactly the same; in a similar vein, Heraclites (c.535–475 BCE) once noted that one can never step into the same river twice.[1] In short, bringing these two problems together, the question becomes: how can we possibly hope to recollect the past just as it happened when the past no longer exists and our act of recollection is necessarily always in flux? It seems that, even though the ink in my skin is permanently etched there, the *experience* of my tattoo – whether in the present when I look at it or in my memory when I think about when I first got it – is *not* something that is permanent in the sense of being experienced in *the exact same way* every time I look at it, think about it, or remember the pain surrounding its being etched into my skin. Thus, my tattoo is permanent but my memory of it isn't.

Answering this two-fold problem is, in a sense, the only way to give a truly *phenomenological* account of the experience of having a tattoo. Though it had existed in various forms for centuries, phenomenology as an area of philosophy first really came into its own with the German philosopher Edmund Husserl (1859–1938); it concerns itself with the study of the structures of consciousness and the direct experience of the objects of consciousness.[2] Tattoos are permanent and unchanging, and yet the memories associated with them are the complete opposite: constantly changing just as *we* ourselves are constantly changing. Thus, I argue in this chapter that we need to reimagine how we directly experience our own tattoos in a phenomenological manner, dismissing the possibility that the memories we associate with a given tattoo are unchangeable, and dismissing the notion that to look upon a tattoo is to recreate the past precisely as it happened. Instead, we must invert our understanding completely: we must realize that it is the current act of *phenomenological inquiry* into what our tattoos mean to us that carries all of the tattoo's meaning, not a static past lost to the tides of time but what is important to us in the here and now of our present state of mind. In short, our reflections upon our tattoos tell us more about who we are now – in that moment of recollection, in that present inquiry – than they ever could recapture a past just as it once happened.

The Present Time of Things Past

Consider the reflections of Marcel Proust (1871–1922), whose work *Remembrance of Things Past* remains one of the most profoundly significant contributions to literature and a subtle but poignant resource in phenomenology and the philosophy of memory: 'And so it is with our past. It is a labor in vain to attempt to recapture it: all the efforts of our intellect must prove futile.'[3] What was it that so troubled Proust's protagonist in his quest to relive his childhood through memory? The act of recollection seems as commonplace and easily attainable as its object, the memory itself. For example, we can look upon a tattoo of a loved one's name and conjure up that person's face clearly in our mind, or trace the lines on our arm of a naval anchor and remember the camaraderie we found through our time in service. How can it be possible that such a simple and commonplace activity such as this troubles Proust's protagonist? Why are these memories, for him, 'in reality all dead'?[4]

Proust's reflections on memory are subtle and must be excavated carefully; though *Swann's Way* is clearly a novel (of a sort), it is pregnant with more philosophical import than perhaps any other work of its kind. From the perspective of what an individual is experiencing at a given moment – namely, a phenomenological perspective – what Proust is considering is not the impossibility of recollection itself but the impossibility of recapturing, through memory, the past *just* as it was experienced *when* it was experienced originally. The past is past for Proust. It's 'dead' and buried and placed beyond the reach of an intellect that operates in the present – a morbid visualization that resonates with St. Augustine's (354–430) own sort of phenomenological investigation into the existence of the past. Augustine was one of the most profoundly influential philosophers on the topic of memory and recollection: 'When,' he says, 'time is passing, it can be perceived and measured; but when it has passed, it cannot, because it does not exist.'[5]

Indeed, Augustine divided time as it is *experienced* into three separate domains, concluding that 'it is incorrect to say that there are three times – past, present and future.' Rather, we should conceive of time as 'a present of things past, a present of things present, and a present of things future.'[6] This three-fold conception of time as pivoting around a stable point of direct experience in the present was a revolutionary way to solve the problem of the existence of non-present epochs ('past' and 'future') while retaining their significance to human experience. For Augustine, the future has not yet happened, the past has come and gone, and thus neither can be said to properly 'exist.' And yet there is still foresight, planning, and anticipation as much as there is recollection, memory, and reminiscences. This conception of time directly anticipates Proust's dilemma of recapturing the past as it was initially experienced in some long-lost present. 'Thus,' Augustine notes, 'wherever [the past and the future] are, and whatever they are, they cannot be anything except present.'[7]

If the 'present of things future is expectation,' and the 'present of things present is sight,' then it follows, as Augustine rightly notes, 'that the present of things past *is* memory.'[8] The 'present of things past' is not to be conflated with the past itself, which, as Augustine notes, is a chimera born of an 'incorrect use of language.'[9] If there is no past in itself, but only the present of things past, what then is the act of recollection and what, subsequently, are the objects of that act? We must turn from an investigation of the past *as* past to an investigation of the past *as it is experienced* from the present. This is the phenomenological result of Augustine's revolutionary conception of time and the implicit dilemma in Proust's reflections.

Effectively, then, from the phenomenological standpoint of our own personal experience, we can eliminate the need to posit things like 'future' and 'past' as separately existing. Indeed, *all we have* is the present, a fact that has profound ramifications for the very act of recollection. To give one example, after returning from a particularly long tour of duty with the US army, my dear friend Kalju decided to commemorate his time and experiences in service by getting a rather beautiful rendition of the famous 'crossed rifles' tattoo across his forearm. The moment of getting the tattoo was already distanced from the actions and adventures that it represented – and is all the more so now, years later. What our exploration of Proust's and Augustine's phenomenological attitudes toward time and memory aim to show is that the tattoo isn't a bridge through which, upon looking at it, we can conjure back to mind memories of events, people, and places magically secured in some pristine, unchanging mental realm. What is conjured, rather, is made up of bits and pieces of a profoundly dynamic and multifaceted initial experience, but *created*, then and there, through a *present* inquiry, reflecting some *present* desire.

At any given moment, we are bombarded by innumerable sensations (sights, smells, noises, and so on), and from this manifold we piece together a meaningful experience. Thus, even in the initial moment that we are attempting to recollect, there has already been some choice and selection. What is important presents itself from this *gestalt* of experience, a foreground of interest against an ambient background. The act of recollection, itself a present moment of experience, is no different: it selects from a multiplicity of potential data what it desires to explore at that moment. Thus, I asked my friend Kalju what his experience had been, initially, after originally getting the tattoo to commemorate his time in the army. He said that when he first got the infantry tattoo it was as a place to 'put' his army experience, both the good moments and the bad. Aspects that were negative could be put out of his mind without fear of losing them entirely as the tattoo provided a physical anchor for his thoughts. It was a 'box,' he said, that he could put his army experiences into, 'storing' them for reflections at a later time. Asking him again, years later, what the tattoo meant to him then, he said that at some point it became more of a symbol of impressive accomplishments, and that it acted as a reminder that he must continue to lead as significant a life as he could. He said that the crossed rifles stood for an organization that he was proud to have been a part of, and experiences that he was glad to have had. He notes now, later in life, that since he has this emblem on his arm permanently he has to spend the rest of his life living up to what it represents, lest he become just a 'fool,' in his own words, meaninglessly 'wearing old symbols, like pants that don't fit anymore.' The ink didn't change, but the meaning it elicited for Kalju over the years changed dramatically. Gravitating around the fixed and immutable point of the ink itself are his present inquiries and his present concerns, which are, in effect, read into the ink and combine with the manifold of sensations from his time in the army to construct for him something fresh, new, and, most importantly, infused with *present* meaning and significance. How he finds himself interpreting the tattoo, at a given moment, speaks more of that given moment than it does about the events of the past.

Both the act of recollection and its object are found in the present, the only time that actually 'exists' for Augustine and the only possibility for experiencing the past for Proust. Augustine's conception of the past and his articulation of the act of recollection are intimately related:

> Although with regard to the past, when this is reported correctly what it brought out from the memory is not the events themselves (these are already past) but words conceived from the images of those events, which, in passing through the senses, have left as it were their footprints stamped upon the mind ... when I recollect the image of my boyhood and tell others about it, I am looking at this image in time present.[10]

This is why, simply put, it is a 'labor in vain' to try to recapture the past as it was initially experienced as present rather than, as Augustine suggests, and Proust laments, the past as represented in memory through a present act of recollection. The present inquiry constructs 'words conceived from the images of those events,' not the events themselves, and, since the past is both 'dead' for Proust and no longer existing for Augustine, our present recollections are necessarily different from the events of the past as they were initially experienced.

Proust echoes this notion of 'images' and 'picturing' the past through the act of recollection when he says, 'we picture [one of these moments] to ourselves, we possess it, we intervene upon it, almost we have created it.'[11] What is this *creation* that Proust associates with the act of recollection? Surely we're not merely fabricating past events through a present inquiry? For Augustine, the events having 'passed through the senses' have left their 'footprints' in the mind and these footprints, these images, provide the necessary substructure for the act of recollection in the present act of inquiry. However, the individual that performs the act of recollection necessarily alters what is now the dead past (but was once experienced as a present event) when he or she pieces together these footprints. To look upon a tattoo is to bring it to life, to infuse it with present meaning, to construct something fresh, far more than it is to reconstitute, in a sense, 'the dead.' Pieces of the event, in other words, may be represented quite well, but the meaning and import that the event currently has for us is constantly shifting and dependent not on the past but on the present. We are not who we once were; what is important now to us is not necessarily what was important to us at the time of the event, and, subsequently, what caught our attention then (and likewise what receded into the

CLANCY SMITH

background) may no longer catch our attention now. As William James famously notes:

> Often we are ourselves struck at the strange differences in our successive views of the same thing. We wonder how we ever could have opined as we did last month about a certain matter. We have outgrown the possibility of that state of mind, we know not how. From one year to another we see things in new lights. What was unreal has grown real, and what was exciting is insipid. The friends we used to care the world for are shrunken to shadows; the women, once so divine, the stars, the woods, the waters, how now so dull and common.[12]

On the one hand, the objective conditions are no longer the same: this both Proust and Augustine acknowledge readily by relegating the past into the realm of the deceased and non-existent. Subjectively, on the other hand, the individual engaged in recollection has likewise changed, and this is the subtler, but perhaps more significant and more profound, consideration that James so eloquently fleshes out in this passage from the *Principles of Psychology*. Rather than simply observing *what* we remember when we gaze upon our tattoos, let us likewise attune ourselves to *why* we are remembering what is being remembered and not something else. What is it, namely, that captures our attention at the moment of inquiry, the present moment of gazing upon the ink, about the past, as we are experiencing it in that present moment? For recollection, far from unearthing the dead events lost forever to the tides of time, may well be able to tell us just as much, if not more, about what we are experiencing at the present moment of reflecting upon our tattoos.

Thus, when we combine James' psychological insights with the reflections on time and memory as we've explored them, we can begin to understand how the static ink of a tattoo is a dynamic marker but cannot hope to ever fully encapsulate an entirely protean self-consciousness, always changing, growing, and developing.

For example, it is common to get the name of one's beloved tattooed onto one's skin to commemorate what, one hopes, will be a lifelong love affair, one as permanent as the ink itself. As we've seen (keenly through James' examples: 'the women, once so divine … ') in the aforementioned scenario, it is precisely *only* the ink that is permanent; our desires, thoughts, feelings, hopes, and aspirations are all entirely protean. Even if we do, in fact, remain in love with the individual represented by our tattoo, that sensation will change and grow, diminish and rekindle, in a constant cycle of flux and generation. Of course, all too often, we've heard the tales and seen the grim reminders about how such relationships don't necessarily endure, providing a tragic but poignant example to our exploration here: a tattoo that at one time conjured up feelings of love and admiration may come, one day, to elicit quite the opposite effect.

Consider a different sort of example; in Tony Kaye's film *American History X*, Edward Norton plays the protagonist, Derek Vinyard. A neo-Nazi in his youth, Derek chose to represent his sentiments of racism and hatred by permanently etching the traditional symbols of neo-Nazism into his skin, not the least subtle of which was a massive black swastika across his chest. As he matured and came to realize the errors of his ways, he struggled to discourage his younger brother from following him down the same twisted road. One of the most poignant moments in the film finds our protagonist years later staring mournfully at his own chest in a mirror, tracing the lines of his tattoo, an expression and gesture that reflect his regret at the permanence of the ink, which, in turn, demonstrates precisely James' point: our successive experiences with the same events are never twice the same and even the most potentially stable aspects of our lives, our very beliefs, are subject to complete transformation. Vinyard's experiences when getting the tattoo – and then, again, after his transformation – are profoundly different, and yet the ink (tragically, in this case) will forever remain exactly the same.

Memory as Presently Constructed

John Dewey (1859–1952), one of the most prominent American philosophers in the classical tradition of *pragmatism* (a philosophical school that focuses on the dynamics of human development, education, and experience), discusses the objects of experience in his famous essay entitled 'The postulate of immediate empiricism.' There he notes: 'what something is ... is what it is experienced as.'[13] As such, if we take any object of experience, in order to explain what it is, one must only describe how it is experienced. A memory is no different from any other object of possible experience. Thus, in order to know what a memory is, for Dewey, all we need to do is describe what it is experienced as, an experience that necessarily takes place in a present moment of inquiry. Therefore, a memory, *any* memory, is simply the object of a present inquiry. For, what are we doing if not engaging in precisely the type of inquiry that Dewey's philosophy hinges upon when we ask ourselves 'What does this image etched upon my flesh of my loved one's name mean to me?' or 'What is the importance to me now of this military emblem on my arm?'

The normal association, as Maurice Merleau-Ponty (1908–1961) points out in *Phenomenology of Perception*, is to assume that present experiences are given meaning and made understandable by an appeal to experiences past, provided they are suitably similar. The problem comes in the form of an odd paradox:

> Before any contribution by memory, what is seen must at the present moment so organize itself as to present a picture to me in which I can recognize my former experiences. Thus the appeal to memory presupposes what it is supposed to explain; the patterning of data, the imposition of meaning on a chaos of sense-data. No sooner is the recollection of memories made possible than it becomes superfluous, since the work it is being asked to do is already done.[14]

In order to conjure memory, what mental faculties exist must first coordinate the present experience into a picture suitably similar that is then capable of evoking memory. Hence, the onset of memory is a redundancy; its materialization is not the tether binding present experience to past meaning; it is the residual aftereffect of present experience itself. 'Nowhere, then, does it work from past to present,' Merleau-Ponty concludes, 'and the "projection of memories" is nothing but a bad metaphor hiding a deeper, ready-made recognition.'[15]

Merleau-Ponty, familiar as he was with *gestalt* psychology, articulates the difference between 'figure' and 'background'[16] – what does and does not leap from the *gestalt* of our experience and presents itself as something, pragmatically speaking, that is 'attention-worthy.' Memory is not rushing from the past, arising from some pristine torpor within the mind, toward the present experience and constructing an association with this new, encountered object. Why we conjure one memory and not another is based, simply but profoundly, on what does and does not present itself at a given moment of recollection as 'attention-worthy.' That is, *why* we remember one association with a tattoo and not another at a given time has far more to do with what we're going through now, in that moment of reflection, and far less to do with what happened in the past itself. Memory is not a 'self-subsistent picture of the past.'[17] If anything, 'memory of the past' is none other than the object of a current inquiry, constructed in the present by what we currently find worthy of our attention, that interests us and occupies our thoughts, and thus not a 'self-subsistent picture of the past' but a constantly changing image that is infused with new meaning, taking on new angles and dimensions, never twice the same.

Constantly being Imbued with New, Present Meanings

Consider, then, any number of different sorts of tattoos and the implications of this inversion of our general conception of how we experience our past through them. The crossed rifles of the army infantry or the anchor of the navy can at one moment commemorate a significant life experience, and at others a regret for time spent away from home, exhilaration regarding adventures abroad, pride, sorrow, grief, friends lost, or accomplishments in the service of one's country. As another example, tattoos received in concentration camps – the rough scrawls of numbers symbolizing barely more than brands or barcodes – can, for survivors of such atrocities, act as painful reminders at one moment of friends and family lost, and at others of anger and outrage, of endurance and survival.

The initial event and the memory as it is being remembered *now* are, necessarily, different experiences altogether, constantly changing as we ourselves change and thus, too, constantly being imbued with new, present meanings. This is the bittersweet tragedy of Proust's remembrances and the unfortunate reality that we all must face: the experience of memory can never duplicate the experience of the event itself. What I add to such claims is, simply, that it *can* tell us far more about who are we are at the moment of recollection by implicitly reflecting our present desires and interests if we are keen enough to interpret why it is that we are remembering something one way, one event, one feature, and not any of the innumerable others.

Thus, as I look once more upon the tattooed recreation of my friend's epitaph, in this present moment of inquiry, asking myself, in effect, 'What does this tattoo mean to me right now?' I can say that it fills me with a sense of bittersweet joy as I'm reminded of the afternoon we spent together talking, drinks in hand, discussing how best to live 'the good life' as Buddy Holly's 'Not Fade Away' played softly in the background. How I must interpret this present recollection, given our recent explorations, is not that I've somehow magically reconstituted that past moment precisely as it happened, but that in the infinite sea of potential recollections (from the moment I met my friend, to the moment he died; from the cold stone of his grave, to the abstract thoughts of mortality) I am, for some reason, choosing to remember *this* moment out of that innumerable sea of potential other moments. Something in me *now* is deciding this; something in my present state of mind, through my present desires and concerns, has constructed this object of inquiry out of this infinite manifold of possible sensations. It has driven me to create this image as I reflect upon the ink, ink no different than it was when I first got it. It is the 'good life,' perhaps, that currently captures my interest and aids in constructing this memory. Indeed, it is a notion of the good life that necessarily includes the company of good friends. In fact, because of this specific recollection, I may just this very moment invite some friends over, ensure that we find ourselves with drinks in hand, and spend the evening in conversation. I may even put on a little Buddy Holly, to help us all along.

NOTES

1   William James, *The Principles of Psychology*, 2 vols. (New York: Henry Holt Publishers, 1890).

2   Good introductions to phenomenology include David Smith and Ralph McIntyre, *Husserl and Intentionality: A Study of Mind, Meaning, and Language* (Dordrecht: Springer, 1982) and David Smith and Barry Smith (eds.), *The Cambridge Companion to Husserl* (Cambridge: Cambridge University Press, 1995). See also David Woodruff Smith, 'Phenomenology,' in Edward N. Zalta (ed.), *Stanford Encyclopedia of Philosophy* (Fall 2009, http://plato. stanford.edu/entries/phenomenology).

3   Marcel Proust, *Swann's Way* (New York: Modern Library College Editions, 1956), p. 92. See also Thomas Lennon, 'Proust and the phenomenology of memory,'?*Philosophy and Literature* 31, 1 (April, 2007): 52–66.

4   Proust, *Swann's Way*, p. 92.

5   Augustine, *The Confessions of Saint Augustine*, trans. Rex Warner (New York: Signet Classic, 2001), p. 265.

6   Ibid., p. 268.

7   Ibid., p. 266.

8   Ibid., p. 268, emphasis added.

9   Ibid., p. 268.

10 Ibid., p. 266.

11 Proust, *Swann's Way*, p. 37.

12 James, *The Principles of Psychology*, p. 166.

13 John Dewey, 'The postulate of immediate empiricism,' *The Journal of Philosophy, Psychology, and Scientific Methods* 2, 15 (July 20, 1905): 393–399.

EXPRESSIONS OF FREEDOM

'Aren't tattooed people just following the crowd? Are the tattoos everyone pretends to be symbols of rebellious freedom really the mark of a person enslaved to what's "cool"?'

(Jonathan Heaps, p. 136)

CHAPTER 10

TATTOOS ARE FOREVER

Bodily Freedom and the (Im)possibility of Change

A Philosopher's Worries

In approximately one week I will be experiencing the painful sensation of having dozens of needles simultaneously piercing my arm, leaving permanent ink traces in the dermis of my skin. But I am no newbie here; once next week's section is finished, my left arm will be completely covered in ink, and this is not to mention a few scattered tattoos I have elsewhere. Although this is not nearly as much ink as some people I often see at tattoo conventions, that's arguably quite a lot for someone in the philosophy business. Being an exception to the rule, at colloquiums and conference dinners I always attract a lot of curious looks and polite questions about my tattoos. Fortunately, in my experience people have always been very nice, their curiosity arising out of a true philosopher's sense of wonder, as they enquire about the meaning of the artwork or my personal reasons for these particular motifs.

Tattoos – Philosophy for Everyone: I Ink, Therefore I Am, First Edition.
Edited by Robert Arp.
© 2012 John Wiley & Sons, Inc. Published 2012 by John Wiley & Sons, Inc.

One particular night during a conference dinner, a fellow philosopher – let's call him Toby – approached me with a mixture of curiosity and perplexity, and, as usually happens, started asking me about my tattoos. As drawings were shown and stories told, he became more and more interested, enquiring about everything from motives to pricing, pain, and aftercare. After hours of engaging conversation, we finished our dessert and he offered me his concluding thoughts for the evening's subject matter: 'I really like tattoos,' he said, 'but I am not sure if I could ever get one.' The confession surprised me; 'Why not?' I asked. 'If you find them so beautiful and interesting, what keeps you from getting one?' 'Well, it is just that … they are forever. Once it's done, you can't change it anymore. So I can never decide if I should just give in to my impulses, or stay away from them in order to avoid future regrets. What do you think?'

He stared at me with a blank look on his face, as if waiting for me, a fellow philosopher, to ease his concerns, to offer him precious insight into the mind of someone who has already chosen to adorn his skin with permanent artwork. But, disappointingly, I returned his blank look. Not because I had no thoughts on the matter – philosophers, it should be noted, always have an opinion about all possible subjects of conversation, even if we really have no idea what we are talking about – but because I had *too many* things to say, too many points of view, advantages and disadvantages to consider, and I could not decide what to tell Toby in order to alleviate his worries. Should he be impulsive and finally get that tattoo he had always wanted? How careful should he be in ensuring he will not regret it in the future? If Toby is afraid, should he commit himself to a change to his body that is irreversible?[1]

After coming home frustrated and with too much dessert in my stomach, I decided Toby deserved an answer. I could not give him one at the dinner because the way in which he posed his question introduced a false and simplistic dichotomy, imposing a *mere* choice between (a) being too impulsive and (b) being too careful. In order for the problem to be tractable, I felt I needed to overcome this dichotomy and introduce more elements into the story. Toby's worries were of course legitimate, but the elements he gave me with which to build a reply were lacking substance. So this chapter will be dedicated to developing Toby's worries into a philosophical problem, and to finally offer him a solution.

The problem, as I see it, can be put in terms of the relationship between freedom over one's own body and the permanent effects of a particular change effected in the body. How should we see the interplay between these two factors? How should permanence constrain our actions, and

❦   FELIPE CARVALHO

what role does freedom over one's body play in it? Each element in Toby's dichotomy reveals different ways of conceiving this relationship, as this chapter will make clear. After showing how neither one helps us to deal with Toby's worries in a satisfactory way, I will propose a new way of seeing the relationship between permanence and bodily freedom, with elements extracted from my own experience as a philosopher who, through frequent visits to tattoo conventions, has been able to learn valuable lessons from the tattoo community.

Being a Hedonist … and Regretting It

Recall that Toby's first worry was about being 'impulsive' – letting go of his fears, doubts, and inhibitions, and allowing himself to engage in an action for the sake of the immediate pleasure it would give him. Let's call this line of reasoning *hedonist*, from the Greek work *hedon*, meaning 'pleasure.' The hedonist, as the name suggests, ultimately seeks pleasure and happiness manifested in an ability to make choices that will maximize personal fulfillment.[2] This kind of person lives for the moment, takes opportunities as they come, and doesn't give too much thought to the future, as long as the capacity to make present choices brings immediate joy and pleasure. If the hedonist were present at the table in my conversation with Toby, s/he would simply tell him to go ahead and do it; if getting a tattoo is something Toby would like, something that would make him happy, by all means he should just do it. 'Seize the day!' s/he might say, gulping down a glass of wine. 'Take opportunities as they come! You philosophers take yourselves way too seriously!'

But here I side with Toby. What if Toby gets a tattoo he will later come to regret? Surely this is a legitimate worry that must be taken into account. If our choice is based upon a purely hedonistic worldview, the mere possibility of future regret plays little role in constraining our present choices. As the hedonist sees it, we cannot have freedom without regret; if we are free regarding our present choices, that means that the possibility of making a bad choice (or at least a choice that at a later time might be considered bad) is always there. But, if regret is seen as a constitutive part of freedom, we just have to accept it as an occasional hazard and go on with our lives, abandoning regret as a significant constraint on making particular choices. Being free to choose also means being open to mistakes, so if we want freedom we must also accept regret.

Besides, the hedonist tells us, it is hopeless to take future regret into account when making a particular choice in the present. We cannot predict how, or if, our standards will change in the future; even our predictions about possible future changes are made within the context of our *present* standards, which of course might change. And, if we cannot move outside our present standards in order to make a choice, our present standards will always be the relevant ones in evaluating a certain course of action. So, if a tattoo is appealing to you now ... well, just go ahead and do it, the hedonist says, because these are the only standards you have available for choosing.

So here is the picture the hedonist offers us regarding bodily freedom and permanent choices: what counts as freedom toward one's own body has to do with one's capacity to make free choices that will bring one pleasure and fulfillment. The fact that a certain choice is irreversible, as in the case of tattoos, is only seen as a constraint if we acknowledge a role for future regret in how we make choices. But, as all choices are necessarily made within our present context, and this context is what counts in evaluating the action as good or bad, or free or not free, then everything speaks in favor of Toby getting a tattoo, if at the moment he finds them appealing and believes they will make him happy.

But this view, almost childlike in its simplicity, cannot give a satisfactory answer to Toby's worry. After all, one of his main concerns is the possibility of regret, and, even if we acknowledge the hedonist's plausible claim that regret is part of freedom and we can never escape it completely, the idea that we should make our choices in a way that at least *minimizes* the chance of future regret is also very appealing, something the hedonist ignores. Future regret might have devastating psychological consequences, especially if the choice made was an irreversible one. If all we have to go with is the present appeal of a certain choice, this might lead us to too many bad choices, risking, for example, permanently having your first girlfriend's name on your skin as the result of a fiery, but short-lived, adolescent passion you once had. And this result is unacceptable – especially if your wife's name is Mary and your tattoo says 'I Love Becky ... Forever and Ever!'

Indeed, it seems there is a problem with the hedonist's reasoning. Her/his own claims on regret can be used as an argument against her/his own view, once we accept the principle that we should make our choices in a way as to minimize the chance of future regret. If the hedonist is right in claiming that we can't know how, or if, our taste standards will change, then, if we make an irreversible choice *now*, any change whatsoever in our standards might lead us to regret this choice at a future time.

FELIPE CARVALHO

As we want to minimize regret, we should stick to reversible choices and avoid those that are permanent, as these will bring a risk of future regret that is simply too high.

To conclude, even if Toby does occasionally feel the impulsive pull of the hedonist, his view is just too extreme to be plausible, and the relationship between bodily freedom and permanence is too simple to deal satisfactorily with Toby's concerns about future regret. Hedonism might work for very simple choices, whose consequences are not so important or long lasting; if you are in doubt as to whether you should have one last drink, the worst thing that can happen from choosing like a hedonist is a bad hangover tomorrow. But, when it comes to irreversible choices, the hedonist gives us very little to go with.

Mill's Will

So, we may decide to pursue another line of thought, based on a conception of freedom found in the writings of philosopher John Stuart Mill (1806–1873). In the present context, I will call this view Millian, although I do not claim that these are exactly Mill's views on the matter. The Millian, as we shall call this person, is reasonable and always ponders about choices in a careful manner, choosing a certain course of action that will best suit her/his motivations according to certain principles s/he takes to be valid. According to the Millian, the hedonist got it all wrong in his conception of the relation between bodily freedom and permanence. What constitutes freedom is not merely the capacity to freely make present choices but the fact that one's choices should not preclude one from being free in the future. To support this view, the Millian quotes his philosophic hero concerning freedom:

> [A person's] voluntary choice is evidence that what he so chooses is desirable, or at the least endurable, to him, and his good is on the whole best provided for by allowing him to take his own means of pursuing it. But by selling himself for a slave, he abdicates his liberty; he forgoes any future use of it, beyond that single act. He therefore defeats, in his own case, the very purpose which is the justification of allowing him to dispose of himself. He is no longer free; but is thenceforth in a position which has no longer the presumption in its favor, that would be afforded by his voluntarily remaining in it. The principle of freedom cannot require that he should be free not to be free. It is not freedom, to be allowed to alienate his freedom.[3]

Of course, Mill here is talking about slavery, which is a bit too extreme to be compared with tattoos; but his idea – that even if one freely chooses to be a slave it would not constitute a free act due to its preclusion of future freedom – has a general argumentative form that might be used in the context of the present discussion. The thought is that, although one may freely choose to X, if one chooses to permanently and irreversibly commit oneself to X-ing, one by this very act loses his future freedom, as he is no longer free to choose between X-ing and not X-ing. By parity of reasoning, although permanently getting one's skin marked with tattoo ink may be a free choice, in doing so one is no longer free regarding what to do with one's skin. As the Millian sees it, what constitutes bodily freedom is not the capacity to *choose* freely but to *remain* free; hence, it is something that is constrained by the future impact of present choices. As a permanent and irreversible commitment to change is something that directly affects the individual's future freedom regarding the object of change, it should in principle be avoided. The Millian would then tell Toby to refrain from getting a tattoo, suggesting that he should fulfill his desire through other acts that are reversible and do not preclude his future freedom toward his body. If Toby wants to minimize regret and keep his freedom, he should adopt Millianism and stay away from tattoo parlors and tattooed philosophers with funny ideas in their heads.

But is the Millian right? If the problem with the hedonist was that he was leading us to a path where we might make too many bad choices, now the worry is that the Millian might be granting us *too few* choices, putting us in a position where we might miss too many opportunities to be happy and fulfilled. Many opportunities in life do not come by very often, and if we don't take them as they come we might be victim of another form of regret not addressed by the Millian – the regret of not having taken certain opportunities in life, because at the decisive moment we were too concerned with possible future consequences of our choices.

Besides, the idea that we should avoid an action merely because of its being irreversible cannot be right as it stands. To illustrate with an example, one of my best friends in school used to be called 'Dumbo' because of the rather large ears he had as a small child. After years of embarrassment and bullying, as a teenager he finally decided to undergo plastic surgery in order to make his ears smaller, getting rid of his childhood trauma once and for all. Now, many years later, his ears can no longer be changed back to look like Dumbo's, but I doubt the impossibility of change is something my friend is concerned with. Contrary to what the Millian says, I assure you that, despite having committed himself to an irreversible change, he now feels much happier, and freer, than he did when his self-consciousness made him a shy and reserved child with few friends in school. So it cannot be a general principle that one should avoid permanent changes. In my friend's case, and many others, the fact that one is now less free regarding the object of change is greatly outweighed by the fact that one is much happier and self-fulfilled after committing oneself to the irreversible change. This is something that needs to be taken into account but that is missing from the simple Millian conception of bodily freedom and permanence.

Too Little and Too Much

Be as it may, even if both positions, in their extremes, have failed to deal with Toby's worries in a satisfactory way, I believe they have both said something right about the relation between bodily freedom and the impact of irreversible choices. They express different intuitive pulls: on the one hand, the impulse to do as we please and get a tattoo 'in the heat of the moment,' when we know it would make us very happy to do so; and, on the other, the Millian tendency to ponder about our choices and think about future consequences of our acts, where the possibility of regret scares us into *not* getting a tattoo. Both of these are valid points that should be taken into account in any informed decision about getting a tattoo.

The hedonist is too childish in his/her simplicity, too inconsequent in how s/he views choices and the relation between freedom and permanence. There is just *too little* role for permanence in his/her picture, which downplays regret and the importance of a principled basis upon which to make an informed decision about one's tattoos. This is the opposite problem faced by the Millian, who gives *too much* of a role to permanence, positing it as a general principle and overlooking the fact that we can many times be happy and free through choices that are themselves irreversible, as my friend's example illustrates. We need a middle path here, and the clues to finding it, I'll argue, are in a place few philosophers look – in the heart of the tattoo community.

Motif, Meaning, Motive, and a Middle Path

When I was around eighteen, I had an image of tattoos that is quite different from the one I have now, which is the result of attending tattoo conventions, reading articles in tattoo magazines, and numerous conversations with tattoo artists and tattoo lovers in general. When I was younger, there didn't seem to be anything special about the way in which one chose to get a tattoo. Sure, it was more difficult to get the money, but, once one had decided on a certain artwork with some sort of personal meaning involved, all one needed to do was find the nearest tattoo parlor and agree on a price. Let's call this (represented in Figure 10.1) the *simple picture* of the tattoo process.

There is nothing wrong with the elements in this picture *per se*, but we need to complicate it a bit in order to address our concerns. Remember, we want to be able to make permanent choices that will bring us happiness, but we want to do so in a way that will minimize regret, and the simple picture in itself does nothing to address this. If, in step (1), you choose the name of that short-lived teenage passion as motif, according to present standards that seem right to you, then all you need to do is find the nearest tattoo parlor and execute your decision. But there is of course a very high chance that the future will bring you regret. Even if later you may look at your tattoo and say 'Well, that was once meaningful to me' (as people often say about their bad tattoos), this brings little comfort when twenty years later you still find yourself with *her* name on your arm, or an enormous 'peace and love' symbol on your back.

One suggestion to slightly complicate the simple picture is to add a further element in the relation between (1) and (2). Another important problem with the picture is that it makes the choice of the tattoo artist something quite arbitrary, almost like choosing a mechanic to fix your car – all you need is to do some price research, get a few recommendations, verify that the shop meets certain minimal standards

(1) Choose a motif ⟶ Personal reasons
(family, ideology, activity)

(2) Go to the tattoo parlor

FIGURE 10.1 The simple picture of the tattoo process.

FELIPE CARVALHO

and that the mechanic has an acceptable technical level, and ultimately settle for the best compromise between these factors. But this leaves the idea of the tattooist *as an artist* completely out of the picture, reducing him or her to the level of a mere technical executer. Thus, we miss the fact that the overwhelming majority of tattooists are true artists, original painters whose tattoos can be seen as genuine paintings on canvasses. In many cases this is literally true, as a lot of tattooists also paint in one form or another, and these paintings can then be (or not) laid out as a tattoo.

Seen in this way, the tattooist is no longer a mere intermediary between one's idea for a motif and the final product on one's skin, but a crucial element in the decision process that influences one's choice of motif. In the tattoo community, it is not uncommon to hear phrases like 'I want to get so-and-so's art on my arm,' or 'one of so-and-so's surrealist figures would be great on my chest,' and the like. This shows great appreciation for the tattooist as an artist, as choice of motif is influenced by one finding a personal and meaningful connection with the way in which the tattooist expresses him/herself in his/her artwork. Thus we come to the revised picture shown in Figure 10.2.

In this picture, part of the appeal of having a tattoo is not only to express a motif that is dear to you but also to have someone's original artwork on your skin – someone with whom you feel a great connection as an artist, someone who expresses very well the way you feel about your motif. Now the relation between (1) and (2) is no longer merely technical, and all aspects of the process are now interconnected. This is already a great improvement on the simple picture we started with, but in order to ensure we are dealing with our concerns in an effective way I would like to add yet another element.

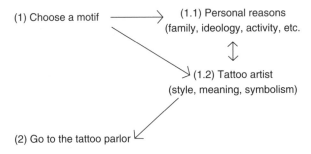

FIGURE 10.2   A more complex picture of the tattoo process.

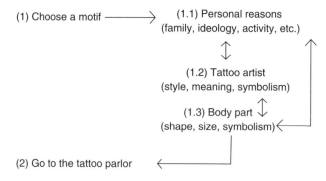

FIGURE 10.3   A final, revised complex picture of the tattoo process.

In the tattoo community, very often people do not choose a motif merely based on personal meaning, artist, and artwork. The choice of motif is very often modulated by *where* on their body they want that particular artwork, which in turn modulates the choice of the artwork itself. Depending on things like shape, size, and symbolism of the body (for example, getting a particularly emotional motif near one's heart) as well as how the chosen site of the body interacts with the tattooist's artwork, one may decide to get a tattoo in one particular part of the body as opposed to another, or change the artwork to adapt to that body part. This reveals a very complex interplay between choice of motif, the tattooist's art, and seeing one's own body as a canvas, as a frame shaped in a certain way that may hold beautiful and meaningful art. So, we arrive at the second and final revision to the simple picture, shown in Figure 10.3.

And now we finally have something to tell Toby. One of the problems with the simple picture was that the step between choosing a motif and going to the tattoo parlor was too simple and straightforward; hence, if one as a teenager decided one was in love, with all the force and phenomenological certainty characteristic of adolescence, there was nothing in the picture that constrained one's choice in having one's teenage sweetheart permanently marked on one's skin. Thus, a false and simplistic dichotomy arose between doing it anyway 'in the heat of the moment' (the hedonist's recommendation) and denying the action as an action-*type*, as the only way to avoid this kind of risk altogether (as the Millian recommends). But the revised

FELIPE CARVALHO

picture, with all its elements, allows us to steer a middle path between the *inconsequentialism* of the hedonist and the excessive *precautionism* of the Millian.

In the revised picture, tattoos can be seen as expressions of bodily freedom through a view of the body as canvas for meaningful and personal art. But, of course, the principle that we should minimize regret demands us to be careful in the choice of motif, hence the added ingredients in the revised picture. Their presence introduces a more complex interplay between motif, artist, and the body, ensuring we take more factors into account in arriving at a principled choice, as one element constrains the others in the decision process. Although this picture will not completely eliminate regret, the fact that tattoos represent an irreversible choice will actually invite us to deepen our relationship with our own body and the artwork (and artist) that will adorn it, acknowledging a proper role to all. Once we do so, permanence will no longer *keep* us from making choices; its role will be instead to help us make more principled ones.

A Philosopher's Worries Again

If this is a view that speaks to Toby, as it did to me many years ago, then by all means he should get a tattoo, according to the principles suggested by the revised picture. Of course, this requires one to get into the right frame of mind, and admittedly not everyone will come to see the relationship between one's bodily freedom and permanence in the way suggested here. But, as long as this view looks appealing to some, I can only hope it might serve to reduce the great number of bad tattoos and purely hedonist choices out there. And that means: no teenage sweetheart's name on your skin, please! Sorry Becky…

NOTES

1 Throughout this chapter I will assume that tattoos, once made, cannot be removed. Even if there are nowadays laser procedures that are able to remove tattoo ink, they only work in limited cases, and with less-than-optimal aesthetic results. In other words, you may remove that tiny butterfly on your ankle, but I am stuck with my entire left arm covered in ink.

2 See Michael Flocker, *The Hedonism Handbook: Mastering the Lost Arts of Leisure and Pleasure* (Cambridge, MA: Da Capo Press, 2004). See also the many articles referenced in Andrew Moore, 'Hedonism,' in Edward N. Zalta (ed.), *Stanford Encyclopedia of Philosophy* (Fall 2009, http://plato.stanford.edu/entries/hedonism).

3 John Stuart Mill, *On Liberty* (Indianapolis, IN: Hackett Publishing Company, 1978).

CHAPTER 11

BEARING THE MARKS

How Tattoos Reveal Our Embodied Freedom

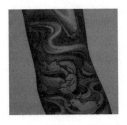

Fingers Running Up and Down the Back of My Arm

The question of the moment should have been whether I wanted the *carnitas* or the *chili verde* burrito, but instead I was wondering whose fingers were running up and down the back of my arm. Looking over my shoulder, I noticed an elderly woman and her middle-aged daughter standing behind me in line at the Mexican cafe. They were discussing in hushed tones the tattoo that runs from below my elbow to the cap of my shoulder. When the pair discovered they'd been caught caressing the triceps of a perfect stranger without permission, both looked up and smiled. 'We like your tattoo. What's up here?' the elderly woman asked, pushing up my t-shirt sleeve. My face made the mercurial expression of someone rolling his eyes while smiling with patient exasperation. Then I rolled up my sleeve to point out the lanterns, trees, and clouds that make up the upper third of my tattoo. This, after all, was not the first time a stranger had presumed to comment on, and touch, my tattoos as though we were old friends.

Tattoos – Philosophy for Everyone: I Ink, Therefore I Am, First Edition.
Edited by Robert Arp.

People with visible tattoos, often without meaning to, invite questions, opinions, pokes, and prods from complete strangers. Also, it can't be avoided that tattoos, like political bumper stickers, occasion the silent judgments of others. When people do ask questions, they range from the innocently inane – 'Does that hurt?' (not presently, thank you) – to the minimally invasive – 'What does it mean?' (what do *you* think it means?). There is one question, though, with which the tattooed person is most awkwardly saddled:

> 'Aren't you afraid of being stuck with that tattoo, perhaps when tattoos aren't cool anymore?'

Lurking behind this question is the suspicion that you, the tattooed person, don't really want your tattoo. No, with sufficient years and the changing of the times, you'll realize that your skin art is more like a Flock of Seagulls haircut that will never grow out. It's a question asked leaned back, with arms crossed and looking down one's nose to note dryly: 'Ah, a tattoo. How rebellious – in a conformist sort of way.'[1] The asker suspects that you didn't so much choose to get a tattoo as fail to choose *not* to get a tattoo. There resides – nestled behind a logical fallacy called a 'loaded' question – as in, 'When did you stop drinking and driving, Mr. Smith?' – a serious question about why we tattoo ourselves. Why would someone do something so permanent and unusual? Would anyone do such a thing if they weren't somehow pressured or influenced by a trend or a fad? Aren't tattooed people just following the crowd? Are the tattoos everyone pretends to be symbols of rebellious freedom really the mark of a person enslaved to what's 'cool'? Suddenly, the tattooed person and the philosopher are people stuck with the same question: Do we really *freely* choose to act in certain ways – for example, to steal from the candy store, to *not* take a second piece of cake, to take the shorter route home, or to get a tattoo? Or, are we determined by circumstances beyond our control to act in certain ways, as if we're caught up in some big, invisible force that makes our decisions for us?

Am I Really Free?

'Am I really free to get a tattoo?' asks a tattooed philosopher, raising a colorful arm to scratch her head in wonder. Though the tattooed person asks that question about only a very specific example, the philosopher

JONATHAN HEAPS

(tattooed or not) asks the question regarding freedom about human life in general.[2] Picture a tattooed philosopher on the sofa with a cup of coffee, wondering as follows:

> It *seems* like I choose to get a tattoo freely. Sure, sometimes other things limit the options from which I get to choose. Still, for the most part, I am the author of my actions; or, at least, of the intentions behind my actions. And yet, this morning in the newspaper, I read an article about a scientific study that says some of my actions and even my thoughts (even *this* thought?) are the product of a process determined by biological laws, specifically laws associated with genetics. Doesn't my *nature* – in terms of genes causing me to act one way or another – determine my character, beliefs, opinions, motivations, intentions, and actions? And aren't those genes determined by chemical laws? And aren't those chemical laws *ultimately* determined by the laws of physics? Thus, am I only a very complex arrangement of atoms behaving according to the laws of physics? Further, I had no control over the circumstances into which I was born, and the people who raised me and influenced my life growing up (parents, guardians, teachers, role models, and the like). All of this environmental influence and pressure surely has had a direct effect upon my character, beliefs, opinions, motivations, intentions, and actions. So, it's not just my nature, but doesn't my *nurture* (the environment and its lasting effect upon me) also determine who I am? And hasn't that nurture further determined how I have acted, do in fact act now, and will act in the future? How can I be the thing freely choosing my actions, given the determining influence of *both* nature *and* nurture? Are my actions determined just like the growth of a tree or the instinct of an ant? If so, the experience of myself as free (and maybe the experience of myself at all?) must be an illusion. And yet, since this has been such an unsettling little daydream, I'm going to *choose* to think of something else now – or, was I *determined* to think of something else now?!?

Perhaps then our tattooed philosopher turns on the television or leans back to take a nap, while we are left wondering whether the action of turning on the television, or leaning back to nap, was wholly free or wholly determined!

Hopefully the philosopher doesn't give up on this problem so easily, and neither should we. The problem is usually presented as the conflict between freedom and determinism. The rest of this chapter will take a look at that conflict and how tattoos don't just bring up the problem of freedom but help to answer it, too. First, we'll look at the idea of determinism and how it invites us to worry about the state of our freedom.

Then, we'll talk about a well-known solution to the conflict between determinism and freedom offered to us by the German philosopher Immanuel Kant (1724–1804), who probably didn't have any tattoos.³ Along the way, I'll suggest a way of thinking about our tattoos that helps to address the problem of freedom. Lastly we'll see how tattoos show us that our freedom is both real and compatible with the world that science explains to us.

Determinism

Professional philosophers make their living by cutting up big philosophical problems into much smaller ones. So, earlier, when I was talking about determinism, a philosopher ought to have asked, 'Yeah, but what *kind* of determinism?' I have in mind *causal* or *material* determinism. Material determinism assumes a world made of little bits of matter arranged in more or less complicated combinations and relationships: electrons and neutrons arranged in atoms, atoms arranged in molecules, molecules arranged in cells, and cells arranged into organisms. Those different levels of arrangement aren't just cosmically erratic chaos. Instead, the laws of cause and effect determine them. Those laws tell us how change is understandable. The laws of science help us to understand the particulars of cause-and-effect change. For example, when one thing happens, for example applying heat to a pan full of water, and then something else happens, for example the water evaporating, the laws discovered by science articulate the cause-and-effect relationship between those two events. These short chains of cause and effect can – causal determinism assumes – be linked together into one big deductive chain of related events.

The cause-and-effect chain should, in theory, include every thing and event in the universe. Every physical thing is caught up in an enormous, stupendously complicated *system*. Human beings, for better or worse, don't get to be innocent bystanders in this cosmic billiards game of bits of stuff bumping into and affecting other bits of stuff. We have bodies and bodies are made of matter. In our bodies are brains and the material stuff of brains seems to have a causal relationship with how and what we think. Those brains are in bodies that are in the universe controlled by the system of laws that science articulates to us. The past all happened according to the cause-and-effect chain of those laws and the unfolding chain of the past and present has already determined the future's path. Like one of those woven finger traps, the harder you tug and pull at this chain, the tighter you discover its destiny to be, says the causal determinist. When you dig way down deep, the universe of existing stuff is just a bunch of atoms arranging and rearranging themselves according to laws that we can discover but can't do a single damn thing about.

Imagine again a tattooed and an un-tattooed person. Imagine the latter insinuating that the tattooed person's decision to get inked was really a non-decision. Remember the suspicion that getting a tattoo is just yielding to the external force of what's 'cool.' If the causal determinist is right, a certain irony emerges from this scene. The suspicious, un-tattooed fellow would be right, of course. The desire, decision, and action to go get that Japanese-style sleeve or traditional sacred heart is really just an expression of the incredibly complex interactions of atoms, molecules, and proteins that make up a human body. The experience the tattooed person had of getting tattooed is just another effect of all the ongoing atomic, molecular business of the universe. The ironic bit, however, is that the decision to passive-aggressively insult the tattooed person with an impertinent question about their freedom wasn't really a decision either. It, like me writing this sentence and you reading it, was just one more expression of a universal system of causally determined interactions between little bits of stuff.

Kant, Freedom, and Alternate Natures

Of course, if the causal determinist is right, trying to make someone feel bad for going along with a fad is a complete waste of time, as is trying to defend yourself against such suggestions. What's more – as Kant, among other thinkers, realized – criticizing or praising any action as bad or good is pointless if every single little thing is just the manifestation of predetermined cause and effect. If we, as material beings, just *happen* to act one way or another as a part of the system of natural events, what would it even mean to say that anyone *does* anything? We aren't the cause of our actions and so we aren't responsible for them. We just happen to act one way or another, and we can neither start nor stop our own actions. Morality doesn't mean anything in this kind of deterministic system. Obviously, that's hard to believe and even harder to accept. Kant offered a brilliant way of getting philosophers out of the conundrum that they and the physicists had gotten themselves in. It was brilliant, and it involved an alternate universe. Well, sort of.

Technically, it involved an alternate *nature*, but what Kant meant by nature is not just trees and bees and tattoo sleeves. Rather, 'nature is the existence of things under (a system) of laws.'[4] All the stuff and events of the physical universe, then, constitute a nature under the laws of physics. In his *Critique of Practical Reason*, Kant suggested that, because the physical world is ruled by a closed system of physical laws, human freedom and morality are real, but in an *alternate nature* that has a different system of laws. That nature Kant calls 'rational nature.' Rational nature, according to Kant, has its own laws and beings that, as much as they are rational, are ruled by those laws. This is the 'internal' nature of our reasoned thinking. Just like sensible, physical nature, there is in rational nature a law of causality, but it's not a deterministic kind of causality as is found in physical nature. The causality comes from rational decisions *freely* made by rational beings, namely us. In other words, Kant's argument is that rational human beings are free, but in an alternate nature that is totally invisible, but can be found in our thinking.

For Kant, freedom is autonomy; a rational human being gives him or herself the laws under which he or she is ruled, and so we are *auto nomos* (which is Greek for 'self-lawed' or 'self-ruled'). In other words, when we make decisions according to rational law, we are acting freely because we become the source of the principle of our actions. The person who is accused of getting a tattoo as part of a trend or fad is being accused of abandoning this sort of autonomy. Some other force is giving the reasons for the faddish tattooed person's decision, and not that person's own authentic self-legislation.

Kant also argued that, when we fail to make decisions with our rational law, we inevitably decide in accord with what he calls our *inclinations*. Those inclinations are, at root, expressions of our biological existence. Basically, when we aren't ruled by our rational nature, we're ruled by our animal nature. When humans are free in the rational realm, they are choosing independent of the interference of biological (and thereby physical) nature and its laws. In terms of our tattoo-related example, the tattooed person faces the suspicion that they abandoned their independence as a thinking, rational person to more base influences. They might have gotten tattoos only to intimidate competitors and attract sexual partners, much like a peacock with its colorful tail.

Though this solution hangs together well enough philosophically, it is also unsatisfying to most of us. It seems like offering an amputation to cure how determinism ails us. We're only left with half of our humanity. This solution also makes the relationship between decision, choice, and action awfully tricky. Certainly, we can make autonomous and independent decisions, but, if the laws of rational nature determine those, was there really a *choice*? Conversely, we can make decisions determined by our inclinations in physical nature. Either way, our decisions are under a kind of determinism. It isn't clear how choice works in Kant's solution. Also, once we've decided, it is only the deciding that matters morally, because there is no way to change things 'out there' in the physical world. Physical nature is already fully determined by its laws. Freedom and morality, it seems, have become cut off from physical-world action. Kant's solution to determinism seems to work by quarantining whole portions of human life off from one another.

What, in the world of tattoos, would all this mean? Let's say that you have been thinking about getting a tattoo. You, rationally, determine that getting a tattoo wouldn't violate the moral law in any way, so you decide, 'Yes, I am going to get myself a tattoo.' This much you have done freely and morally. However, jump ahead to sitting in a chair and having an artist put a needle and ink to your skin. None of that experience has anything to do with your freedom or choice, but is instead subject to the determinism of the laws of physical nature. It's as if one's decisions and one's actions are only coincidentally related. You decide to get a tattoo and somehow the physical world intuits that decision and gives you a tattoo. Two parallel natures, one rational and one physical, just *happen* to be, more or less, corresponding. Certainly, Kant would say, you are the cause of your decision to get a tattoo, but you can't at all be considered the cause of your physically getting the tattoo. Still, this correlation seems too uncanny to let us be content with Kant's solution.

'Nature' Isn't a System

The big problem with both determinism and Kant's clever solution is that they misunderstand what science tells us about the physical world. Both of them assume that, because nature *contains* many laws and systems, *all of* nature is a system of laws. Now, there is good reason to want to think of nature as a system of laws. A system of laws is fixed and certain, so fixed and certain that you can move backwards and forwards through its parts and events like you can move backward and forward through a really big math equation and it will all make sense. You could understand or predict any one part from any other with enough time and brainpower. Science has shown us, however, that nature is fluid and its events can be predicted only in terms of probability, not certainty. I am not saying that the laws of science aren't true and don't explain the relationships between things and events in nature. I am, however, saying that they explain those relationships in an if-then kind of way. If you put a pot of water over a powerful enough heat source, then the water in it will boil and turn to water vapor. The laws of science will tell you what 'then' to expect when you have some 'if,' every time. What they won't tell you is when and where those 'ifs' will show up.[5]

Where and when the 'ifs' (*conditions*) of 'if-then' (*classical*) laws of science show up is the business of statistics. Statistics, however, doesn't deal in certainty; statistics deals in frequency and probability. Much like the classical laws of science explain how systems hang together, real statistical frequencies explain non-systematic things, such as the distribution of blades of grass in a one-foot-by-one-foot square of lawn. Non-systematic events are only related by a shared time and place, so you can't string them together into big chains of cause and effect like you can the stuff of classical laws. You can, however, discover the real frequency of those events, which is an average from which future events won't diverge systematically. If the events *are* diverging from that frequency systematically, well, that means you've got the wrong frequency and it's time to do some more observing and calculating. That, after all, is what statistics is all about.

Because causal determinism and Kant's theory of freedom both start from the assumption that science explains a completely systematic world to us, they miss the more complicated and encouraging reality that the universe is an open world into which events and things emerge more or less probably. Let me say that again, because it is going to be very important for how we talk about tattoos and freedom in the last bit of this chapter: The world is not a closed-off system determined by air-tight cause-and-effect laws telling the physical stuff of the universe how to move around. Nature, the world, and the universe are unfolding fluidly and improvisationally, like a cosmic jazz concert. If we start from determinism, like Kant does, we're going to come up with otherworldly solutions to the problem of freedom because that's not the character of the real world. This, of course, doesn't answer our question for us. We still need to know if we are free. And, if we are free, in what way.

Embodied Freedom: It Develops!

The week I turned eighteen, I got my first tattoo. Though I was a little nervous about how much getting tattooed would hurt, I laid myself down on the tattoo artist's table resolutely. I had *decided* that I was getting this tattoo as soon as I was legally allowed. Of course, there were limits and conditions on getting my first tattoo. I had to arrange an appointment, a price, and a design with an artist. I had to save the money and wait until I was old enough and come up with an image. I also had reasons for getting this tattoo. I'd wanted a tattoo since I could remember. Ultimately, it wasn't because all these conditions came together at once and it wasn't even for these reasons that I got that first tattoo. I got that tattoo because I decided I would.

When it comes right down to it, I am the 'if' to the 'then' of my first tattoo. All those other things were influencing factors, to be sure, but I was the decisive one. For that reason, it was my free choice and I was, at root, responsible for it. Getting that tattoo demonstrated both my freedom and my moral responsibility.

However, freedom and responsibility are not the disconnected, otherworldly versions found in Kant's ethical philosophy. Real freedom is an *embodied freedom* that needs the lower stuff of chemistry and biology but isn't determined by them. In fact, it determines them. I can choose when and how much to feed myself so that all the biological processes that keep my mind operating are functioning. I can choose to sleep enough or not at all or somewhere in between. However, if I don't eat or sleep enough, I might not stay conscious. If I'm not conscious, I sure won't be able to make more decisions until my blood sugar comes up or I get some rest. I can choose to hold my breath until I pass out, but, once I'm out, I'm not making any more choices. This is freedom and responsibility that is intimately related to the biology and chemistry and physics that supports it. Embodied freedom rests on those lower systems as if on a scaffold or skeleton. If the conditions of those systems start to veer from the span of a certain average, the higher things of thinking and choosing will start to fall apart.

Being conscious and thinking, though sufficient preparation for the exercise of embodied freedom, is only potentially freedom. What do I mean? Well, though I am clearly capable of choosing to receive and heal a tattoo, I might have been *unwilling* to go ahead with it. You can picture someone sitting in the lobby of a tattoo shop, their knee bouncing as they tap their foot nervously, quietly trying to talk themselves into going through with this new piece of body art. Maybe they are unwilling to face an unknown but probably painful sensation. Maybe they are unwilling to face up to a (relatively) permanent addition to their appearance. Whatever is holding them back, they aren't willing to sit in the chair and get inked. Even though they may have already paid the deposit, may have taken the day off work, or may be embarrassed to have given up on the idea, they just cannot decide to get a tattoo. Though this person is *essentially* free to get the tattoo they have picked out and saved up for, they *effectively* are not. They lack the willingness or the *effective freedom* to follow through.

Real, effective, embodied freedom is something that has to be developed. Expanding our willingness develops our freedom. When I got my first two tattoos, I was only willing to get tattoos that had deep, symbolic meaning. One day, one of my tattoo-artist friends offered to give me a small free tattoo so that he could start to get his skills back after a ten-year hiatus from tattooing. Without too much deliberation, I decided on a small umbrella and he put it on the lower outside part of my right leg. This was my first purely aesthetic ('meaningless') tattoo. Both the tattoos I've received since have been large pieces I got for almost entirely aesthetic, and not symbolic, reasons. My willingness to get tattooed for different reasons has been expanded. Much like the coalescing of 'ifs' makes some 'thens' more statistically likely in physics, chemistry, and biology, this new willingness makes certain decisions more likely. By making a series of decisions in this small way, I have developed my freedom.

The Response Part of Responsibility

Kant brought to our attention that the absence of freedom means the absence of moral responsibility. What does moral responsibility look like for people who have embodied freedom that must develop to be fully effective? It means we must be making ourselves into the kind of people willing to make the kinds of decisions demanded by the real, unfolding universe. This is the 'response' part of responsibility. Let's say you've just got a big traditional dagger tattooed on your forearm, and a day later your tattoo is red, swollen, and painful to the touch. You realize something has gone wrong in the healing process. You've transcended your mere biology to choose with freedom and authenticity getting a tattoo, but now your biology is saying 'Something's not right here!' The facts of physics, chemistry, and biology are demanding that you respond with decisive action. Now, let's say you, because of a phobia, are unwilling to go see a doctor about your increasingly painful tattoo. In this case, then, you aren't sufficiently free to meet the demands of being a responsible person. Because of unwillingness and irresponsibility, you are probably going to have some serious infection-related health issues. We need to develop our freedom so that we are willing to do what is responsible when the facts require it of us. If we aren't willing to do what the facts require, then things will tend to go poorly.

What about our original concern? We've shown how we are *capable* of making free decisions in cooperation with our biological, chemical, and physical underpinnings. How, though, can we figure out if *this* decision I made to get *this* tattoo was a really, authentically free decision or if it was a manifestation of an unwillingness *not* to get a tattoo? After all, because we have to live and make decisions before we know *how* to live and *what* decisions to make, it is entirely possible that some (even a great deal) of our decisions are constrained by an unwillingness to have done otherwise. Unfortunately, there is really only one remedy for this kind of concern and this essay can't help you out with it too much. Socrates, one of the few philosophers almost everyone has heard of, exhorted people with the divine words 'Know thyself,'[6] and, on this count, I do the same.

The only way in which you can uncover phobias, personal limitations, and other forms of unwillingness in yourself is to ask difficult, probing questions of yourself. Socrates also famously said that 'the unexamined life is not worth living,'[7] and here we've uncovered one of the reasons that he was right about that. If you don't examine yourself ruthlessly, you cannot develop in yourself the freedom to become what you most essentially are: an embodied, thinking, morally responsible person. Whether you're getting tattoos, voting, or making any other important decisions, it is important to take seriously not just the factors at work outside of you in the world but also the factors at work in the 'inner world' of your motivations, beliefs, and desires. Not only will you be liberated from constraining unwillingness, but you'll also be more likely to do what is right when circumstances demand it of you. As an added bonus, if someone challenges you on some important decision, you'll be able to look him or her in the eye with confidence and take full responsibility.

In the Space Created by that Fluid Emergence

So many of our decisions are automatic that sometimes it takes choices that fall slightly outside the norm to raise important questions for us to ponder. The decision to get – as well as bare – a tattoo can be one of those choices. In this case, we saw how the suspicions of the common-sense person raise the question of freedom for the tattooed person. Then, material or causal determinism suggested to us that the problem of freedom includes the suspicious person as much as the tattooed person. We tried to answer the problem of freedom along with Kant, but found that his answer divorced the rational part of human life from the fullness of our existence in bodies. We questioned whether determinism was even a real characteristic of the world in which we live. Science, and statistical method specifically, showed us that physical things and events are much more fluid and emergent than they are pre-determined in the sense that determinists and Kant suggest.

In the space created by that fluid emergence, I suggested that humans exercise real freedom, but a freedom that rests atop a whole host of physical, chemical, and biological 'if-then' systems. That embodied freedom is well-illustrated by how a person must cooperate with their body to pick out, receive, heal, and wear a tattoo. So, if you've got a tattoo, next time you catch a glimpse of it in the mirror, remember that it is evidence that you, in your body, are really, truly free. Don't forget, though, that your freedom must be developed and that your ability to meet your moral responsibilities depends on you making that development happen.

NOTES

1 See the episode, 'Simpson Tide,' *The Simpsons*, Season 9, Episode 19. Original Air Date: March 29, 1998. In that episode, after Bart gets his ear pierced, Lisa says: 'An earring. How rebellious – in a conformist sort of way.'

2 Philosophical questions, issues, ideas, and arguments concerning whether things in the universe – including humans – are free or determined are found in the Western philosophical area known as 'philosophy of freedom,' which is a discipline under the umbrella of 'metaphysics.' See, for example, the relevant articles in Michael Loux and Dean Zimmerman (eds.), *The Oxford Handbook of Metaphysics* (Oxford: Oxford University Press, 2003); also Alfred Mele, *Motivation and Agency* (New York: Oxford University Press, 2003); Randolph Clarke, 'Incompatibilist (nondeterministic) theories of free will,' in

JONATHAN HEAPS

Edward N. Zalta (ed.), *Stanford Encyclopedia of Philosophy* (Fall 2009, http://plato.stanford.edu/entries/incompatibilism-theories); and Carl Hoefer, 'Causal determinism, ' in Edward N. Zalta (ed.), *Stanford Encyclopedia of Philosophy* (Fall 2009, http://plato.stanford.edu/entries/determinism-causal).

3   See Immanuel Kant, *Critique of the Power of Judgment*, trans. Eric Mathews and Paul Guyer (Cambridge: Cambridge University Press, 2001), p. 115. Kant uses the case of New Zealanders with tattoos to argue that tattoos are neither art nor beautiful.

4   Immanuel Kant, *Critique of Practical Reason*, trans. Mary Gregor (New York: Cambridge University Press, 1997), p. 42.

5   These sections on the relationship between classical and statistical knowledge borrow heavily from Bernard Lonergan's *Insight*, ed. Robert Doran and Frederick Crowe (Toronto, ON: University of Toronto Press, 1992), vol. 3. Also see John Dupré, *The Disorder of Things: Metaphysical Foundations of the Disunity of Science* (Cambridge, MA: Harvard University Press, 1993) and the papers in Harold Kincaid, John Dupré, and Alison Wylie (eds.), *Value-Free Science: Ideal or Illusion?* (Oxford: Oxford University Press, 2007).

6   Plato, *Phaedrus*, in John Cooper (ed.), *Plato: Collected Works* (Indianapolis, IN: Hackett Publishing Company, 1997), 229E.

7   Plato, *Apology*, in John Cooper (ed.), *Plato: Collected Works* (Indianapolis, IN: Hackett Publishing Company, 1997), 38A.

SHEET VI

EXPERIENCES AND STORIES SURROUNDING TATTOOS

'Tattooing is a practice of writing, an activity or performance that always exceeds its original inscription, through which stories are told, and in virtue of which a better understanding of the relationship of human selves to human embodiment under particular conditions/within specific contexts is made possible.'

(Wendy Lynn Lee, p. 155–156)

CHAPTER 12

NEVER MERELY 'THERE'

Tattooing as a Practice of Writing and a Telling of Stories

Story One: Sewn into My Skin is Written into My Story

Some visible tattooing of not-terribly-feminine themes (geckos and Chinese pictographs), in black, in the unlikely venue of a fiftyish, white, female, academic body. Or Marxist, feminist, environmentalist, animal welfare activism inscribed as such in ink. Or conversation starter/ice-breaker. Or, this mommy's not interested in your fucking rules of appropriate civil behavior. Or, yawn … fads come, fads go; one day's 'cool' is another's 'whatever.' Any of these describe my tattoos depending on the audience, the location, the lighting, and the season – even my own disposition toward them, myself, and the world at the moment. I often forget about my tattoos, and wonder what people are looking at, when they're looking, if they're looking.

Not that forgetting means their significance has faded. No: my ink is so deeply woven into my life, into my sensibilities about the world, that forgetting it is more like taking for granted I have things like legs, eyes, and arms. Fortunate me. It's a special luxury to be able to forget them, and I like telling their stories – including the part that's not about the

Tattoos – Philosophy for Everyone: I Ink, Therefore I Am, First Edition.
Edited by Robert Arp.
© 2012 John Wiley & Sons, Inc. Published 2012 by John Wiley & Sons, Inc.

meaning but the pain. Indeed, the pain is about the meaning, and vice versa – somehow. Tattooing is violent; it hurts, it can make you vomit, it involves blood. I have ink sewn into my skin, perforating it, permanently disfiguring it, re-configuring the terrain of my body. Better to say, 'I'm inked.' But what does this mean? What does it mean to say I chose this disfigurement? Chose it freely? Against the wills of others (my kids), against the 'look' of my profession?

Does it matter that I paid for my ink? That, as 'tats' have become advertised as not just for sailors, bikers, circus performers, or gang members anymore, they've gotten pricier? What kind of product is something so intimately featured on its buyer's body? Intimate doesn't mean 'like a pacemaker.' No one depends on their tattoo as they depend on a pacemaker (or on kidney dialysis, or even a prosthetic). But are tattoos more like cars, houses, gym memberships, or jewelry – just another decorative expression of our capacity to consume? None of these, I'll argue, comes close to capturing what it means to be inked because neither capture the story 'told' by a tattoo of the intimate relationship between a tattooed subject and her or his embodied experience. Whatever else is true about tattooing, tattoos are never 'merely there.'

Story Two: Tattooing at Auschwitz – Ink, Terror, Death

Some concentration camp prisoners at Auschwitz were tattooed – those registered for work, those not dispatched directly to the gas chambers. These tattoos, whose origins were profoundly different from my own stories of celebration, commemoration, or resistance, were intended to identify the bodies of the worked-to-death when indelible marker failed:

> Initially, the SS authorities marked prisoners who were in the infirmary or who were to be executed with their camp serial number across the chest with indelible ink. As prisoners were executed or died in other ways, their clothing bearing the camp serial number was removed. Given the mortality rate at the camp and the practice of removing clothing, there was no way to identify the bodies after the clothing was removed. Hence, the SS authorities introduced the practice of tattooing in order to identify the bodies of registered prisoners who had died.[1]

Tattooing at Auschwitz signified the capacity for work and the presumption of death. Like a model number inscribed onto a machine-bit, it chronicled the transformation of some 400,000 human beings into disposable tools:

> A special metal stamp, holding interchangeable numbers made up of needles approximately one centimeter long was used. This allowed the whole serial number to be punched at one blow onto the prisoner's left upper chest. Ink was then rubbed into the bleeding wound.[2]

'Not desired,' 'not sought,' 'not saved-up-for,' 'not-beautiful,' 'not chosen' seem grossly inadequate to capture this ink. Even words such as 'unthinkable,' 'horrific,' 'inhuman' seem bland in light of the computational efficiency of dispatch recorded onto the bloodied surfaces of these human bodies.

How can words such as 'story' encompass a program so systematically brutal and dehumanizing? What sense can be made of language such as 'writing' to describe a number so punctured? How could the Auschwitz tattoos be anything other than 'merely there' for these prisoners? 'Willfully forgotten' or 'paralyzing reminder' might seem far more forthright than 'story.' My claim, however, is that the meaning of the Auschwitz tattoos – all tattoos – *exceeds* their original circumstances, and that they do so regardless of the desires, intentions, feelings, or attitudes of those who ink them, have them, see them, or remove them. A tattoo is not *only* never merely there; it is *performative* – it *does* something. It tells a very important kind of story.

The Auschwitz tattoos dispatched thousands of concentration camp prisoners to a trajectory of labor, exhaustion, and, nearly always, death. They distinguished between those recognized as living and those destined for the gas chambers and therefore effectively dead. But these origins can't adequately capture the experience signified in the ink, not because those tattooed necessarily knew its purpose but because the content of the tattooing, impersonal and efficient for the Nazis, signifies a world, an experiential context, for Holocaust survivors. Tova Friedman, for example, refuses to have her tattoo removed:

> Sometimes [she] meets someone who believes the Holocaust never happened. That's when she shows them her tattoo on her arm, 'A27633,' a mark she was branded with as a 5-year-old girl at Auschwitz. Four million perished at the German concentration camp.[3]

Friedman related her experiences as a Holocaust survivor:

> 'They told me I no longer had a name,' said Friedman … 'Some people told me I should have got rid of the tattoo,' she said. 'I respond by saying that it

was nothing I did. The world should be ashamed, not me. Sometimes you are going to meet people who say the Holocaust didn't happen... That's why it's so important for me to talk. Most of them didn't make it. By telling you my story, I also tell you their stories. I just don't want them to be forgotten.'

For Friedman, 'A27633' isn't merely a reminder of Auschwitz; it exceeds the story of a little girl who survived a concentration camp. That's why she tells her story. Her tattoo tells the story of her family, the dead, Auschwitz. Even more: it confronts those who would deny the Holocaust occurred.

Freidman's story connects her as an embodied experiencing subject to the history of the 'tortured body,' a history I argue that's told in resistance to 'the institutions and practices reinforced in the violence acted out against' subjects like Friedman:

> The tortured body speaks through the subject's attempts to protect herself, through her compliance, and through the physical space she occupies while she endures being beaten. Her very comportment signifies the institutions and practices reinforced in the violence acted out against her. Even in death, her body signifies her as an individuated thing whose identity is past or spent, and whose treatment in death is as much prescribed by law as her actions in life. Far from mute, bodies materialize subjects such that identification by others – particularly those responsible for acts of violence against them – is made possible.[4]

'A27633' defies those who claim the Holocaust is a conspiracy or a hoax; the tattoo demands accountability. It refuses shame; it connects the particularity of subjects to the practices, institutions, and historicity of its advent. But, if storytelling is the right way to think about tattoos like Friedman's – tattoos we might otherwise be tempted to see as fixed, alienated, the first to be removed – it is the right way, I suggest, to think about all tattooing.

Story Three: Tattooing as a Practice of Writing, Unwriting, Inscription, and Counterinscription

Consider the performative tattooing of self-identified radical feminists, the Suicide Girls:

> Tattooing is a form of radical feminist identification. Jaylin, a Suicide Girl, is a part of an alternative genre of feminist actors who perform the pain of

beauty in order to upset beauty's hegemonic control on women's bodies. The tattoos ... speak to the contradictory performances of gendered actors in light of [Judith] Butler's theories on agency to highlight the ways in which agents subvert imposed subjectivities ... Beauty is thus not only a system of control, but also a means by which the individual can resist power structures through positive articulations of one's agency. Tattooing is a radical form of feminist self-identification.[5]

Conceptual (and contextual) light years away from serial numbers punctured without consent onto the bodies of concentration camp prisoners, the Suicide Girls embrace ink as a symbol of liberation from heteropatriarchal beauty standards. Harlow argues that tattooing offers a strategy for subverting a femininity conceived as a 'system of control' and oppressive 'power structures.' The chosen tattoo both denies heteropatriarchal images of beauty and reclaims 'beauty' via the appropriation of tattooing as a feminist value. As Margo DeMello argues, for feminist scholars such as Judith Butler 'the body is both the site for the inscription of power and the primary site for the resistance to that power – the body itself entails the possibility of counterinscription.'[6]

SuicideGirls.com has 2,167 members, 276,005 uploaded photographs, 17,809 articles, and 35,497,439 comments, boasting 'a community that celebrates ALTERNATIVE BEAUTY and alternative culture from all over the world.' Membership is selective: 'You MUST attend a SGPhilly event, or have a glowing recommendation to join. If you are not an active member of the website, or without profile pictures, don't even bother applying.' Cited by the *Los Angeles Times* as a 'nationwide art sleaze phenomenon,' the photographs posted by the Suicide Girls open a Pandora's box of questions about what constitutes a feminist response to heteropatriarchal institutions, what role ink plays, and what role the sexually charged imagery of web-entrepreneurs such as the Suicide Girls plays in resistance to heteropatriarchal industries such as pornography, prostitution, marriage, and the marketing of beauty.[7]

I am less concerned here, however, with these issues than I am with what a Suicide Girl appropriation of tattooing might mean for how we understand tattooing; or, better, how we might most usefully understand what tattoos do as a kind of storytelling. One philosophical claim runs as follows:

Tattooing is a practice of writing, an activity or performance that always exceeds its original inscription, through which stories are told, and in virtue of which a better understanding of the relationship of human selves to human embodiment under particular conditions/within specific contexts is made possible.

Tattoos are, in other words, a dynamic site or venue for the ways in which the circumstances of human embodiment inform self-identity. They function as such regardless of their content or particular circumstance. They are a specific kind of site in that they involve a writing on/in the body. Ink inscribes and counter-inscribes, but its meanings can change – indeed, *will* change insofar as they are permeated by the experience of their embodied subjects but not necessarily controlled by those subjects.

This isn't to say that tattooing is rightly conceived as a conversion of body to text. Tattoos do not textualize embodiment. Bodies aren't 'books,' but selves are storytellers. Embodiment is experienced as the venue of a performance; a prison; a site of pleasure or pain; an instrument of violence, bravery, or comfort; as the self's activity as an agent; or, alternatively, as a subject denied agency. Tattoos are not read inasmuch as they are witnessed; they are not merely presented but rather performed as an activity of inscribing. Whatever their content, however unique or generic, however badly or well inked, however their stories are told (truthfully or as complete fabrications), tattoos tell a story or stories of the relationship of a human being to their body in a way that, unlike piercing or even branding, entails and discloses aspects of the evolving (or deteriorating) particularity of that contextually situated, embodied self.

Tova Friedman's tattoos tell as vibrant a story about Friedman as do those of the Suicide Girl Jaylin about her. This would be true regardless of whether Freidman at some point determined that she no longer wanted to tell her story of being a little girl at Auschwitz, had her tattoos removed, and fabricated a story about a fire accident to explain the scarring. It would be true if Jaylin adopted an oppressive form of fundamentalist Christianity, had her tattoos removed, and also fabricated a story to explain the scarring. If such comparison makes us uncomfortable, this is at least in part because the performative aspect of a tattoo – even one removed – is so powerful. It demands that stories be told, even when they're not true, even when their tellers fabricate alternatives.

The sense in which telling is a kind of doing is also the sense in which stories are not merely accounts. Accounts do typically include a narrative, but they are also presumed to correspond to events at least believed to have actually occurred. Nothing necessitates a 'truth value' for a story, including those we might tell about our tattoos. An account is fixed in the sense that, once settled, it is conceived as unchangeable unless by some discovery relevant to the facts (themselves conceived as fixed). *The Holocaust Encyclopedia* offers an account of tattooing at Auschwitz, but it can't exhaust the stories of its victims. What, however, may most tellingly distinguish accounts from stories in the case of tattooing is that while accounts offer a narrative of the facts regardless of the status of their subjects, the stories told by tattoos are never so detached. Even when they might seem to have nothing to do with the identity of their subjects, where their subjects might disown or remove them, tattoos remain performative, perhaps more so in these cases than in any other – including that of the Suicide Girls.

Why? To *desubjectify* was the point of tattooing at Auschwitz. The Nazis' aim was to negate the subjectivity, particularity, and humanity of individual persons.[8] In converting subjects into instruments, a Nazi guard with a punch-gun seems far removed from the performance of the Suicide Girls' pain-as-beauty. For Harlow, Suicide Girl tattooing is a form of self-expression, a vehicle of resistance through which a woman can transform herself from being (seen as) the sexualized, objectified instrument of male manipulation into an agent of her own aspirations. She subjectifies herself through the performance of 'the pain of beauty.' Deliberate, aesthetic, provocative, personal, and unique, Suicide Girl tattooing seems to be everything Auschwitz isn't. Here is a story we might then be tempted to tell: via ink, Jaylin tells the story of her emancipation from heteropatriarchy. She counter-inscribes herself against stereotypical beauty standards as an agent of her own decisions. The concentration camp prisoner, however, is denied agency through a number inked onto skin against their will. For Friedman, a tattoo is an obituary. Tattooing subjectifies in one case, and desubjectifies in the other. Is it that simple? Is that the right story? No.

Auschwitz and the Suicide Girls involve institutions premised on the threat of violence. Walter Benjamin distinguishes violence as a means from violence as an end and argues that all 'violence as means is either lawmaking or law-preserving. If it lays claim to neither of these predicates, it forfeits all claim to validity.' He then goes on to develop an aetiology of violence arguing that violence is not merely artifactual to the breaking of law but rather informs its creation and preservation in law, which codifies the use of force under particular circumstances and in particular spaces.[9] Both Nazi fascism and heteropatriarchy are premised on this threat for those who fail to conform to the law. 'A27633' encodes the law on Friedman's body, reminding her of its institutions, inscribing a direct threat of violence should she break it. Such violence desubjectifies her (for the Nazis). It is thus hard to imagine anything more dissimilar than Jaylin's performance, but this isn't because Jaylin doesn't pay for her transgression of the heteropatriarchal law. Being denied employment, stereotyped as queer, or assaulted by men to show her what a 'real woman' 'wants' are all risks Jaylin takes in the deliberate inscription of her subversive story.

The dissimilarity consists not in Jaylin's relationship to the law but in her relation to the violence deployed to enforce it. Unlike Friedman, Jaylin occupies a position where she is empowered to subvert the violence spent to desubjectify Friedman. Her performance satirizes the law. She solicits violence as a kind of politically empowering aphrodisiac; she occupies a position from which she can say 'no' to the tattooist. She chooses the themes of her tattooing. Even if she were to choose a random numerical code, say 'A27633,' and have it 'punched' onto her chest wall to symbolize her rejection of corporate America, her identification with Holocaust survivors, or her love of numbers, it could not but tell the story of her agency, at least at that moment, despite any (and legitimate) claim she might make to subjection under heteropatriarchy:

> Suicide Girls performances blur the boundaries between beauty and beast. Jaylin speaks to the horror of the beauty hegemony in visual screams of pain on stage. Bringing the blood to the surface, let the red drops fall, let it spill, let it stand for pain, let it express that which is real and unspoken. A multiplicity of powers emerges, reclaiming the dead as free to name themselves. To start speaking about pain is to inscribe meanings upon a history that wrote woman as passive … Jaylin speaks her gender in a way that goes against the institutional norms of a Playboy world.[10]

Jaylin takes herself to be undermining an institution that objectifies and demeans her. Yet her relationship to her performance is also mediated by other institutions elided in it. The theater is rented, the tattooist engaged for the performance and paid. Invited people drive, take buses, and bicycles to see it. There might be music, a disk jockey, dancers. There is lighting and ink ready to go in technicolor under clean, safe, controlled conditions. However much it is a subversion of heteropatriarchal beauty standards, it's not obvious that a Suicide Girl performance is a rejection of, say, corporate capitalism or Western standards of safety, health, and hygiene.

I'm not suggesting that the Suicide Girl strategy to reinscribe heteropatriarchal 'woman' as 'text devoid of meaning' isn't a valuable feminist counter-narrative; it may be. But I'm not convinced it exceeds law-giving or enforcement in any way that makes Jaylin's tattooing a radical performance of agency. Insofar as Friedman tells her story for those who 'didn't make it,' so that they 'won't be forgotten,' the embodied self disclosed through her tattooing may offer the more compelling story of resistance – and a critique of Benjamin: 'For those for whom being a coherent subject is fraught with the intrusions of a destabilizing materiality, embodiment is a witness – even the undesired witness manifest in the blood, color, or wear which identifies gender, race, and class.'[11] Friedman 'reclaims the dead as free to name themselves' in the minds of her audience, even in the minds of Holocaust-deniers. Her story *exceeds* law-making and law-enforcement because it resists the Nazi extermination-narrative and the Aryan 'law' of racial superiority. It cannot be contained as a violation of the law because what it interrogates in every witness of A27633 is the legitimacy of the law itself. Does as much follow from the stories of the Suicide Girls? Not obviously.

Story Four: 'Real' Tattoos and the Excesses of Meaning

Consider this, offered by the anonymous male blogger 'spiderz':

> A genuine tattoo tells a story. They're symbolic of the important moments in your life, no matter how well done. If they don't tell a story that grabs you emotionally, then they're just there for decorations ... that makes them not a valid tattoo. There has to be some emotional appeal or they're not ... a real tattoo. It could be the most beautiful tattoo in the world, but if it's for pure decoration, it might as well be wallpaper in your grandma's house. On the flipside, you can take the ugliest tattoo, put a powerful story behind it and it suddenly becomes an extremely beautiful piece of work.[12]

Although spiderz recognizes a connection between tattoos and stories, his criteria for what counts as 'valid' is problematic. It is, however, the way in which his criteria are problematic that reveals something important about how the context of tattooing can inform our conceptions of ourselves as embodied human beings.

According to spiderz, tattoos are 'symbolic of the important moments in your life, no matter how well done. If they don't tell a story that grabs you emotionally, then they're just there for decorations.' Fair enough.

But, while it's true that Auschwitz tattooing constitutes an 'important moment,' that Freidman's story grabs us emotionally, and that Auschwitz tattoos fall into spiderz's category of ugly tattoos turned beautiful, it defies credulity to suggest that failing these criteria renders such tattoos merely 'decorative.' This isn't because the utilitarian can never be decorative; it's because the conditions of the Auschwitz tattooing defy spiderz's apparent assumptions about tattooing as a freely chosen performance. He claims that tattoos 'tell people what you are and what you believe in.' But little could be further from the truth for Friedman, except, I think, in the following respect: though not freely chosen, her tattoos signify, by contrast, what its victims were as Jews and what they believed in as Jews – simply because, according to the Nazis, they were Jews.

Such is what makes little girls like Friedman candidates for extermination and the stuff of stories like this:

> Students listened intently as [Friedman] described how she was transported to Auschwitz for three days in a cattle car by train without food, water or any privacy... She told how all the prisoners were stripped and had to walk naked by the Nazis to see if they were healthy ... Some people didn't pass inspection ... They were shot or taken to the crematorium. We smelled the smoke and the burning flesh ... Hunger was unbearable ... All I thought about was food. I forgot about my mother and father. I forgot I belonged to anybody.

However horrific the conditions, Friedman refuses to be desubjectified by them. Instead, she reclaims herself as an embodied human *agent* capable of making choices through the telling of her story. She confronts the disbelievers in her audience not merely with evidence but with the embodiment of Nazi brutality. She reappropriates the integrity of the relationship between herself and her body as that of a Holocaust survivor through her tattoo – despite the fact that her tattooing does not fit spiderz's criteria for what makes a tattoo meaningful: being chosen.

The fact that Friedman had no say in the original tattooing does not by itself imply that there is nothing about it that is not freely chosen – even if 'freely chosen' means 'removed.' The Auschwitz tattoos remain performative even for the dead insofar as they offer identification to others. They tell the story of that person to others. Such tattoos are 'beautiful' not necessarily because they exhibit aesthetic qualities but because they may be the only way to identify the body of someone who had a family, an occupation, aspirations, worries, a life – someone who was loved, someone who can no longer make choices. It doesn't matter whether such identifications are accurate; the 'powerful story' behind 'the ugly tattoo,' as spiderz puts it, needn't be true. It needs to be believed – and this is possible even for a misidentified body. The story of this tattooing is heartrending, but what could make clearer the intimacy of the relationship of human selves to human bodies than the search for a number that identifies the body of your mother, your father, your sister, your brother?

There is no necessary connection between the content of a tattoo and its being 'real' or 'genuine.' There is no necessary relationship between 'freely chosen' and 'meaningful.' There is no guarantee that 'meaningful' will mean the same thing to others, or even to oneself over time. There is another sense, however, in which a tattoo might be said to desubjectify a subject, and this sense applies perhaps more obviously to the Suicide Girls than to Friedman. On the one hand, 'tattooing signifies a violence through which one can take possession of oneself and one's presentation to others as tattooed; this may be so especially under those conditions where one's choice of theme is originally composed (not flash or 'off the wall').'[13] Such is the upshot of Harlow's argument. On the other hand, however, 'tattooing both subjectifies and de-subjectifies in that however it's experienced as chosen, it identifies its bearer with a subculture distinguished by class (economic underclass), sex (male), and ethnicity (predominantly white).'[14] To whatever extent, in other words, that such tattooing is identified with this subculture, it can desubjectify those who choose it as a form of self-expression regardless of their intentions.

Consider the association on the Internet of the Suicide Girls with pornography. While Harlow insists that performances like Jaylin's depict a feminist claim to emancipation, what a Google search of 'Suicide Girl' produces are websites tailored for the male consumption of female bodies. *Encyclopedia Dramatica* satirizes Suicide Girl outrage at the site's sale of photographs to 'hard core' porn sites:

> Despite promoting themselves as 'art' pushers, the makers of Suicide Girls have a habit of selling the rights of the photos to hardcore porn sites. This sparked a lot of drama when the models were aghast to find themselves being referenced as cock hungry maniacs in dark corners of the web.[15]

Wired describes the ensuing 'exodus' of models as 'battering' to the Suicide Girl reputation as an artsy-feminist website.[16]

It's not my mission to weigh in on whether the Suicide Girls represent a genuine feminism, much less whether pornography consumed primarily by men can be squared with feminist sexual emancipation. My argument is that, whatever the aims of the Suicide Girls, one of the ways in which their use of tattooing exceeds any message of emancipation is as pornography for the men of a primarily white, heterosexual, working-class subculture. 'Owl Eyes,' of the blog 'Boner Killer,' argues: 'all that is different is the women are put in leather outfits and covered in cliché tattoos like pin up girls and stars ... it's NOT underground or alternative in 2010 to have tattoos.'[17] For her, Suicide Girl tattooing amounts to an advertising gimmick, a sales pitch for porn: 'I don't see how this is "alternative" when the women are still portrayed as nymphomaniacs awaiting [sic] to please a man.'[18]

Tattooing can thus exceed its original intention and promote the consumption and anonymity of subjects desubjectified. Such is what Jean Baudrillard might describe as an example of the ecstasy of communication:

> *We no longer partake of the drama of alienation, but are in the ecstasy of communication*. And this ecstasy is obscene. Obscene is that which eliminates the gaze, the image and every representation. Obscenity is not confined to sexuality, because today there is a pornography of information and communication, a pornography of circuits and networks, of functions and objects in their legibility, availability, regulation, forced signification, capacity to perform, connection, polyvalence, their free expression ... it is the obscenity of that which no longer contains a secret and is entirely soluble in information and communication.[19]

Baudrillard returns us to Auschwitz: while the purposes are perhaps incommensurably different, the obscenity is the same. The Auschwitz tattoos signify an 'excess of communication,' converting human bodies into 'information and communication.' Obscenity is thus no more 'confined to sexuality' than is any strategy that alienates embodiment from self. An excess of communication isn't necessarily an excess of meaning; it renders 'meaning' a place-holder for any story, including contradictory stories about the emancipation of the feminist self or 'alternative porn bullshit,' or even the Holocaust denier's fatuous stories of Jewish conspiracies and deceit.

Meaningful comparison, however, ends here. For, what distinguishes Tova Friedman from Jaylin is that Friedman demands an end to alienation, an end to the obscenity of reckless communication. Whereas Suicide Girl photographs may be entirely soluble into a 'communication' where the challenge to beauty stereotypes is demoted to a titillating feature of pornographic advertisement, Friedman's story directs us back to A27633 as a site of resistance and demand for hope.

A Final Story: My Geckos

All tattoos are real tattoos, but this doesn't guarantee that all are meaningful, or that the ways in which a tattoo discloses the story of an embodied self emphasize the story we want to tell. Tattoos can erect a phalanx against an invasive world and invite an intimacy – they can fight and flirt, all at once. They involve violence, sexiness, and the repulsive. Tattooing is a practice that spills over the boundaries of its intended meaning – however merely decorative or profound – effectively interrogating that meaning, reinscribing it, changing it up. Tattoos signify not only a story of their origination but the ongoing story of me or 'me.' Via location, visibility, color, size, content, and/or juxtaposition, tattoos aren't ink on skin; they enflesh a life whose ongoingness is inscribed in them. They embody what is enforced upon us without our consent, or, as in the case of the Suicide Girls, with consent that remains suspect. Once they're inked, they're mine. They solicit my stories. I can have them erased. They can pick me out in a line-up. They can persist after my death. Whatever else is true, they're never merely there.

NOTES

1 'Tattoos and numbers: The system of identifying prisoners at Auschwitz,' in *United States Holocaust Memorial Museum Holocaust Encyclopedia* (http://www. ushmm.org/wlc/en/article.php? ModuleId=10007056).
2 Wendy Lynne Lee, 'On the (im)materiality of violence: Subjects, bodies, and the experience of pain,' *Feminist Theory* 6, 3 (2005): 288.
3 All quotes relating to Tova Friedman's story are taken from John Burdick, 'Holocaust survivor keeps stories alive. Woman was sent to Auschwitz at 5 years old.' *The Holland Sentinel* (October 19, 2002, http://isurvived.org/ StoryAlive_Holocaust.html).
4 Lee, 'On the (im)materiality of violence.'
5 Megan Jean Harlow, 'Suicide Girls: Tattooing as radical feminist agency,' *Advances in Communication Theory and Research* 2 (2009; http://www.k-state. edu/actr/2009/12/20/suicide-girls-tattooing-as-radical-feminist-agency-megan-jean-harlow/default.htm).
6 Margo DeMello, Bodies *of Inscription: A Cultural History of the Modern Tattoo Community* (Durham, NC: Duke University Press, 2000), p. 173.
7 See http://www.vanishingtattoo.com/suicide_girls_galleries.htm.
8 Lee, 'On the (im)materiality of violence,' p. 293.

9   Walter Benjamin, 'Critique of violence,' in Marcus Bullock and Michael W. Jennings (eds.), *Walter Benjamin: Selected Writings, Volume I, 1913–1926* (Cambridge, MA: Harvard University Press, 2004), pp. 236–252.

10 Megan Jean Harlow, 'Suicide Girls.'

11 Lee, 'On the (im)materiality of violence,' p. 290.

12 spiderz, 'Tattoo philosophy and passion,' *The Experience Project* (October 15, 2008, http://www.experienceproject.com/stories/Have-Tattoos/344314).

13 Lee, 'On the (im)materiality of violence,' p. 293.

14 Ibid.

15 'Suicide Girls' (http://suicidegirls.com).

16 Randy Dotinga, 'SuicideGirls gone AWOL,' *Wired* (September 28, 2005, http://www.wired.com/culture/lifestyle/news/2005/09/69006).

17 Boner Killer, '"Owl eyes" and "alternative" porn – Suicide Girls and barely rotten girls: Sexualizing violence, embracing white male supremacy and reinforcing gender roles' (September 2, 2010, http://bonerkilling.blogspot.com/2010/09/alternative-porn-suicide-girls-and-half.html).

18 Ibid.

19 Jean Baudrillard. 'The ecstasy of communication,' in William McNeill and Karen Feldman (eds.), *Continental Philosophy: An Anthology* (Malden, MA: Blackwell, 1998), pp. 441–446.

CHAPTER 13

SOMETHING TERRIBLY FLAWED

Philosophy and 'The Illustrated Man'

There is no perfect beauty that hath not strangeness in the proportion.

(Sir Francis Bacon)

A Bad Sign?

Why talk about tattoos philosophically? The *anthropological* study of tattoos as universal social and symbolic features is familiar. For thousands of years, tattoos have stood for status and identity in a great diversity of cultures. Then, as today, tattoos have functioned as both metaphor and reality for 'how the body is both inscribed by culture and counterinscribed by individuals.'[1]

And yet tattoos are a study in opposites unlike any other form of bodily scarification. Signifying singular experiences, shared trials, and remembrances, they are deeply personal. At their best, they are distinctive, unique pieces of bodily artwork. They may be beautiful or strange, or both, but, like the classical music and sculpture of 'high art,' a correct reaction to tattooing 'marks the beholder with aesthetic properties and elevates him or her in society.'[2] Beyond most people's appreciation of

Tattoos – Philosophy for Everyone: I Ink, Therefore I Am, First Edition.
Edited by Robert Arp.
© 2012 John Wiley & Sons, Inc. Published 2012 by John Wiley & Sons, Inc.

high art, though, 'tats' have a mystique that is equally rooted in primitive attitudes toward spirit and body as well as a uniquely subversive modern counter-culture that believes the primitive to be superior politically, culturally, and spiritually to today.[3] Inscribed as they are, not so much *on* but *into* the body, they nonetheless represent private ideas or feelings, yet in public and (mostly) permanent ways.

Tattoos, of course, are both expressive and symbolic, and so have a social character. Anthropologist Mary Douglas underscores this interpersonal dimension of tattooing: 'The human body is always treated as an image of society,' she writes, 'and there can be no natural way of considering the body that does not involve at the same time a social dimension.'[4] However, unlike many other socially valued goods – fashion, money, influence – tattooing, as the unique fusion of an individual's body and an inked pattern, is not 'fungible.' It can't be traded in for other goods, and I can't trade the social recognition (or disdain) that I earn by having a tattoo for other social goods, much less give it away to someone who needs it more than me. Tattooing also signifies a depth of commitment on the part of the soon-to-be-tattooed that easily outweighs that of trying a new hairstyle or buying different types of clothes.[5] The possibility of a conscientious and self-organizing 'tattoo community' means that this type of bodily scarification has expanded beyond the monopoly of interest that the working-class 'bikers,' 'sailors,' and 'scratchers' had in tattoo culture.[6] It was probably this culture that Truman Capote was allegedly referring to when he claimed, after interviewing one hundred killers over a decade, 'There's something really the matter with most people who wear tattoos ... I know from experience there's something terribly flawed about people who are tattooed above the little something Johnny had done in the Navy, even though that's also a bad sign.'

Perhaps some philosophical reflection can help to advance our understanding of and appreciation for the tattooing art past Capote's hasty generalization. Yet I don't think philosophy can do this alone, however, since it has a long and disastrous history of downplaying the importance of the lived body to the quality of human experience.[7] So, as an untattooed philosopher, I intend to press into service American literary great Ray Bradbury (b. 1920). The title of one of Bradbury's more famous fictions, 'The Illustrated Man,' hearkens back to loud and lusty carnival sideshows, and has become synonymous with the love of tattoos. This particular short story of Bradbury's – as well as his later tale 'The Illustrated Woman' – offers an opportunity to peek underneath the hem

KEVIN S. DECKER

of the freak-show tent to catch a glimpse of what tattooing really represents in the deep identity of Americans. The goal is not only to increase your understanding and appreciation of the distinctive art form of tattooing with its important counter-cultural dimensions. Because Bradbury's tattooed men and women appear in a universe whose boundaries are those of fantastic 'weird fiction,' what follows could raise your *apprehensiveness* as well.

Pictures of the Future on Your Skin

The larger story of how Bradbury came to pen tales of tragic, tattooed protagonists is itself an odd one. In his short stories, Bradbury creates his own brand of 'magical realism,' a deeply philosophical literary mode more commonly associated with Latin American writers such as Gabriel Garcia Márquez (b. 1927) and Isabelle Allende (b. 1942. Magical realism 'employs various techniques that endow all things with a deeper meaning and reveal mysteries that always threaten the secure tranquility of simple and ingenuous things.'[8] But, in Bradbury, this never occurs at the sacrifice of wider social significance. In 1950, Bradbury cared deeply about the possibility of atomic war, the misuses of technology, and race tensions, and all these factors are reflected in his stories from the 1950s. His idea of the sideshow's illustrated man is attractive not just because of the strange fascination that tattoos typically incite in us but also because of the promise of knowing something certain about the future. Bradbury's haunting twist to tattoos that tell the future is that they typically portray grim events that drive the characters that see them into a manic state, thus turning the tattoos into self-fulfilling prophecies.

In fact, Bradbury produced two fictional creations entitled 'The Illustrated Man.' The first was a short story published in *Esquire* in 1950 that presents us with Mr. William Philippus Phelps, a carnival sideshow attraction whose tattoos cover his body and bewitch audiences with their vivacity. The second is a set of stories, originally published from 1947 to 1950 and collected in the anthology *The Illustrated Man* by Doubleday in 1951. According to the editor of the critical edition of Bradbury's works, both the book's 'framing narrative' of weird stories unwinding from a sideshow freak's tats and the earlier short story focus on three perennial Bradburian themes: 'preoccupation with the temporal paradox ... the grotesque body, [and] the loneliness of the outsider.'[9]

The short story is, like many good weird tales, full of madness and murder. It begins,

> 'Hey, the Illustrated Man!' a calliope screamed, and Mr. William Philippus Phelps stood, arms folded, high on the summer-night platform, a crowd unto himself ... He was an entire civilization. In the Main Country, his chest, the Vasties lived – nipple-eyed dragons swirling over his fleshpot, his almost feminine breasts. His navel was the mouth of a slit-eyed monster – an obscene, in-sucked mouth, toothless as a witch. And there were secret caves where Darklings lurked, his armpits, adrip with slow subterranean liquors, where the Darklings, eyes jealously ablaze, peered out through rank creeper and hanging vine.[10]

Phelps is an unhappy character from the start. True, things were not always this way, and Phelps was not always the illustrated man. Phelps and Lisabeth meet and fall in love while working at a carnival. After marriage and a brief but happy honeymoon period, they begin to fight constantly and, suffering from psychological compensation, Phelps becomes morbidly obese. Searching for any lure that may bring his wife back into his charms, Phelps seeks out an unusual tattoo artist in the country who is, in fact, one of Bradbury's beloved witches: 'she was a thing sewn tight into whispers and silence.'[11] The tattoo witch, despite her sewn-shut eyes, ears, and nose, instantly captivates Phelps when she shows him a picture of himself on her palm, a tattoo that has been there since before her visitor was born.[12] The witch inscribes him with needles and 'vials of tattoo milk – red, lightning-blue, brown, cat-yellow':

> 'I know the Deep Past and the Clear Present and the even Deeper Future,' she whispered, eyes knotted into blindness, face lifted to this unseen man. 'It is on my flesh. I will paint it onto yours, too. You will be the only *real* Illustrated Man in the universe. I'll give you special pictures you will never forget. Pictures of the Future on your skin.'[13]

But what is a witch without a curse? Two of Phelps' new tattoos are covered with gauze, not to be unveiled at the carnival until one and two weeks have passed, respectively. 'The Future is in these pictures,' the witch warns. 'You can't look now or it may spoil them. They are not quite finished. I put ink on your flesh, and the sweat of you forms the rest of the picture, the Future – your sweat and your thought.'[14]

❦ KEVIN S. DECKER

Never a Tattooed Man Like This

The Illustrated Man wows the crowds every night, because 'there had never been a tattooed man like this':

> Mr. William Philippus Phelps was a museum jolted to life. Fish swam in seas of electric-blue ink. Fountains sparkled under yellow suns. Ancient buildings stood in meadows of harvest wheat. Rockets burn across spaces to muscle and flesh. The slightest inhalation of his breath threatened to make chaos of the entire printed universe. He seemed afire, the creatures flinching from the flame, drawing back from the great heat of his pride, as he expanded under the audience's rapt contemplation.[15]

Phelps' 'sheathing' makes him the new star attraction of the carnival, but Lisabeth is less than impressed. When he catches her looking at other men filing in for the night's show, his hands, decorated with roses, 'shrivel.' When the gauze finally comes off the first of Phelps' hidden tattoos, we have to wonder if more than just his sweat has gone into the pattern: 'It was a picture of his wife, Lisabeth, and himself. And he was killing her.'

From Lisabeth's perspective, this is a monstrously unfunny joke; the other carny folk are not amused, and the audience certainly can't be shown the image. Phelps, in his desperation to rid himself of the image of what he begins to creepingly perceive as his inevitable role as a murderer, sees a 'skin man' in vain. He takes to his chest in his own bathroom with 'peroxide, acids, silver razors, and squares of sandpaper' and 'work[s] steadily for an hour.'[16] Bradbury omits any description of the intense pain both procedures must have caused Phelps, all in the service of ridding himself of a terrible secret that he had never even asked for. Lisabeth has no sympathy for his plight – indeed, there's never any evidence in the tale that she has ever felt the slightest bit of love for him. 'I've hated you for a long time now,' she tells him. 'Good God, when you started putting on the fat, you think anyone could love you then?'[17] The Illustrated Man's only defense is that he would never harm Lisabeth, and, of course, that he didn't know the content of either of the witch's hidden tattoos. But yet he cannot help but think: *'Or did I know? Who made this picture, me or the witch? Who formed it? How? Do I really want her dead? No! And yet....'*[18] Phelps feels violence welling up like never before. Lisabeth attacks his chest tattoo – and, wrapping his hands around her throat, he puts reality in perfect sync with the witch's 'curse.' As he does so, perhaps Phelps remembers the self-sewn witch's final words to him as he chokes the life out of Lisabeth. 'I will sit here for the next two weeks and think how clever my pictures are,' she had whispered to Phelps' back. 'For I make them fit each man himself and what is inside him.'[19] It is as if an inevitable series of events led from the Illustrated Man's tattooing down to Lisabeth's murder, as if the witch's inscriptions were borne by the hand of fate.

Tattoos and Human Nature

Now, it would be a disservice to Bradbury to finish this summary by revealing his ending. First, the questions of what Phelps does after the carnies discover his crime, of his fate, and of what tattoo lays under the second swatch of gauze are best presented in the context of the delirium and terror of Bradbury's prose itself. Second, we already have enough details from the tale to venture a speculation about tattoos and human nature.

At the time of Bradbury's writing, the subculture of tattooing was quite limited and there were two primary motivations to get a tattoo: because you wanted to display traditional American values – 'God, mother and country' – or because you were trying to make a living (however tenuously) as a sideshow tattoo attraction. Some of the early tattooed men on display in this way were marketed through a fabrication that they had been captured by primitives and forcibly tattooed – as John Rutherford claimed about the Maori in 1828 and James O'Connell accused the inhabitants of Micronesia at about the same time.[20] For audiences, the display of the outlandish, all-over tattoos, together with the nightmarish tale of savage capture and coercion, must have made a potent mix.

In this regard, 'The Illustrated Man' strikes a nerve that points to a reason why people have engaged in philosophy in the West for two thousand years, and in the East for even longer. In the story, do the witch's clairvoyant inscriptions predict Lisabeth's fate or actually make it happen? Questions about fate have their own niche in philosophical thought experiments. Alvin Goldman (b. 1938), for example, conjures a scenario called the 'Book of Life' in which he finds an 'old dusty tome' with his name on it in his local library. Everything Goldman has ever done is recorded faithfully in the book, right up to the present moment. As 3:03 on the library clock rolls around, Goldman looks at the entry for 3:03 in the book, at the same time thinking that the book is remarkable. 'The entry reads: "He continues to look at me, meanwhile thinking

KEVIN S. DECKER

how remarkable I am."' Goldman repeatedly tries to refute what the book tells him he will do in entries about his own future, but each time he fails.[21] It seems as though Goldman has no free will, that he is living in a world in which even his future actions are pre-determined.

Perhaps fortunately, complete Books of Life are not found laying around dusty libraries, and the question of the truth of causal determinism is still highly debated by philosophers. However, French social theorist Michel Foucault (1926–1984) could be read as translating Goldman's book into readily accessible *social* and *bodily* categories. Foucault believes 'that our selves are not fixed ontological identities ... but are instead socially constructed roles that we play with respect to others.'[22] Specifically, Foucault is interested in how *power* socially constructs not only identities but also how we treat the body itself. The institutions of society and the practices of culture foster 'the power and knowledge relations that invest human bodies and subjugate them by turning them into objects of knowledge.'[23] While Foucault focuses on how prisons, asylums, and social attitudes toward homosexuality change the very nature of what we conceive of as 'the body,' we might extend his analysis to all sorts of themes that lie at the intersection of body and culture: anorexia and bulimia, the problem of homelessness, workplace aesthetics and 'cubicle culture,' and more.

In 'The Illustrated Man,' Phelps' rare and beautiful inscriptions on his body raise him from the oblivion Lisabeth has consigned him to. At least the leering crowds of the sideshow appreciate him. They give him a degree of control over his own 'Book of Life.' But the same inscriptions present excerpts of Phelps' own future. The irony here is that his attempt to seize his own life back, to 'write himself,' comes at a dark and tragic cost. While we all know that the end of our earthly existence will occur upon the death of our body, the message that Bradbury seems to be conveying is that *the body is also our fate* between birth and extinguishment. And, like Foucault, 'The Illustrated Man' offers the disquieting idea that the inscriptions on that body – the social meaning of our fundamental appearance to others – is not under our control.

Covered with Rare and Significant Beauties

Pretty grim, no? Well, there's irony in the fact that no stronger contrast to Bradbury's dark and pessimistic 'The Illustrated Man' can be found than in the story called 'The Illustrated Woman.'[24] Light and upbeat, this 'better half' of Bradbury's tattoo stories was originally published in his 1964 collection *Machineries of Joy*. The story's unusually playful narrator weaves the story of a meeting between psychiatrist George C. George and a new patient, Emma Fleet. At four hundred and two and a half pounds, Fleet is, like 'Illustrated Man' Phelps, morbidly obese. But Emma isn't interested in losing weight; if anything, she'd like to '*gain* another one hundred or two hundred pounds.'[25] The problem is that she has been fully tattooed from neck to toe: her tattoo artist has no further frontiers to conquer.

She tells her story. Years before, Emma, clocking in at only two hundred and fifty pounds, caught the eye of the Guess Your Weight man at a Labor Day carnival:

> There I was alone with three Kewpie Dolls, a fake alligator handbag and nothing to do but make the Guess Your Weight man nervous by looking at him every time I went by and pretending like at any moment I might pay my money and dare him to guess.[26]

The Guess Your Weight man – Willy Fleet – offers the girl a free prize just for letting him estimate her mass. He is smitten with her, not in spite of her size but *because* of it:

> 'You're not fat,' he said. 'You're large, you're big, you're wonderful. Michelangelo would have loved you. Titian would have loved you. Da Vinci would have loved you. They knew what they were doing in those days. Size. Size is everything.'[27]

Willy Fleet, only three feet tall and weighing 'probably sixty pounds in the rain,' knows of what he speaks. For Fleet is a master tattoo artist who has been searching a lifetime for the right 'canvas' to exercise his craft on. Emma marries him, and accepts the honor. 'Ten thousand cozy busy hours' were spent together, Emma says, as Fleet inscribed first her arms, then

> half a year on my right leg, eight months on my left, in preparation for the grand explosion of bright detail which erupted out along my collarbone and shoulder blades, which fountained upward from my hips to meet in a glorious July celebration of pinwheels, Titian nudes, Giogione landscapes and El Greco cross-indexes of lightning on my façade, prickling with vast electric fires up and down my spine … Dear me, there never has been, there never will be, a love like ours again, a love where two people so sincerely dedicated themselves to one task, of giving beauty to the world in equal portions.[28]

KEVIN S. DECKER

And so it went, 'year after year,' until Fleet finished, then falling down at Emma's feet to sleep for forty-eight hours straight.

Four weeks later, Emma and Willy are standing at the city limits of Splitsville. The psychiatrist diagnoses the husband as having an artist's case of 'baby blues,' or post-natal depression. Emma is worried that Willy's canny eye may be wandering off toward some new, perhaps even larger 'canvas.' Dr. George C. George comes quickly to his conclusion: 'You must destroy the Masterpiece,' he says. What was the Illustrated Man's most frustrating failure – to start over – could be Emma's salvation. She is overjoyed, and, spontaneously whipping off her coat, says she wants to 'share the Masterpiece' with the doctor. 'He gazed at the continental vastness of the woman. Upon which nothing whatsoever was stitched, painted, watercolored, or in any way tattooed. Naked, unadorned, untouched, unlined, unillustrated.'[29]

After Emma leaves, Dr. George realizes that he really has solved the Fleets' problem, if by a kind of 'idiot grace.' The charm of Willy and Emma, 'the Illustrated Woman,' is that they share a mutually beneficial delusion, one that the psychiatrist has just unintentionally rewritten:

> By prescribing for a half-seen cause he had made a full cure, yes? Regardless if she believed or he believed or both believed in the Masterpiece, by suggesting the pictures be erased, destroyed, the doctor had made her a clean, lovely and inviting canvas again, if *she* needed to be.[30]

Is the 'Masterpiece' a testament to Emma's imagination, to Willy Fleet's powers of description, or to both? Whatever the truth, 'The Illustrated Woman' exemplifies an idea that cultural inscriptions can, with the right sort of effort, be redrawn. Dr. George's 'prescription' reflects the idea that no one's fate is set in stone, if we are willing to accept the trade-off that *everyone* might be deluded, at least a little, as Emma and Willy seem to be.

Creativity, Creativity, Creativity

The key to saving the Fleets' marriage is found in the suggestion of potentially infinite combinations of invisible 'tattoos' that Willy can inscribe and reinscribe on his doting wife. It might occur to feminist critics examining the story to point out Emma's passivity, the ulterior motives behind her husband's embrace of her girth, and the wider meaning of a man's 'inscribing' his wife with his own chauvinistic cultural values. All these criticisms might be legitimated, but nonetheless it should be stressed that Emma and Willy had, for most of their time together, been extremely happy with the 'you scratch my back, I'll scratch yours' nature of their relationship. Willy's creative activities and Emma's creative imagination feed off each other in a charming way.

Maybe this sort of creativity, of both act and appreciation, is what relates members of the tattoo community – artists as well as their 'canvases' – through such a strong bond. After all, tattoos come in all shapes, sizes, colors, and motifs, but simply having one communicates a surplus of meaning to others who are also tattooed. Postmodern cultural critics such as Nikki Sullivan, examining tattoos, have favored an interpretation that 'the tattoo is not simply reducible to a symbolic representation of the truth of the subject, but rather that the tattoo is indispensable from the subject and can be understood as a process (rather than an object).'[31] This process points at possibilities for tattoos enhancing self-understanding and public meaning, possibilities that are 'plural' in nature. In other words, the possibilities for our lives to interweave with tattoos in ways to give them new meaning 'is constantly (re)negotiated in and through relations with others and with a world,' Sullivan writes.[32] As one long-time tattoo artist puts it in plainer language, 'There's a certain emotional feeling that reflects the moment that you put [the tattoo] on, and it's still there, and if tattoos do that, then they've served the wearer. If they're just there for decoration, then it's like a paint job on a car, it doesn't tell you much.'[33]

Perhaps the specter of Michel Foucault's 'socially subjugated bodies' and Alvin Goldman's Book of Life (albeit now 'illuminated' via the tattoo-parlor descendants of careful monk copyists) may seem to still be with us. Emma's 'tattoos' will always reflect an alien perspective, one as much imposed upon her helpless body as it is definitive *of* her identity to all who see her. Her body is, perhaps, always her fate. But not all philosophers would agree with Foucault's view of power relations or Goldman's suggestion that we can live well without free will. George Herbert Mead (1863–1931) made the notion of the creative social self the center of his resistance to the problem of fate written on 'The Illustrated Man's' sleeve. 'There is always a mutual relationship of the individual and the community in which the individual lives,' Mead says, and the nature of the relationship is adaptive.[34] Like the relationship between Willy and Emma, the interactions between individual people and the cultural forces that shape them are reciprocal ones. Mead

KEVIN S. DECKER

explains the nature of the links flowing between individuals and society in terms of 'taking the attitude of the other.' He explains:

> The individual experiences himself as such, not directly, but only indirectly, from the particular standpoints of other individual members of the same social group ... For he enters his own experience as a self or individual, not directly or immediately, not by becoming a subject to himself, but only in so far as he first becomes an object to himself.[35]

With his example of a team game (baseball, for example), Mead demonstrates that an individual playing the game is really also playing each of the other participants' games as well. Excellent team players internalize the habits and capacities of their mates. What Mead is claiming is that our selves, our identities, aren't 'givens,' but instead are constructed out of both interactions with others and our efforts to see ourselves *as we are seen by others*. Sometimes the effort is conscious, as when Dr. George helps Emma to realize that, if Willy sees her as a blank 'canvas,' he will return to her. In other cases, it is less conscious, like the dispiriting effect that Lisabeth's venomous criticisms of Phelps have on his character. In 'The Illustrated Man,' when the first hidden tattoo is revealed, suddenly the entire sideshow crowd sees Phelps as his wife's murderer and, when he recognizes this fact, it fuels his self-doubt: where did the idea to kill her come from? Bradbury suggests that the delirium of the carnival atmosphere is as much at fault in Phelps' crime as anything.

Creativity, for Mead, is the source of 'enlargement and enrichment of the community,' and comes from a most unexpected source.[36] Its origin is not found in the deepest regions of the human mind, he writes, but rather in a creative individual's embrace of a 'larger society' than the one they currently belong to. 'Such an individual is divergent from the point of view of what we would call the prejudices of the community; but, in another sense he expresses the principles of the community more completely than any other.'[37] How could this be so, since it seems to be a self-contradiction? Remember that, according to Mead's view of how we become selves, our identity is knit from 'taking the attitude' – that is, the values, norms, ideals, habits, advice, and wisdom – of others. The creativity of individuals comes from expanding the possibilities already present in the surrounding culture. There couldn't be a stronger contrast with the power politics of Foucault when Mead cheerfully opines, 'To the degree that we make the community in which we live different we all have what is essential to genius, and which becomes genius when the effects are profound.'[38] Mead's ideas clearly reject the proposition that 'my body is my fate,' suggesting that those who embrace tattooing with a creative spirit are making a sound difference to their community.

Can't You Recognize the Human in the Inhuman?

The lights have gone down and the tents are being rolled up. What's left to say?

By entertaining the possibility that unasked-for horrors could assail a downtrodden protagonist like William Philippus Phelps, and by venturing that Emma and Willy Fleet could turn the absurdity of their relationship into a mechanism for producing infinite diversity in infinite combinations, Ray Bradbury's stories use the trope of tattooing to 'carnivalize' the idea of wearing one's identity on one's skin. 'Carnivalization' (as odd as the idea may sound) has been suggested as Bradbury's form of literary 'laughter at static hierarchies of meaning.' One interpretation of Bradbury's entire *oeuvre* suggests that the idea of 'carnival' is the best way to understand Bradbury's aims: 'Through the art of carnivalization, horror is transformed into the sublime ['The Illustrated Man'] and the absurd rendered comic ['The Illustrated Woman'] … the terror and horror of existence [have been] 'polarized' and filtered by art.'[39] Both the horrific and the absurd, confronted and transformed in this way, are that much easier to deal with.

If tattooing represents plural '(re)negotiations' of self identity, then this form of human expression belongs in the sideshow of Bradbury's carnival. It encourages us to see our 'modern primitives' as producing '"category turmoil," which challenges the necessity and fixity of all forms of identity.'[40] As a form of social creativity, tattooing has a deeply philosophical significance inscribed, as it were, in its flesh.

NOTES

1 Margo DeMello, Bodies *of Inscription: A Cultural History of the Modern Tattoo Community* (Durham, NC: Duke University Press, 2000), p. 9.
2 Tobin Siebers, 'Introduction: Defining the body aesthetic,' in Tobin Siebers (ed.), *The Body Aesthetic: From Fine Art to Body Modification* (Ann Arbor, MI: University of Michigan Press, 2000), p. 8.

3   Victoria L. Pitts, *In the Flesh: The Cultural Politics of Body Modification* (New York: Palgrave Macmillan, 2003), p. 126.

4   Mary Douglas, 'The two bodies,' in *Natural Symbols: Explorations in Cosmology* (New York: Routledge, 2003), p. 79.

5   Eric Gans, 'The body sacrificial,' in Tobin Siebers (ed.), *The Body Aesthetic: From Fine Art to Body Modification* (Ann Arbor, MI: University of Michigan Press, 2000), p. 177.

6   DeMello, *Bodies of Inscription*, p. 5.

7   See Kevin S. Decker, 'Knockout! *Killer's Kiss*, the somatic, and Kubrick,' in Jerold J. Abrams (ed.), *The Philosophy of Stanley Kubrick* (Lexington, KY: University of Kentucky Press, 2007), particularly pp. 93–99.

8   Alberto Ríos, 'Magical realism: Definitions' (http://www.public.asu.edu/~aarios/resource bank/definitions).

9   William F. Touponce, 'Introduction: The pulp origins of a literary style,' in William F. Touponce and Jonathan R. Eller (eds.), *The Collected Stories of Ray Bradbury: A Critical Edition, 1938–1943* (Kent, OH: Kent State University Press, 2010), p. xvi.

10 Ray Bradbury, 'The Illustrated Man,' in *Bradbury Stories: 100 of His Most Celebrated Tales* (New York: Harper Perennial, 2003), p. 383.

11 Ibid., p. 384.

12 This 'dust witch,' or a character very like her, is resurrected as a minion of the insidious carnival master Mr. Dark in Bradbury's *Something Wicked This Way Comes* (New York: Harper Voyager, 1999).

13 Bradbury, 'The Illustrated Man,' p. 385.

14 Ibid., p. 386.

15 Ibid., p. 387.

16 Ibid., p. 391.

17 Ibid.

18 Ibid.

19 Ibid., p. 386.

20 DeMello, *Bodies of Inscription*, p. 56.

21 Alvin I. Goldman, 'Actions, predictions, and books of life,' *American Philosophical Quarterly* 5, 3 (1968): 143–144.

22 Richard Shusterman, 'Somaesthetics and care of the self: The case of Foucault,' in *Body Consciousness: A Philosophy of Mindfulness and Somaesthetics* (New York: Cambridge University Press, 2008), p. 35.

23 Michel Foucault, *Discipline and Punish*, trans. Allan Sheridan (New York: Vintage Books, 1995), p. 28.

24 Ray Bradbury, 'The Illustrated Woman,' in *The Stories of Ray Bradbury* (New York: Alfred A. Knopf, 2010), pp. 731–741.

25 Ibid., p. 732.

26 Ibid., p. 734.

27 Ibid.

28   Ibid., p. 737.
29   Ibid., p. 740.
30   Ibid., p. 741.
31   Nikki Sullivan, *Tattooed Bodies: Subjectivity, Textuality, Ethics, and Pleasure* (Westport, CT: Praeger Publishing, 2001), p. 19.
32   Ibid.
33   'Leo,' quoted in DeMello, *Bodies of Inscription*, p. 193.
34   George H. Mead, in Charles W. Morris (ed.), *Mind, Self and Society from the Standpoint of a Social Behaviorist* (Chicago, IL: University of Chicago Press, 1934), p. 215.
35   Ibid., p. 138.
36   Ibid., p. 216.
37   Ibid., p. 217.
38   Ibid., p. 218.
39   Jonathan R. Eller and William F. Touponce, *Ray Bradbury: The Life of Fiction* (Kent, OH: Kent State University Press, 2004), p. 39.
40   Pitts, *In the Flesh*, p. 127.

KEVIN S. DECKER

ETHICAL CONCERNS

'Tattooed men who are not behind bars are either latent criminals or degenerate aristocrats. If someone who is tattooed dies in freedom, then he does so a few years before he would have committed murder.'

(Adolf Loos, *Ornament and Crime*, 1908)

CHAPTER 14

THE VICE OF THE TOUGH TATTOO

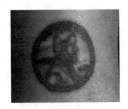

Nature has surrounded our soul with the body as with a sort of garment; the body is its cloak. But who has ever reckoned the value of clothes by the wardrobe that contained them? The scabbard does not make the sword good or bad. Therefore, with regard to the body I shall return the same answer to you – that, if I have the choice … the good involved will be my judgment regarding these things, and not the things themselves.

(Lucius Annaeus Seneca, *Moral Epistles*)

Of Ouija Boards and Bar Owners[1]

There are mummified bodies of women in ancient Egypt that are tattooed with pattern of dots around their abdomens. During pregnancy, the dots would expand into a wider pattern, one that kept pace with the pregnancy itself, forming a kind of visual net. Historians have speculated that these tattooed 'nets' have an analogous significance to the beaded nets we've found placed over mummies.[2] Was the idea a metaphorical kind of protection? Were the nets meant to hold everything precious in? How beautiful, if so.

Tattoos – Philosophy for Everyone: I Ink, Therefore I Am, First Edition.
Edited by Robert Arp.
© 2012 John Wiley & Sons, Inc. Published 2012 by John Wiley & Sons, Inc.

I mention mummy tattoos for a reason. At some level tattoos are expressions of a culture, and I can no more analyze, pin down, or even identify the motives for these expressions in other contemporary cultures than I can in ancient ones. In this chapter, my interest is in assessing the morality of the motives I understand and recognize, ones I hear voiced and can relate to in my own, American, culture. And yet, even within my culture, some discussions are above my pay grade; for example, women with full-sleeve tattoos seem to be doing something rather subversive in a cultural context. The complexity of that means they're out. I have to narrow it down to the cases of tattoos that are simpler, and ones about which I can plausibly assume an easily stated motive.

Here are some examples of the tattoos I want to talk about in this chapter. One of my best friends has a workable Ouija board on his back. Another has the expulsion-from-the-family-warranting tattoo of 'pay up' on the palm of his hand. I used to live in Tucson, Arizona where even our visitors – who were full of tattoos themselves – would make comments about how many tattoos people in Tucson had; for example, large eighteenth-century ships on young women's chests. We met girls who would even get boyfriend's names scripted as their eyebrows. I've known more than two people with that 'full skeleton tattooed on the external part of my body' thing going, as well as two dudes with 'Mama Tried' on their necks. And, memorably, I was even present for a branding of – why? *Why?* – an image of the face of the owner of a local bar on a friends' arm. Even the missteps seem informative: a Rasta lion that came out as a large, dark ink spot, as well as countless 'cover ups' of embarrassing things such as tiny little dancing bears turned into something larger and tribal.

I am going to limit myself to discussing late-twentieth-century, early-twenty first-century, American-style tattoos, of the sort had by people I've met and mentioned above. Eventually, I'll have to narrow this down still further to what I will call the 'tough tattoo'; but, first, let me suggest that the following reasons for condemning tattoos are pretty bad as reasons go.

Bad Reasons for Condemning Tattoos

(1) *Getting a tattoo is a shallow way to assert one's individuality.* Or, in other words, getting a tattoo does not make you as much of an individual as you think it does. I don't see this as a legitimate criticism. Little things represent us – common things represent us as much as anything else.

(2) *Once you get a tattoo you are stuck with it. You are not thinking about your future if you get a tattoo.* Do people get tattoos to place a stake in time, to memorialize something, from the shallow to the deep? Sure. Critics might mock this for aesthetic reasons. The tattoo owners might do the same (Kid Rock teases himself a little for the Paul tattoo on his shoulder). But there is something nice about putting a stake in time, for any reason. What real objection is there to this? If it's irrational, what standard do we use to determine that it is so? Who says we must always be prudent as measured by those at a later stage of life? That's silly. The idea that young people will have their tattoos into old age is trotted out a lot, but, having now seen seventy-somethings with tattoos all over, I'm not sure their arms would look any worse without them. Who cares? There is even something nice about giving up on future vanities. Yeah, it might look weird in your nursing home gown, but couldn't we, with confidence, figure that at eighty we won't really care how we look?

(3) *Tattoos are ugly.* Yeah, sure they are. We are always at risk of confusing our aesthetic concerns with moral ones. This is no kind of reason for morally condemning tattoos.

These complaints against tattoos fail to hold up under scrutiny as ethical or moral concerns. When we raise a moral concern we ought to worry about the consistency of our complaint, we ought to think of it as something that objects of our concern might themselves endorse. I will demonstrate how a traditional approach to virtue – an approach along the lines of Socrates (c. 469–399 BCE), Seneca (c. 4 BCE–65 CE), and the ancient Greco-Roman schools of philosophy – can do this. I'll be relying heavily on Seneca's ideas in this chapter.

Some Moral Compliments

To be fair, let me toss out some compliments to tattooed people that are consistent with a traditional approach to virtue.

(1) *How great to undermine our Puritan inheritance.* As just mentioned, so much of what we count as moral really isn't defended as moral. To the extent that we are surprised by well-dressed, well-mannered serial killers, we need to become more conscious of how we confuse moral worth with mere, or misplaced, social standards. Our Puritan inheritance is something we ought to become conscious of, and assess for ourselves, because it works in us to discriminate against people. Having bad teeth, for example,

surely isn't a sign of not being accepted by God. Yet one very resilient bit of discrimination reveals itself when it comes to the hiring rates of people with very bad teeth. How could tattoos help here? If enough decent people get tattoos, or become unconventional in some other way, it might get us to refocus on what immorality actually is. This could serve a very helpful purpose. I mean this as a serious compliment to those who are tattooed.

(2) *Tattoos are cool.* Being cool is often mocked by stuffy ethicist types. But traditional virtue ethics has, I'd argue, always valued 'being cool.' Aristotle basically describes how to be Cary Grant cool and does assimilate it to ethical advice. Why? The riskiest people are the ones who fly off the handle and get caught up in the moment too quickly. If you are getting tattooed in pursuit of 'cool,' well, you may be more generally interested in a mannered approach to things. This could be a good way to develop yourself. It at least shows some effort to develop yourself. I'll tentatively give credit for this.

My Complaint

So where is my complaint? It isn't over how ugly or unconventional (or conventional) tattoos may be. I don't care about aging with tattoos or limiting your options in other ways with them (though to my friends I have bemoaned the fact that they will now never be president). What is there *really* to object to, if tattoos are cool and get us to reassess outdated cultural assumptions?

I honestly can't find anything wrong with tattoos that aren't designed to give the owner a certain swagger: cartoon characters, ink portraits of children, initials, and Latin sayings are all okay, according to this criterion. What do I find morally worrisome? Tattoos that are meant to make the owner look like a *badass*, or *tough* gal, or *tough* guy.

Why are these different? It has to do with an incompleteness in one of American culture's takes on a certain rebellious posturing. I don't mean actual criminality, though there is a thread running through history regarding tattoos as a sign of outlier status: the 'tattoo elegy' of the second century BCE describes the practice of tattooing pictures of mythical sinners being punished on wrongdoers, and historians point out that accused criminals used to have a description of their crimes tattooed on their body.[3] But the modern-day parallel to the practice, the arm that marks years in prison (or murders) with crude tattoo counts, is not my topic.

I can't talk about the tattoos that actually reveal bad behavior. What I'm talking about is the posture we take when we get tattoos that look tough.

I read an interview about a European woman who, as a student, had been travelling the U. S. happily before encountering the very worst the U. S. has to offer – a homicidal drifter, who easily found odd jobs where he wanted. He easily hid after murdering this woman's traveling companions; she was the sole survivor of the attack. Of course every country has predators like this, but the woman made this observation in the interview: that the U. S. promotes a type of 'outlaw' culture, granting harbor to men (and women, too) who, through some outward signs, signal to us that they are no good.

I saw what she meant, and only realized it after reading her interview. How complicit I had been! Did I think tough guys looked cool? Probably. Did I think they might have hearts of gold under their tough exterior? I hoped so. Did I have tough friends periodically and think it was a good thing? Yes. Does my husband still talk about kicking people's asses for the smallest slight to me? Yes.

How many of us laud a kind of rebelliousness here without making any distinction between those who are 'rebels' because they murder and rape and those who are 'rebels' for other reasons? This is wrong and lazy, and too many people get tattoos for reasons related to this thinking. And it's not good. Traditional virtue ethics helps me to sort this out. As I will explain, it will get us to focus on the norms we do maintain (even without realizing it) and suggest that we stop endorsing such norms that are irrational and harmful.

Now, I won't be arguing that having tough gal or tough guy tattoos in itself leads to anything bad. I've even thrown out a compliment in regards to overturning our Puritanical assumptions about morality (Puritanical thinkers are lazy, too!). I'm suggesting that the motivation one might have to get a non-humorous, badass tattoo – if you are an American female or male (in the culture I recognize) – is immoral (indicative of a vice) because it's unreflective in this sense: Wanting that type of tattoo is a way to appropriate tough gal or tough guy imagery from a subculture that already exists, and a good person should want no part of this subculture. In fact, getting a tough tattoo contributes to a vicious, rather than a virtuous, psyche.

I'm no sociologist, but I am banking on the idea that we can agree that there is a subculture of people who have tattoos as a sign that they are in fact bad people. I need to know nothing about this culture itself, as my focus will be on (good people's) motivations for getting a tough-guy tattoo. So, again, I will argue against only the non-humorous tattoos of American women/men who have not been repeatedly convicted of crimes (if you are in fact a predator, again, this argument obviously won't convince you). Tattoos designed to make you look badass – despite how fuzzy or blued the ink, and despite how effectively or ineffectively the impression of badass-ness is conveyed – are not a good idea, from a virtue ethics, moral perspective. Let me get started with the argument.

Traditional Virtue Ethics

If every good is in the soul, then whatever strengthens, uplifts, and enlarges the soul, is a good; virtue, however, does make the soul stronger, loftier, and larger. For all other things, which arouse our desires, depress the soul and weaken it, and when we think that they are uplifting the soul, they are merely puffing it up and cheating it with much emptiness. Therefore, that alone is good which will make the soul better.

(Lucius Annaeus Seneca, *Moral Epistles*)

I want to argue that getting a tough tattoo is immoral from the virtue ethics perspective. What is virtue ethics? It is an approach to ethics first formulated by the ancient Greek philosophers and then promulgated by many philosophers after that. It holds that ethics is a matter to be determined by considering standard, healthy, rational human psychology (*psyche* is Greek for 'soul,' 'mind,' or 'character'). The virtue ethicists' central idea is that, if one has a virtuous psyche, then not only will one likely perform morally right actions but also these actions likely will have good consequences.[4] And, after all, not only do we want to perform right actions that have good consequences, but we also want to be *virtuous persons* performing right actions that have good consequences. You can get a demon to do the right thing, yielding good consequences; however, he's still a demon.

What is 'virtue' according to the virtue ethicist? It is a good habit whereby one fosters a kind of balance in one's psychological and emotional states. The idea is to promote the 'not too much' or 'not too little,' but the 'just right' in our psyches so that our actions and reactions to situations reflect this hitting of the mean between two extremes. In fact, the extremes are both considered vices, as you can imagine. The virtuous person has cultivated the kind of psyche whereby s/he knows how to act and react in the right way, at the right time, in the right manner, and for

JENNIFER BAKER

the right reasons in each and every moral dilemma encountered. However, the way in which one cultivates a healthy, rational psyche is through choosing actions that are conducive to building that virtuous psyche. So, for example, if one wants to cultivate the virtue of honesty so that one can actually be an honest person, then one needs to act honestly time and time again so that the virtue can 'sink in' to the person's psyche. The more Jimmy actually tells the truth when asked whether he has done something wrong, the more Jimmy cultivates the virtue of honesty. The more Sally lies when asked whether she has done something wrong, the more she cultivates the vice of dishonesty.

Virtue ethicists set forth a general list of virtues, including honesty, courage, prudence, generosity, integrity, affability, and respect, to name just a few. And performing virtuous actions can be quite difficult, at times. Consider the words of an ancient virtue ethicist, Seneca, in his collection of letters we now call *Moral Epistles*, where he notes the connection between reason, a balanced psyche, virtue, and honor:

> In the case of man, it is not pertinent to the question to know how many acres he ploughs, how much money be has out at interest, how many callers attend his receptions, how costly is the couch on which he lies, how transparent are the cups from which he drinks, but how good he is. He is good, however, if his reason is well ordered and right and adapted to that which his nature has willed. It is this that is called virtue; this is what we mean by *honorable*; it is man's unique good. For since reason alone brings man to perfection, reason alone, when perfected, makes man happy … I shall explain what I mean: A good man will do what he thinks it will be honorable for him to do, even if it involves toil; he will do it even if it involves harm to him; he will do it even if it involves peril; again, he will not do that which will be base, even if it brings him money, or pleasure, or power. Nothing will deter him from that which is honorable, and nothing will tempt him into baseness.[5]

Interestingly enough, Seneca is not *merely* giving advice in terms of some virtue ('be courageous' or some such). He also notes that acting virtuously is, for the most part, no easy task:

> Who can maintain this standard [of virtue]? Very few, to be sure; but there are some. It is indeed a hard undertaking, and I do not say that the philosopher can always keep the same pace. But he can always travel the same path.[6]

Virtue Ethics and Tattoos

It is the *path* Seneca speaks about above that we need to illuminate in connection with tattooing. For starters, what if getting a tattoo is too minor for virtue ethics to properly illuminate? Is it really necessary or even good to dwell on something as trivial as a tattoo? Should we obsess over other elements of fashion, similarly? There is a way that virtue ethics simultaneously makes attention to small things significant without giving undue emphasis to small things. It is a little tricky to explain, but Seneca helps us here:

> Do you not see that when you have let your mind loose, it is no longer in your power to recall it, either to propriety, or to modesty, or to moderation: but you do every thing that comes into your mind in obedience to your inclinations? To what things then ought I to attend? First to those general (principles) and to have them in readiness, and without them not to sleep, not to rise, not to drink, not to eat, not to converse (associate) with men; that no man is master of another man's will, but that in the will alone is the good and the bad. No man then has the power either to procure for me good or to involve me in any evil, but I alone myself over.

Now, what are these general principles? Traditional accounts of virtue use as their standard for rightness an account of practical rationality, or what Seneca means by *reason*. Practical rationality, in such accounts, is what sets the standard for virtue – not anything you can see or might just assume. According to any such account, we will not have coherent beliefs about our behavior without engaging, consciously, in this process. The process is that we must analyze what it is we are doing (and not just 'go with the flow'), and we need to assess whether what we have committed ourselves to matches what actually gets done. The principles of virtue ethics are not rationalistic formulas.

Let me provide some of the examples of the principles we would find through this process, according to ancient virtue ethicists:

- Educate your daughters like your sons.
- Attend to your children's illnesses even when it is painful to you.
- Avoid crowds that encourage you to act or think badly.
- Put yourself in another's shoes.

See how easy they are to understand? They are not fancy – they are common, and what makes them special is how we regard them if we are

JENNIFER BAKER

ethical: as claims that need to be assessed (i.e., don't just take any old saying to be right) and internalized so that we follow them with ease.

When it comes to tattoos, let's use traditional virtue ethics in the way it was used in the past: as a means of endorsing particular norms that have been carefully thought through. You will have to accept the reasoning for yourself, if it is to be effective. Here is the advice Seneca gives about clothing and homes, for example:

> Observe yourself, then, and see whether your dress and your house are inconsistent, whether you treat yourself lavishly and your family meanly, whether you eat frugal dinners and yet build luxurious houses. You should lay hold, once for all, upon a single norm to live by, and should regulate your whole life according to this norm. Some men restrict themselves at home, but strut with swelling port before the public; such discordance is a fault, and it indicates a wavering mind that cannot yet keep its balance. And I can tell you, further, whence arise this unsteadiness and disagreement of action and purpose; it is because no man resolves upon what he wishes, and, even if he has done so, he does not persist in it, but jumps the track; not only does he change, but he returns and slips back to the conduct which he has abandoned and abjured.[7]

The suggestion is this: go for a match between the motivations and norms of which you become conscious. Given our starting places, changes will need to be made in both directions. We will not begin, as children especially, being motivated to tell the truth in the right situations. But we should aim to find an account of honesty, a set of norms we could articulate in a rough fashion, that we are motivated to follow. Some norms we pick up are not capable of existing alongside others that we have ('I'm not hurting anybody'; 'If someone does that to me I'll call the police') or with our motivations ('People should donate their time').

Another example is 'be nice,' an instruction that misleads many well-meaning people into not pushing for the exercise of contrary norms. Notice how this account includes a check on even very common norms. Many young people, perhaps especially young women, can labor under the norm 'be nice.' If it becomes apparent that this norm is costing opportunities, or if a person finds they just cannot be motivated to 'be nice' all the time, this is the signal to rethink. Could society be wrong to hold 'niceness' as a standard for goodness? Yes, of course. Our ethical norms have to work for us; virtue ethics justifies them because they do.

No one method of success in practical reasoning is prescribed. We have distinctive and personal projects. We have different degrees of risk aversion. Our prospects differ. We endorse different epistemic norms. (The list goes on.) The process we will be engaging in will be unique. Trial and error is also an anticipated part of this process. One can try, for example, to care less about one's family or to put in less time at work. One can try to identify with just the job, or just one's children. The process of analyzing these mismatches can facilitate some revision of the norms to which we had previously been committed. These commitments will have to be, in order for us to understand our behavior in relation to them, related to each other. Thus, what we do, when we decide to tutor children, is determine that what we were doing with our time before was less worthy than this. As we become conscious of this choice, we generate two new norms: one about the activity we were doing instead of tutoring children and another about tutoring the children. As Seneca explains:

> Men do not know what they wish, except at the actual moment of wishing; no man ever decided once and for all to desire or to refuse. Judgment varies from day to day, and changes to the opposite, making many a man pass his life in a kind of game. Press on, therefore, as you have begun; perhaps you will be led to perfection, or to a point which you alone understand is still short of perfection.[8]

To 'press on' is not just a matter of analyzing and revising beliefs and behavior – testing the ranking of commitments that make our lives go better as a whole. It is discovering that we are not motivated by a set of concerns – one for work, one for family – but are motivated by what integrates these and all of our other worthy commitments successfully. So, to discuss the morality of the kind of tattoos I'm talking about, we need to identify norms and think about motivations.

Tough Tattoos ... What Lies Beneath

Let me propose this: being tough is considered a good thing by people who get tough tattoos, and people who get badass tattoos do so, in part, to look tough. Fair enough? The norm in question is, 'If I get this tattoo, I will look tough, and that is good.'

Well, using traditional virtue ethics, I first want to argue that no decent person can simply sign on to 'being tough is good.' This is far too imprecise, far too general, and it lets in far too much. Much of Shakespeare works as a representation of Seneca's own suggestion that, once you let in some approval of violence, you let it all in. In other words, to justify a bit of violence is to approve of a range of violence you never thought to.

Second, being tough seems to be an inaccurate description. How tough are we really? Let me try to get at the idea that we are not tough from two different angles. If I may, I will start with a story and admission: I once had a friend I adored who was regarded as 'very tough.' Hipsters would move out of our favorite seating in the bar when he would approach and (in his mind) innocently ask if we could sit there. One evening, he defended me in some dumb argument (over philosophy of all things) with a bartender by making the (tough) bartender say he was a 'bitch' after having called me one. Lovely, right?

Well, I must have signaled that I approved of this kind of behavior, because he was eager to tell me soon after that he had a story for me: some guy had looked at his friends and him funny, and they had repeated kicked him in the head for it. I still feel sick thinking of it. I remember the sinking of his face as he realized I was not going to enjoy the story. Another time, perhaps previously to this, a woman started flirting with my boyfriend and he (and his friends) told me I should do something. A bottle got smashed for me (I assume!) to use as a cutting weapon. I learned my lesson: If tough guys are cool, then how much cooler are killers? It has to be thought through. To be ethical, we have to pay better attention to the norms we approve of willy-nilly.

Finally, allow me to question how tough *any of us* actually are. We die easily, we die by surprise, or we die even if our heads hit the ground too hard. We have children that keep us in a constant state of fear and worry, about whom no dirge can capture the depths of our love and concern. By this I want to suggest that tough-guy tattoos are a misrepresentation.

So, back to tattoos. My first contention is that people should not get tough-guy tattoos before thinking very hard about the norm that underlies 'looking tough.' I imagine the self-examination we'd go through – if following traditional virtue ethics as an approach – would go as follows.

(1) Are you trying to look tough? Why? Is that something that you think makes you more valuable? What is it that makes you valuable?
(2) Do our tough tattoos properly reveal our loyalties? Are murderers as cool as culture takes them to be? Are they as suave as the movies depict? What does it mean to ally one's self with the outlaws?
(3) Do our tough tattoos properly represent us? Are we so tough?

Traditional virtue ethics lets you get around these points I've tried to raise. If you want a tough, badass tattoo, just think about why. What is your motive? Is it consistent with what you need from others? Is it consistent with your actual status here among us? Examine your life and motives. To paraphrase what is perhaps Socrates' most famous observation, we ought not to live a life we don't subject to examination. And, Seneca might conclude:

> When you wish to inquire into a man's true worth, and to know what manner of man he is, look at him when he is naked; make him lay aside his inherited estate, his titles, and the other deceptions of fortune; let him even strip off his body. Consider his soul, its quality and its stature, and thus learn whether its greatness is borrowed, or its own.[9]

NOTES

1   The pictured tattoo is the only type of which the author approves. Physicist Laura Penny's penny.
2   See, for example, Niels Lynnerup, 'Mummies,' *American Journal of Physical Anthropology* 134, 45 (November, 2007): 162–190.
3   For good introductions to the history of the tattooing arts, see Jane Caplan (ed.), *Written on the Body: The Tattoo in European and American History* (Princeton, NJ: Princeton University Press, 2000); Steve Gilbert, *The Tattoo History Sourcebook* (New York: Juno Books, 2000); and Maarten Hesselt van Dinter, *The World of Tattoo: An Illustrated History* (The Netherlands: Mundurucu Publishing, 2007).
4   See, for example, Aristotle, *Nicomachean Ethics*, trans. Martin Oswald (Upper Saddle River, NJ: Prentice Hall, 1962). See also Cora Lutz, *Musonius Rufus 'The Roman Socrates'* (New Haven, CT: Yale University Press, 1947); Alasdair MacIntyre, *After Virtue* (Notre Dame, IN: Notre Dame Press, 1981); the papers in David Carr and Jan Steutel (eds.), *Virtue Ethics and Moral Education* (New York: Routledge, 1999); and Rosalind Hursthouse, *On Virtue Ethics* (Oxford: Oxford University Press, 1999). See also Rosalind Hursthouse, 'Virtue ethics,' in Edward N. Zalta (ed.), *Stanford Encyclopedia of Philosophy* (Fall 2009, http://plato.stan ford.edu/entries/ethics-virtue).
5   Lucius Annaeus Seneca, *Moral Epistles*, trans. Richard Gummere (Cambridge, MA: Harvard University Press, 1917–1925), volume 1.
6   Ibid.
7   Ibid.
8   Ibid.
9   Ibid.

CHAPTER 15

TO INK, OR NOT TO INK

Tattoos and Bioethics

Knowing the Difference Between One's Ass and First Base

If you're looking for the shortest answer to the question 'Will my doctor tell me getting ink is ethical?' then here it is: you have a two out of three shot at getting 'probably yes.' If that was the only bit of information you were looking for from this chapter, then go in peace and please just remember to tell everyone that this was a great read.

If you're looking for a slightly more informed answer that still won't get all academic-y on you, then this is it: if your doctor is older than fifty-five, s/he will most likely tell you that it is wrong; if they are between the ages of fifty-five and thirty-five, they will most likely tell you they have no problem with it; and, if they are younger than thirty, they may even *show you* their tattoo! I know this because I walked around for weeks and asked people their opinion of the medical ethics of tattooing. I thought I would see a difference between medical and non-medical professionals, different levels of

Tattoos – Philosophy for Everyone: I Ink, Therefore I Am, First Edition.
Edited by Robert Arp.
© 2012 John Wiley & Sons, Inc. Published 2012 by John Wiley & Sons, Inc.

education, professionals and non-professionals, or anything but what I in fact found. In the end, the only indicator of opinion on the ethics of tattoos was age. What that means is, even if the survey's findings about doctors' views are true for most people on the planet, they have nothing to do with medical ethics. Even when pressed to respond to the question of the *ethics* of tattoos, the answers I got from rank-and-file medical professionals closely conformed to their personal opinion, which closely conformed to their particular age. I believe that this inability to separate medical ethics (or bioethics) from opinion represents a very unfortunate reality: most rank-and-file medical professionals don't know their ass from first base when it comes to bioethics. If you've taken the time to pick up this book and read the first few chapters, you have probably put more serious thought into the concept than most of us medical types over the age of forty. From a bioethics perspective, tattooing is completely fine, but you will have to continue reading to find out why.

Self-Important Dork

First, an introduction might be in order. My name is Dan Miori, I am a physician assistant, and I work in palliative care, a field that deals with end-of-life situations on a regular basis. I help patients and their families through some tricky decision-making on life-sustaining treatment. Because of this intersection of medical care and personal values, I also work on the ethics committee at my hospital. Although I am careful not to offer my ethical opinion on my own medical decision-making (e.g. '*I* think that thing I did was completely ethical!'), I do ethics reviews on a regular basis as a part of my job. I hesitate to introduce myself as a clinical bioethicist because it just about screams 'self-important dork,' but the fact of the matter is that I am one. The reason I said that rude stuff about medical professionals and their understanding of bioethics wasn't because I am one of those crusty cynical types – I tend to have a fairly optimistic view of humanity. It's because I spent a large chunk of my career ignorant of the fact that there was more than *my* one view of the practice of medicine. Ethically speaking, I didn't know my ass from first base, and it tainted the advice I gave. Most of us clinicians didn't get much training in ethics other than an overview course that, if our feverish student prayers were answered, was taught by someone who graded more on class participation than homework. Unless we went out and learned more on our own, that's also where our training usually ended. Understanding that there is a difference between answering a question from a personal perspective, from a professional perspective, and from a bioethics perspective is important. This involves understanding the difference between personal ethics, professional ethics, and bioethics.

Personal Ethics and Professional Ethics

Personal ethics are precisely that – my reasons for making my decisions with regard to my personal behavior. Do I drink the last cup of coffee and not make a new pot? Do I ask someone 'what's wrong?' when s/he sits down at my lunch table with a big sigh and acts all pouty, or do I start talking about the weather? These are the values that each of us uses to get through our day. While you would hope a medical professional has higher standards than average for making these personal decisions, the reality is that we make our decisions for the same reasons you do: to get through our day with as little disruption as possible. We would probably help you out in a jam if it didn't hurt us too much, but if you start a bar fight for a stupid reason we will most likely sit and watch you get your ass handed to you.

Professional ethics, conversely, concern the reasons behind the decisions we make about our professional behavior. Economists don't have a formal written code of ethics for some reason, but then again neither do prostitutes. Lawyers and politicians do have a written code of ethics, so go figure. We medical types always have been a bit more uptight about ethics than a lot of other professions. While many fields lay claim to some standard of ethical behavior, those standards are mostly with regard to how they behave toward their customers. We have to worry about hurting someone with poorly-thought-through actions.

Most, if not all, fields in medicine have a great deal of similarity in their professional ethical approach to their job; but all fields share a commitment to putting our patient first and not causing suffering. Hippocrates of Cos (c. 460–370 BCE), a physician who lived in ancient Greece, came up with some rules for the practice of medicine that worked so well they lasted till about halfway through the twentieth century. (The original Hippocratic Oath also included an injunction against having sex with your patient's slaves – not something you would think you'd need to tell someone.) In addition to a written code, physicians and physicians' assistants also have a Latin motto, *primim non nocere*, which means 'above all, do no harm' (we figure using that the magical powers of a dead language reinforces our commitment). You might think that we have these because we ascribe to a higher calling, but, having spent the last thirty years working in hospitals, my opinion is that it's because we need reminding. In addition to taking good care of our customers and avoiding harming them, we medical professionals also offer advice on making decisions about medical treatment – advice that contains our professional opinion and at the same time respects our patient's autonomy in making their own decisions. Autonomy is also part of the reason why you should be able to get that tattoo, but more on that later.

It's important to note that the obligations to provide good advice and to behave professionally are really two different things. As a patient, there may be times when your choice may cause you some kind of overt harm – smoking, drinking excessively, or ritual scarification – and our solid best advice from any perspective is 'don't do that.' However, there are times when you may want to do things we wouldn't do, like spending the weekend in a sweat lodge, driving in a demolition derby, or getting a tattoo. Then we most certainly need to help you to weigh the pros and cons, but if we are doing our job right we can't really tell you not to do any of these things.

The Philosophical Foundations of Bioethics

Before discussing this bioethicist's views on tattooing, it would be reasonable to define the field of bioethics and the methods an ethicist would use to evaluate a decision such as 'to ink, or not to ink.' Bioethics can be thought of as a type of practical philosophical application, where philosophical positions are actually put into practice when making decisions concerning matters such as physician-assisted suicide, abortion, contraception, and use of animals for research in the realms of biology, medicine, and clinical practice.[1] Bioethics belongs to a branch of philosophy called 'practical ethics.' Practical ethics is heavily informed by 'normative ethics,' where philosophical positions such as utilitarianism, deontology, virtue ethics, and others are put forward that are supposed to act as a base from which to make a well-informed, practical decision. Normative ethics is the field good old Socrates (c. 469–399 BCE) started up back in Athens before he went on trial for corrupting the young men of Athens and not believing in the Greek gods.[2]

DANIEL MIORI

Clinical Bioethics and Some Major Players

Clinical bioethics came into its own with the technological revolution in the last half of the twentieth century. This was a time that saw great changes in every aspect of life, including, without question, regarding the medical treatment available to us. This era produced devices to help us breathe, to filter our blood, and to make our heart beat, and devices that could buy the time to allow fixable problems to be fixed. This is all good and many people are alive today, perhaps even someone reading this book, because of this marvelous technology.

One problem that arose almost immediately, however, was that sometimes people didn't get better and didn't get worse. Sometimes they just stayed very, very sick, kept alive by these technologies. We were left with the decision as to whether to continue a life attached to machines or to stop those machines. Personal ethics concerns making that decision with regard to myself, and professional ethics concerns making that decision in a way that will help but not hurt my patient. In the case of life-sustaining treatment, we often didn't have a good medical recommendation to make about those machines – no recommendation that would provide a clear benefit, anyway. We were left with the job of helping non-medically-trained patients and families as they struggled through the decision-making process based on their personal values. This caused a re-examination of how we go about offering that help, and gave rise to the field of bioethics.

Clinicians fretted, philosophers puzzled, families suffered, and we all came to a better understanding of the various biomedical dilemmas we faced. The rules and methods we had weren't necessarily helpful, but we did what we could and we got better at figuring out the questions and the best answer for each case. One of the people whose work gave rise to clinical bioethics as we know it today is Daniel Callahan, who has a Harvard-trained Ph. D. in philosophy. His career – from co-founding The Hastings Center to his recent work concerning controlling the cost of healthcare – is well appreciated by this minor player. As I became familiar with his perspective, the thing I most appreciated was his simple humility in the face of the clinical dilemmas he worked through – a humility that usually requires someone screwing up a few patients first.[3] Callahan looked around and called for a new field to deal with the needs he encountered. He also continued his own work – that Hastings Center thing I mentioned earlier is *all about* bioethics – but a good example of the next step is the work of two fine gentlemen named Tom Beauchamp and James Childress.[4]

In 1979, Beauchamp and Childress co-wrote a book entitled *Principles of Biomedical Ethics*, which has been reprinted and updated a number of times and is still one of the gold standard texts on any clinical bioethicist's bookshelf. The important addition these authors made was to provide a way to have that conversation that intimidated Callahan and the rest of us. They offered a set of values as though right out of the pages of Socrates to follow when discussing treatment decisions on a particular afternoon, at a particular hour. Some of those values we already had, such as beneficence (act with your patient's best interest in mind) and non-maleficence (avoid actions that would harm your patient). One value they added was *justice*, as in equal access to healthcare, which may have been influenced by the political ideas of the time. Most importantly, though, and especially relevant to this chapter, they included an important concept – *autonomy* – which is the idea that the decisions you make are important because *you* make them. We need to help you understand the medical implications of those decisions, but at the end of the day it's your decision to make. To ink or not to ink is up to you.

That brings us to a slightly-better-phrased version of our original question: 'Is getting ink a bioethically sound decision?' With what I've covered so far, you could walk away and be able to speak knowledgeably on the subject. If, however, you survived this far and you have just a bit more energy, please continue reading. As a motivator, let me tell you that you will learn some of the reasons your ink gets us old folks uptight (always fun), but, most importantly, you will learn why getting a tattoo may be beneficial. That's right, *beneficial!* You could tell everyone that the answer is 'to ink … because it's good for you!'

Risk Versus Benefit

A well-trained clinical bioethicist would at this point tell you that the bioethics of tattooing is mainly a discussion of two things; namely, (1) risk versus benefit and (2) autonomy. They would then drag you though some long explanation of what that all meant. I'm not an incredibly-well-trained clinical bioethicist, but, since I like to pretend that I am, here goes.

Let's start with risk versus benefit. Traditionally, the risks of tattooing revolve around two main areas, contagious disease and the long-term

DANIEL MIORI

health risks of the pigments used. The risks of contagious disease have historically driven restrictions on tattooing in the United States: New York City, the supposed birthplace of modern tattooing, had a complete ban on it for thirty-six years – from 1959 until 1985 – that was entirely driven by public health concerns over an increase in the number of cases of hepatitis.[5] Those laws were largely ineffective, driving tattooing underground and, sadly, increasing infections from tattoos obtained from illegal, unregulated, fly-by-night shops. However, concerns about the types of pigment used and the changes they caused in the skin's ability to live a long, healthy life were completely rational. Cadmium, chromium, and cobalt (yellow, green, and blue, respectively) provided nice, bright permanent color, but also carried risk to the health of the wearer. Mercury (red) was another element we might now recognize as less than helpful![6] As the dangers became known, however, newer and safer pigments came to market, now almost completely replacing the pigments used even just twenty years ago.

In the end, whether it was safer practices such as sterilization techniques or safer pigments, it was market forces that accomplished what no amount of government oversight could. As a savvier, better-educated consumer sought to get tattooed, the marketplace adapted to attract that consumer. The popularity of tattooing has driven it upscale, creating a cleaner environment where safety is accepted as a necessary cost of doing business. As if to prove that fact, the actual number of cases of hepatitis contracted in New York City has decreased, in spite of the exponential increase in the number of tattoos being performed.

There are other risks that are not as simple to define, non-medical risks that can be described as spiritual or existential. One concern that often came up in my vast and powerful unpublished survey was the risk that the individual getting the tattoo poses to their future self. We know that there is developmental change throughout our entire lives, not just in childhood and adolescence. We will not be the same person at twenty, forty, and sixty. Arguably, the only medical risk remaining to a future self would be from the removal procedure, but the existential risk is worth considering. The field of gerontology specializes in medical care of the elderly and the unique nature of that care. I have a friend who is a gerontologist. He has said that any patient he has asked about a tattoo has always discussed it with regret, characterizing it as the foolish decision of another time, the result of a decision by another person entirely.

One concern that is unavoidable and cannot be controlled is the perception of others. Although annoying, this is usually harmless. There is one important area, however, where we can also consider it a risk. Medical professionals are just as likely as others to fall into the trap of stereotyping (higher calling, close supervision: I stand by my previous statements), and their opinion of you can affect their treatment decisions, which may potentially pose some harm. For years, we were taught that a tattoo was a sign of risky behaviors or psychiatric illness. A review of medical literature from the 1950s to the present clearly shows this predisposition of opinion. In one letter to a medical journal, a cosmetic surgeon described the attitude of his fellow physicians on tattoo removal as, 'Do people who deform themselves deserve anyone's interest or skill to undo the predictable results of their own folly?'[7]

Also, having tattoos with markedly dark imagery has been proposed as a way to identify individuals with borderline personality disorder.[8] Even just having a tattoo has been described as a sign of bipolar mood disorder, believe it or not. In the end, though, the number of crazy people in this country remains stable (high, but stable) while the number of tattooed people is going through the roof. Individuals with psychiatric illness have a higher likelihood of getting tattoos in that same way that they have a higher likelihood of becoming chain smokers or alcoholics. This does not mean that anyone who ever got a tattoo has a psychiatric illness, no more than it would mean that anyone who ever drank a beer is an alcoholic. As tattoos become more mainstream, the likelihood that they will be perceived as the ultimate in antisocial behavior decreases. Real sociopaths may look to separate themselves from the tattooed by choosing less acceptable person options such as having their tongue split, having their teeth sharpened, or attending law school. In the meantime, I would challenge my medical colleges to question their assumptions on the nature of the person who chooses ink.

Autonomy

When asked by your friend, your parents, your partner, or even your doctor why you are getting a tattoo, an appropriate answer would be 'none of your beeswax!' Autonomy is absolutely the trump card. You may suspect that I'm about to say you should have a better understanding of autonomy first. Well, you would be right, but don't worry as this explanation is a short one. The legal understanding of autonomy is in line with what we all think autonomy should be: I want to do it, and it's not

DANIEL MIORI

hurting anyone else; so I should be able to do it – simple as that. Getting a tattoo is covered under autonomy in the form of freedom of expression under the constitution. Try not to get too much of a warm fuzzy glow over that. This is not a case of your kind and benevolent government watching out for you. Signing yourself out of hospital with half-treated pneumonia in the middle of a blizzard is also covered under that legal autonomy thing, and it's almost never a good idea.

Actual autonomy, the kind any real he-man-type bioethicist would swoon over, is made up of three parts, namely intention, understanding, and lack of outside influences. Intention is easy; it's what I just talked about in the last paragraph. You want to get a tattoo, so off you go. Understanding is about fully understanding the procedure, which the artist will be very careful to explain, and that other stuff I droned on about concerning risk versus benefit. In my opinion, though, when it comes to ink, the most important thing to know is what your own outside influences are. That is the real task, and you are the one and only person who can come to that understanding. For that reason, it is worthwhile looking beyond the beeswax answer. You don't want to be one of those old people my gerontologist friend sees who are ashamed of their art (quite frankly even he gets a bit queasy over some of those tattoos). That *understanding* of the reasons you make your decision is what real autonomy is about. If after careful consideration you decide that a tattoo is the right thing for you, congratulations: you have exercised your autonomy. No morning-after shyness; you will walk with your head (or arm, or chest, or butt) held high.

Inside the Outside Influences of Your Ink

Since the reason you are contemplating ink is central to the autonomy of your tattoo decision, it's important to have all those parts of autonomy ready. Not because there will be a test, but so that when you defiantly shout 'None of your beeswax!' you will have a particularly authoritative tone in your voice that will impress the chicks. In addition, if your grandmother asks, you really do need to have some non-shouting-type answers ready. Although there are probably as many reasons to get ink as there are people getting ink, you may gain some insight by reviewing other people's reasons. In an article that keeps an uncharacteristically non-judgmental perspective, Silke Wohlrab, Jutta Stahl, and Peter Kappeler identified ten main categories: beauty and fashion, individuality, personal narrative, physical endurance, resistance, spirituality, group affiliation, addiction, sexual motivation, and none of the above.[9]

Fashion, which I would lump in with beauty and individuality, is the thing that scares the bejeebees out of tattoo artists everywhere. It is, at the same time, the reason so many people walk through tattoo shops' front doors and also the reason so many people wake up the next day, look at their head (or arm, or chest, or butt) and weep. One of the main things the artists I spoke to in preparing for this chapter tell people getting their first tattoo is to make sure that it is what they really want, because it will last forever (or until a painful and expensive surgery). Fashion and beauty are both temporary; tattoos are not. Asserting your independence by dressing just like all the other independent people is actually funny in an ironic way. Getting a mark that will last you a lifetime to be just like all the other independent people – well, that's just sad.

Close identification with a cause or group includes members of the military, sports fans, and Princeton graduates such as George P. Schultz, the U. S. Secretary of State from 1982 to 1989. Mr. Schultz plays his cards close to his chest on the subject, but he is rumored to have his college mascot, the Princeton tiger, tattooed in an unmentionable place. Like fashion, those strong associations can fade with time (right, George?).

Sex isn't really a tough one. I'm kind of a dirty old Freudian at heart, and I think most of the things we desire are sexual in nature, so the idea that tattoos could also be about sex … well, duh! For me, the more interesting part is the people who think they can be dirty old perverts and still come off looking like they aren't. In case you wondered when my next rant about the medical profession was coming, here it is. In an article from *The Journal of Dermatologic Surgery and Oncology* entitled 'Psychological implications of tattoos,' there were twelve photographs: one ear, one hand, two naked butts, two penises, and six pairs of breasts (women's breasts).[10] Granted, all of these things were tattooed (one of the butts had a propeller on each cheek) – but six shots of boobs? Who did they think they were fooling? I'm telling you, close and constant supervision is the only way to deal with these people!

Participation in a criminal or antisocial enterprise is something Wohlrab et al. didn't cover, but I think it crosses over between their categories of addiction and close identification with a group, just a group who happens to be in a gang or lives in a prison. I believe you could also roll a bit of the psychiatrically and socially disturbed in there, too. Some

DANIEL MIORI

great ink is done in prisons, as well as a lot of bad ink. That is also the one place where infections and infectious disease from tattoos is still common.

Personal narrative, physical endurance, resistance, and spirituality are the last batch I would consider as one, and are probably where the real meat of a discussion of freedom of expression lies. Rather than dissect each of these I'd like to use this section to talk about the memorial tattoo. Simple enough to describe, it is a tattoo that marks a passage in life such as a birth or death. Getting a tattoo to reframe a life-altering event is part personal narrative, part talisman (to gain power, or endurance, or resilience), and almost entirely spiritual by any definition. A superficial treatment of memorial tattoos would give the impression that they are a poorly-thought-out sentimental affectation. A closer look, however, shows that they may just be the most useful tattoo there is. This leads me into the concluding section of this chapter. The part I promised you a while ago, when I attempt to build the case for a tattoo that, like broccoli, may be good for you.

Memory Remodeling

About twenty years ago there was a great deal of publicity on repressed memories, particularly repressed memories of child abuse. After much hype and hysteria, it became clear that these people weren't recalling actual events but were rather having disturbing memories implanted – implanted not by nefarious evildoers but by reputable therapists using methods that were thought to be helpful. The resulting investigations of the phenomenon by researchers such as Elizabeth Loftus may have opened new ways to address real traumatic memories.[11] We may be able to restructure those events – for example, the loss of a close friend – into something still painful but less traumatic. One way to do that would be by finding a good therapist; another would involve spending less money and finding yourself a good tattoo parlor. The tradition of memorial tattoos is probably about as old as the art of tattooing. Every artist I've talked to has had remarkable stories to tell of the healing effect of a memorial tattoo. These narratives have come from many traditions, but they are similar in some fundamental ways. The day on which one is tattooed is held to be important, not just in terms of getting ink but also as a spiritual event. The person getting the tattoo is encouraged to bring friends and objects that will evoke positive memories of the event or person to be memorialized. There can even be primitive chanting; for example, saying the Our Father or playing some Fleetwood Mac. The very process of getting the tattoo likely even contributes to the memory remodeling since pain and memory are closely linked. Before public records were kept, business transactions would often be recorded by finding some poor peasant, paying him a few dollars, doing the deal in front of him, and then pounding the living crap out of him so he would always remember the details of the event.

Taking the opportunity to plan your memorial tattoo carefully, surrounding yourself with positive associations, gluing the event in place with the pain of the tattoo, and then carrying that reminder of the positive event with you can turn a painful memory into something more therapeutic. Nobody from the mainstream medical community will be recommending this version of memory remodeling anytime soon, but I think we have already established the fact that those guys don't know everything, and may even require close supervision!

NOTES

1 Good introductions to bioethics include Helga Kuhse and Peter Singer (eds.), *A Companion to Bioethics: An Anthology* (Malden, MA: Blackwell, 1998); Tom Beauchamp and James Childress, *Principles of Biomedical Ethics* (Oxford: Oxford University Press, 2001); Robert Veatch, *The Basics of Bioethics* (Upper Saddle River, NJ: Prentice Hall, 2002); and Helga Kuhse and Peter Singer (eds.), *Bioethics: An Anthology* (Malden, MA: Wiley-Blackwell, 2006).

2 Socrates, in fact, was likely a virtue ethicist. For good introductions to the philosophical field of ethics (or moral philosophy), which at a very broad level can be divided into 'metaethics,' 'normative ethics,' and 'practical ethics' (under which bioethics sits), see Louis Pojman, *Ethics: Discovering Right and Wrong* (Belmont, CA: Wadsworth Publishing, 2005); Emmett Barcalow, *Moral Philosophy: Theories and Practice* (Belmont, CA: Wadsworth Publishing, 2006); and Jamie Carlin Watson and Robert Arp, *What's Good On TV? Understanding Ethics Through Television Episodes* (Malden, MA: Wiley-Blackwell, 2011).

3 Daniel Callahan, 'Bioethics as a discipline,' reprinted in Nancy Jecker, Albert Jonsen, and Robert Pearlman (eds.), *Bioethics: An introduction to the History, Methods, and Practice* (Sudbury, ME: Jones and Bartlett Publishers, 2007), pp. 17–18. See also The Hastings Center's website: http://www.thehastingscenter.org.

4 Helpful hint: if you want to sound like you know your bioethics stuff, pronounce Beauchamp as 'beech-um' – only an uneducated, untrained, uninitiated, *normal* person pronounces it 'bow-champ.'

5 David Silvers and Harry Gelb, 'The prohibition of tattooing in New York City,' *The American Journal of Dermatology* 13, 3 (1991): 307–309.

6 Kris Sperry, 'Tattoos and tattooing, part II: Gross pathology, histopathology, medical complications, and applications,' *The American Journal of Forensic Medicine and Pathology* 13, 1 (1992): 7–17.

7 Alan Rockoff, 'A piece of my mind,' *Journal of the American Medical Association* 27, 14 (April 13, 1994): 1076.

8 Norman Goldstein, 'Psychological implications of tattoos,' *Journal of Dermatological Surgery and Oncology* 5, 11 (November 1979): 883–888.

9 Silke Wohlrab, Jutta Stahl, and Peter Kappeler, 'Modifying the body: Motivations for getting tattooed and pierced,' *Body Image* 4, 1 (2007): 87–95

10 Goldstein, 'Psychological implications of tattoos,' p. 888.

11 Elizabeth Loftus and Giuliana Mazzoni, 'Using imagination and personalized suggestion to change people,' *Behavioral Therapy* 29 (1998): 691–706.

CHAPTER 16

WRITING ON THE BODY
The Modern Morality of the Tattoo

What if Tattooing is Immoral?

How many people do you know with a tattoo? As a reader of this book, you perhaps have a tattoo and have friends and loved ones with tattoos as well. If you're an academic, then you'll no doubt have noticed that tattoos are often revealed as a colorful addendum to campus life. And if, like me, you're an academic at a certain kind of university, then you'll have realized that tattooing is now equally the province of the academic elite and moneyed middle classes, having once been almost exclusively the province of the working class and criminal community.[1] Of course, despite the changing demographic, a university is a place of the young, and youth is one of the other groups with a predilection for decorating the body in Western industrialized society.[2]

Now, you might say that you like tattoos, and I might say that I don't like tattoos, and in expressing this disagreement we're disputing nothing more than a difference of taste. But what if I were to claim that, far from being a matter of personal taste, tattooing is *immoral*? Is this the kind of claim that can be seriously defended in this post-modern, post-moral age, when matters of personal decorum have become a minor matter of manners rather than the substance of morality? This isn't a new idea, but

Tattoos – Philosophy for Everyone: I Ink, Therefore I Am, First Edition.
Edited by Robert Arp.
© 2012 John Wiley & Sons, Inc. Published 2012 by John Wiley & Sons, Inc.

in writing it out and giving voice to the thought it sounds like a boorish anachronism. However, in what follows I shall attempt to explore whether the claim that 'tattooing is immoral' can be defended.

Latent Criminals or Degenerate Aristocrats

The idea that one can approach a lifestyle choice such as tattooing as a moral matter was investigated by Adolf Loos (1870–1933) in his essay 'Ornament und Verbrechen' ('Ornament and crime,' 1908), where he states: 'Tattooed men who are not behind bars are either latent criminals or degenerate aristocrats. If someone who is tattooed dies in freedom, then he does so a few years before he would have committed murder.'[3]

Loos was concerned by the degeneracy that marked the culture of Central Europe at the turn of the twentieth century, and as part of his morality of architecture, style, and manners he argued against decoration and ornament, including decoration and ornament of one's skin. He looked to the 'new' and emerging cultures of the Anglo-Saxon world to set the standards for a modern culture of morality and taste. One hundred years later, we find ourselves in a new *fin de siècle* with a very different cultural milieu. Can Loos' critique be sustained or regarded with any relevance to contemporary, post-modern, pluralist culture?

The present vogue for tattooing, body piercing, and scarification are widespread and have lots of appeal; they are popular in the sense that they are part of a current trend, but it is an open question just how common they are.[4] W. L. Hildburgh's work provides evidence that tattooing and related customs of body decoration and modification were present in the earliest human societies.[5] Anthropologists have long recorded the significance of tattooing within particular cultures in which the meaning of tattooing and other forms of body modification relates to identity, social status, transitions through the lifespan, and cultural memory. As Bryan Turner comments: 'These bodily marks in pre-literate societies were permanent, collective, and largely obligatory. Because they were set within a shared culture of collective meanings, the significance of a tattoo could be read unambiguously.'[6] Something of that surety of meaning has been lost in the contemporary world; although styles of tattooing may borrow their references from traditional motifs found in Polynesian, Japanese, and other Asian traditions, they are also drawn from Celtic designs, from nautical traditions, and from many contemporary cultural reference points including cartoon characters, sport-related designs, cults surrounding films such as *Star Wars*, and so on.[7]

For Loos, tattooing was strongly associated with deviance and criminality. Interestingly enough, other more recent observers also regard tattooing as a sign of disorder and pathology.[8] Contemporary social commentators advance strikingly similar views, as Theodore Dalrymple writes in *The New Criterion*:

> In fact, more than 95 percent of imprisoned white British criminals are tattooed. The statistical association between tattooing and criminality is very much stronger (with the exception of that between criminality and smoking) than that with any of the more conventionally investigated factors, such as broken homes, drug addiction, low intelligence, and poor educational attainment. Show me a man's tattoos, and I will tell you his criminal record: British men, for example, who were incarcerated before the age of twenty-one usually bear a blue spot tattooed over one cheekbone, the criminal's equivalent of the old school tie.[9]

Sociological analyses produce a more nuanced spectrum in which significant meaning-making is seen within a particular social or cultural milieu.[10] Other commentators see the absorption of tattooing and related practices into consumerism as undermining and, in most cases, robbing the practices of any significant meaning – what Bryan Turner refers to as the 'exhaustion of idiom.'[11] Tattooing and related practices might still be regarded as degenerate, deviant, or in equal measure rebellious and subversive when they are practiced to the extreme, but in most cases they are indulged in as any other fashion accoutrement, merely ripples in the stream of consumer culture rather than statements of rebellion and difference. Thus, why should it matter whether a person chooses to tattoo or not? Isn't tattooing an expression of personal autonomy and, if so, shouldn't we be at liberty to tattoo the 'sovereign self'?

Loos and Amorality

Loos takes two broad approaches in his criticism of tattooing; one line of argument considers the wrongness of tattooing as lying with what tattooing implies of the person tattooed, and a second line of argument attacks tattooing directly. So what does tattooing imply? For Loos, if a citizen of the developed world has a tattoo, it implies that s/he is deficient in several ways. The adult is acting as a child – giving in to an urge to express her/himself in a way that is not appropriate for a mature adult. Thus, by implication, moral agents are those persons who ought to act through reason and reflection and aspire to act in ways that reflect a mature and stable character. The child can't be expected to know better and is an *amoral* individual – a term he also uses to describe the behavior of traditional tribespeople: 'The Papuan slaughters his enemies and devours them. He is not a criminal. But if a modern person slaughters someone and devours him, he is a criminal or degenerate.'[12]

While I am very uncomfortable with Loos' emphatic tone and choice of example, the implication of his example is less controversial.[13] The essence of Loos' argument is that we have good reason to consider murder to be the epitome of moral wrong, and, for a civilization that has enjoyed some moral progression, the wrongness of murder – among other things – constitutes one of a widening set of moral baselines. The questioning and challenging of the established boundaries of moral standards has in many cases advanced the 'baseline' or extended the boundary of moral norms to the extent that the new parameter becomes the presumed position from which we start, in terms of personal behavior and the values that underpin important social institutions.[14] With this comes the expectation that citizens ought to comply with such moral positions. This is not to say that moral progress is inevitable; but, minimally, as Thomas Nagel comments, progress starts with something's having become established as 'obvious,' and our setting out from there.[15] For Loos, the amoral individual may be regarded as excusable or non-culpable, though we may nevertheless be justified in seeking to change or control their behavior; however, the 'modern person' is the culpable moral agent who ought to know better and will be held responsible for his/her actions.

Tattooing is Like Murdering?

The challenging thing here is that, although we may agree that Loos' argument holds for murder, or prejudice against race or gender, it is just too much of a stretch to accept that tattooing falls into the same moral category. Tattooing *per se* is just not the same thing as murder or racism – for one thing, murder, racism, and other forms of prejudicial behavior involve abuses of power between individuals, and such acts involve intrusions into the autonomy of others and rob them of individual rights and freedoms. With the exception of enforced tattooing and branding – as happened notoriously in slavery and the Nazi treatment of Jews – tattooing, at least in Western culture, is a voluntary act involving one's own body. Since tattooing is the expression of a relationship one has with one's self, it does not seem to make sense to talk of an abuse of power or an intrusion into autonomy here. The slogan 'it's my body and I can do what I want with it' seems to capture the essence of the act, though this is a claim I shall examine further.

Loos' argument, however, isn't a direct attack on tattooing, but is rather a claim about the moral character of those who indulge in tattooing. Of course, Loos' essay takes the form of a manifesto – he runs fast and loose with bold claims, with scant argument and with empirical claims – for example, the association of tattoos and criminality – for which he offers no evidence. However, recent scholars have supported similar critiques of contemporary tattooing with empirical evidence. As Michael Atkinson reports, social-psychological research tends to seek evidence for tattooing as a form of pathology, the product of a disordered mind, of non-conformity as the product of developmental or cognitive defects.[16] Medical and epidemiological analyses have associated tattooing with youthful impetuousness, irrationality, aggression, and a predilection for other forms of abuse and self-harm.[17] One must be cautious, since space does not allow for a critical review of the evidence; but, it is only really possible to say that the sort of associations between tattoos and immoral and anti-social behavior made by Loos have been sought in research conducted since that time, which says more perhaps about the *presumptions of the researchers* than the 'evidence' their research uncovers. Atkinson again warns that, notwithstanding the more sympathetic sociological approaches of Margo DeMello[18] and Clinton Sanders,[19] there are still many who seek to substantiate the already presumed disreputable nature of tattooing and the assumed pathology of the tattooed.

Here, I find myself in sympathy with Atkinson, as it seems *a priori* unfeasible – but also empirically doubtful – that one can read from a tattoo a meaningful insight into the nature and character of the tattooed individual. However, while we may conclude that contemporary tattooed persons are not a homogenous group, it does not follow that tattooing is immune to moral critique of the kind we have been considering. I have commented upon the potential assumptions of those who take a critical academic interest in the tattooed to be biased, but in the interests of balance the same point can be made of those who take a more sympathetic

SIMON WOODS

approach. In the preface to her book, Margo DeMello[20] comments upon the nature of anthropology and how the imperialistic anthropology of the past has been replaced by a more equitable power structure between researchers and the researched, and she observes that she is as likely to be challenged by her research subjects as she is likely to challenge them. However, the question must arise as to just how possible is it for a well-educated, middle-class, tattooed researcher to engage in critical discourse with her subjects and her data when this is also drawn from middle class, well-educated, tattooed respondents? This is probably unfair, though it raises the possibility that a sympathetic, less critical analysis is more likely from an academic who has already conformed to the cult.

Loos and the Crime of Ornamentation

So what of Loos' second line of argument? Loos argued that it was a crime to add ornamentation to any object, and that the body should be regarded as such a candidate object. The principal problem with ornamentation is that it causes an object to go out of fashion, yet the body must endure, at least for the lifetime of the person whose body it is: 'the form of an object should last, that is, we should find it tolerable as long as the object itself lasts.'[21] Though Loos didn't elaborate on his thoughts about tattooing as a 'criminal' form of ornamentation, there are a number of strands that can be developed in the light of the wider approach he took. For one thing, a tattoo – without painful, invasive, and expensive remedy – is a permanent mark on the body and one that may not be easily disguised by clothing or cosmetics. There has been a long-standing objection to tattooing within Islamic and Judeo-Christian traditions, which regard marking the body as defiling a divine gift.[22] I don't wish to offer an analysis of religious perspectives here, but it's not unreasonable to consider that such traditions have in part informed the common social mores that regard tattooing as rendering a person unsuitable for certain occupations. This observation seems to fit with not-infrequent reports of perceived bias by employers against employees with tattoos, as well as reports of people indulging in tattooing as a form of protest against former employers. What this issue raises is the idea that the body is not only the private self but also operates to a great extent as a public object of scrutiny. With this latter point in mind, one can get a sense that a tattoo may have a shelf life in the way Loos suggests since the person whose body it is will live through many transitions, have different roles, and be subject to the gaze of multiple others over the course of a lifetime. One is left to wonder how a person with the once popular 'LOVE HATE' finger tattoos – now likely to be in their late sixties – would explain them to their grandchildren.[23]

Tattooing and Personal Meaning

For many people who get tattoos, it's not the wider public attitude that matters to them but rather the personal meaning and significance they attach to the tattoo or other body mark. Indeed, for some the tattoo is something to be flaunted in the face of public opinion – a protest, a rebellion, or a public statement. Participants in tattoo-related research frequently comment that the reason for obtaining a tattoo was to mark some special life event, or to express a change in direction such as divorce or leaving a job for a new career. The meanings of tattoos are multiple, as a *memento mori* or as a celebration of love, an expression of family or political values. Some are marks of personal protest arising from frustrating or abusive relationships, some are angry expressions, some are cathartic, and many are attempts to achieve self-esteem and assert individuality.[24]

However, no matter how personal and individual the meaning of a tattoo, there is a sense in which the mark on the body will also have a public reality and meaning – even for those marks seen by few and hidden away. To think otherwise is to be a misguided solipsist. At the very least, tattooing draws upon a *public culture* of tattooing, often derivative of ancient traditions but delivered in a contemporary culture of commerce to the extent that the desire for that *individual* mark will be restricted to a version from the standard catalogue. Reading some of the more articulate testimonies of tattooed persons, one is left with no doubt about the sincerity and strength of feeling of these individuals and their desire to express or show their emotions. Yet, doing so via an irrevocable medium raises the possible comparison with other, more pathological forms of self-mutilation by people who feel that they have no other voice with which to express themselves.[25]

That resorting to tattooing or other forms of body marking may be seen as a disproportionate and inevitably inadequate form of self-expression is given some credence through reference to the desire for tattoo removal. There are empirical data that suggest the 'shelf life' – the period of time in which a tattoo serves to 'express' its intended purpose – is approximately ten years.[26] The desire for a tattoo as an expression of individuality is often undermined by the social stigma associated with it and a desire for removal, but also by a feeling that the time in which the tattoo had its significance has now passed. Although there is a need for more research in this evolving field, there is nevertheless some indication that a desire to express individuality, uniqueness, or a strong emotion through a permanent body mark is later regretted. This latter remark inevitably raises questions about the nature of personal autonomy and the relationship of the self with the body.

Tattooing and Liberal Autonomy

The testimonies of the tattooed, with their claims for individuality, self-expression, and authenticity, are redolent with the usual language of contemporary liberal autonomy.[27] The idea that one may offer a moral critique of tattooing in an age in which the god of personal autonomy erects a barrier around the personal space of every autonomous individual might seem absurd. The liberal canon has been informed by many sources, but John Stuart Mill's (1806–1873) claim in *On Liberty* captures the notion of the sovereign self: 'over himself, over his own body and mind, the individual is sovereign.'[28] This is a notion that is foundational to the deep liberal conviction that the individual has an absolute right to non-interference from the state and from others: 'The only purpose for which power can be rightfully exercised over any member of a civilized community, against his will, is to prevent harm to others. His own good, either physical or moral, is not a sufficient warrant.'[29]

The extent to which the right to non-interference coupled with the right to self-determination is perhaps most profoundly expressed is in the medical context, where a person may refuse life-sustaining treatment knowing that they will die as a consequence. However, the idea that the body is an object – a *thing*, and in particular *my* thing – over which I have absolute rights of disposal is not a settled matter.[30] In the U. K., for example, my right to refuse life-saving medical treatment does not extend to a right to refuse basic care that will keep me clean and fed, nor is it accepted that by mere consent do I render any act on my body either lawful or moral by virtue of that consent.[31] It is recognized that even the 'sovereign self' is subject to the standards of decency and restraint that constitute public concern. There are two issues therefore that are relevant to tattooing. The first concerns the meaning of personal autonomy and the second the status of the body; however, both are related. In relation to the meaning of personal autonomy, the usual liberal account is precisely the one of freedom from interference and rights to self-determination. Although liberals and non-liberals alike acknowledge that we are all engaged in the process of pursuing the best sort of life for ourselves, the liberal view is that no one is privileged over the individual in determining what is good for him or her. The implication of this position is that the best form of political and social order is one that supports maximum individual autonomy, since it is only by maximizing autonomy that individuals are free to pursue and revise their own view about what is valuable in life. This is a position that has become highly pervasive in Western governments, in numerous institutions, and within practices including health care, but sits most comfortably in the world of commerce.

The liberal position is one that seems most antithetical to that of Loos since it may recognize his right to voice an opinion but would deny the implications for constraint and control of social practices that give the opportunity for personal 'autonomous' choices. However, it is possible to respect the importance of individual freedoms yet challenge the extent to which the individual ought to be regarded as the absolute authority and arbiter of his/her own interests, unencumbered with links and ties to others and to social institutions – autonomy is, after all, a relational concept. Recognizing and respecting personal autonomy should not exclude the reasonable and proper challenge to a person's view of their own good; indeed, the fostering of autonomy may require it. The possibility that an improved, better, wiser perspective on our choice of lifestyle may be obtained through reflection, weighing, and reasoned challenge by others suggests a prudent and pragmatic approach that does not entail the abandonment of personal autonomy but rather recognizes the limits to which certain conceptions of personal autonomy are subject.[32]

Since I am a pragmatist and a philosopher who is concerned with matters of public policy, I would suggest that we consider the possibility of more stringent regulation of the 'professionals' who provide tattooing and other permanent body-marking services, at least to the extent that cosmetic dentistry or other cosmetic services are regulated. In particular, I would suggest that there be an expectation for evidence, particularly evidence regarding regret, to form part of the required informed consent. A final practical (but probably unworkable) suggestion is that permanent tattooing be restricted to those over age twenty-five years since the, albeit limited, evidence would suggest that there is a higher prevalence of regret in the under-twenty-five year group.

I have less to say about the relationship of the 'self' to the 'body' in this context, not because it isn't interesting or relevant to our subject but because it would require a chapter, indeed a whole book of its own, to do justice to this aspect. I am sympathetic to the idea that some liberal writers have misunderstood the traditions from John Locke (1632–1704) through Immanuel Kant (1724–1804) to John Stuart Mill that they use to endorse the idea that the person *owns* their body and is thus sanctioned to dispose of it as they will.[33] Just as autonomy is a relational concept, so I would suggest is the body a relational object: it takes its meaning and significance within a public domain and is thus subject to the same relational constraints and opportunities as the self with which it is identical. The implication of this claim is that we may be justly restrained in how we use our bodies.

Attraction and Repulsion

In conclusion, I should state that I am both attracted and repulsed by Loos' diatribe against tattooing. I'm attracted to the boldness of his stance, the certainty of his convictions, and the directness of his approach. I don't like his sweeping generalizations and, to the contemporary ear, almost fascistic opinionating. There should, however, be scope for forthright and public debate on such matters as tattooing and body modification. As a matter of personal taste, I would prefer not to be tattooed, and I respect the decisions of those to make an enduring commitment to their tattoos and body marks. I do believe that in addition to matters of taste there is also a moral matter, for reasons I have merely begun to elaborate here.

NOTES

1 Bryan Turner, 'The possibility of primitiveness: Towards a sociology of body marks in cool societies,' *Body and Society* 5, 2–3 (1999): 39–50.
2 Myrna Armstrong, Donna Owen, Alden Roberts, and Jerome Koch, 'College students and tattoos: Influence of image, identity, family, and friends,' *Journal of Psychosocial Nursing and Mental Health Services* 40, 10 (October, 2002): 20–29.

3 **Adolf Loos, 'Ornament und Verbrechen,' in** *Sämtliche Schriften* (Vienna: Herold, 1924).

4 See Myrna Armstrong, Donna Owen, Alden Roberts, and Jerome Koch, 'College students and tattoos: Influence of image, identity, family, and friends,' n. 1. The authors suggest that three percent of the general population of the United States has a tattoo, but that fifteen to twenty-five percent of those aged between fifteen and twenty five is tattooed.

5 W. L. Hildburgh, 'Images of the human hand as amulets in Spain,' *Journal of the Courtauld and Warburg Institutes* 18 (1955): 67–89.

6 Bryan Turner, 'The possibilities of primitiveness: Towards a sociology of body marks in cool societies,' *Body & Society* 5, 2–3 (1999): 39.

7 See, for example, the historical introduction to Terisa Green, *The Tattoo Encyclopedia: A Guide to Choosing Your Tattoo* (New York: Fireside Publishers, 2003).

8 See, for example, Michael Atkinson's discussion of these analyses in 'Tattooing and civilising processes: Body modification and self-control,' *Canadian Review of Sociology & Anthropology* 41, 2 (2004): 125–146.

9 Theodore Dalrymple, 'Exposing shallowness: On Margo DeMello's *Bodies of Inscription,' The New Criterion* 18 (2000, http://www.newcriterion.com/articles.cfm/demello-dalrymple-2647).

10 Margo DeMello, *Bodies of Inscription: A Cultural History of the Modern Tattoo Community* (Durham, NC: Duke University Press, 2000).

11 Turner, 'The possibilities of primitiveness,' p. 40.

12 **Loos, 'Ornament und Verbrechen,'** p. 167. For Loos, there is an association between the predilection for slaughter and cannibalism and the desire to tattoo and decorate, all of which he regards as indicative of a 'primitive' and amoral state of development.

13 It must be appreciated that Loos was writing something of a manifesto and drawing upon stereotypes and language common to his time. I find much of his style and language offensive, but nevertheless I consider his arguments worthy of consideration.

14 See Michele Moody-Adams, 'The idea of moral progress,' *Metaphilosophy* 30, 3 (1990): 168–185.

15 Thomas Nagel, *The View From Nowhere* (New York: Oxford University Press, 1986).

16 See Atkinson, 'Tattooing and civilising processes.' He cites a number of sources, including Otakar Pollak and Elisabeth Mckenna, 'Tattooed psychotic patients,' *American Journal of Psychiatry* 101 (1945): 673–674.

17 Atkinson, 'Tattooing and civilising processes.' Also see D. Angus Vail, 'Tattoos are like potato chips ... you can't have just one: The process of becoming and being a collector,' *Deviant Behavior* 20, 3 (1999): 253–273.

18 Margo DeMello, 'Not just for bikers anymore: Popular representations of American tattooing,' *Journal of Popular Culture* 29, 3 (1995): 37–52.

19 Clinton Sanders, *Customizing the Body: The Art and Culture of Tattooing.* (Philadelphia, PA: Temple University Press, 1989).

20 DeMello, *Bodies of Inscription.*

21 **Loos, 'Ornament und Verbrechen,' p. 172.**

22 For example, Leviticus 19:28 states: 'Ye shall not make any cuttings in your flesh for the dead, nor print any marks upon you: I [am] the LORD.'

23 Robert Mitchum displayed similar tattoos in his role as a serial killer in the now-iconic 1955 movie *Night of the Hunter.* It isn't clear whether this film influenced, or drew upon, an already established tradition of this form of tattooing.

24 See, for example, DeMello, *Bodies of Inscription* and Atkinson, 'Tattooing and civilising processes.' See also Myrna Armstrong, Alden Roberts, Jerome Koch, Jana Saunders, Donna Owen, and Rox Anderson, 'Motivation for contemporary tattoo removal: A shift in identity,' *Archive of Dermatology* 144, 7 (2008): 879–884.

25 See, for example, Matthew Large, Nick Babidge, Doug Andrews, Philip Storey, and Olav Nielssen, 'Major self-mutilation in the first episode of psychosis,' *Schizophrenia Bulletin* 35, 5 (2009): 1012–1021.

26 Armstrong et al., 'Motivation for contemporary tattoo removal.'

27 See Will Kymlicka, *Contemporary Political Philosophy: An introduction* (Oxford: Oxford University Press, 2002), in which the author outlines the strong liberal position that no one is in a better position than the person her/himself to determine what is good for her/him.

28 John Stuart Mill, *On Liberty* (Indianapolis, IN: Hackett Publishing Company, 1978), p. 7.

29 Ibid., p. 135.

30 For an interesting and extended discussion of this issue, see Donna Dickenson, *Property in the Body: Feminist Perspectives* (Cambridge: Cambridge University Press, 2007).

31 See, for example, the case of *R v Brown* [1994] 1 AC 212, which went on appeal to the House of Lords. The case revolved around a group of men who were convicted for their involvement in consensual sadomasochistic sexual acts. Despite the fact that all the men were consenting individuals, they were convicted for 'unlawful and malicious wounding' and 'assault occasioning actual bodily harm' under the Offences against the Person Act 1861.

32 See, for example, Charles Taylor, *Sources of the Self: The Making of the Modern Identity* (Cambridge, MA: Harvard University Press, 1989), p. 72.

33 Dickenson, *Property in the Body.*

EASTERN AND RELIGIOUS PERSPECTIVES

'The Buddhist practitioner can learn to embrace the pain of the experience of getting tattooed, the healing process and the rest, first as a kind of meditative practice. The pain itself can become the object of meditation as one simply pays attention to the sensations without trying to push them away.'

(Joseph J. Lynch, p. 240)

CHAPTER 17

IS A TATTOO A SIGN OF IMPIETY?

Dispelling a Confusion

In many ways my wedding was a meeting of two worlds: my family and friends come from European backgrounds, while my wife's family and friends come from Asian – largely Korean – ones. My side of the family has, for the most part, a Christian worldview, while my wife's, despite some of its members being Christian, live within a Confucian ethos. Yet, in spite of these differences, nearly all at my wedding shared one thing in common: discomfort with my best man's heavily tattooed arms. Of course, this 'one thing in common' actually springs from sharing *two* things in common: *piety* (a form of justice emphasizing respect for one's superiors) and *ignorance* in respect to what piety looks like in particular circumstances.

That is, both the Judeo-Christian and Confucian traditions insist that it's just or pious that both God and one's parents/ancestors be deeply respected, the reasoning being that, since justice means treating each as they ought to be treated, and since God and one's parents occupy

Tattoos – Philosophy for Everyone: I Ink, Therefore I Am, First Edition.
Edited by Robert Arp.
© 2012 John Wiley & Sons, Inc. Published 2012 by John Wiley & Sons, Inc.

elevated positions, justice demands they be treated piously. None of this I have a problem with. The trouble, however, is that in both the Bible and the *Hsiao King* there are statements linking tattoos, or, rather, choosing to get a tattoo, with impiety – the body of the inferior belonging, in a sense, to the superior: be it one's Heavenly Father (the Bible) or one's earthly father (the *Hsiao King*). Because neither the non-contextualized Bible verses condemning tattoos nor Confucian philosophical reasoning in respect to tattoos are properly understood, the result is a Christian Confucian confusion over the ethics of tattooing. My goal in this chapter is to dispel this confusion.

'You Shall Not Make … Any Marks Upon Yourselves: I Am YHVH'

Jews and Christians alike accept that the Torah, or the books of 'Moses' in the Old Testament, is a part of scripture or instances of what theologians call 'special revelation.' What this means exactly is far from clear; however, what is agreed is that these books and their content – taken either in minute detail or in a more general sense (depending on who you talk to) – have been sanctioned or approved by God. Jews and Christians often claim to be rationally justified in believing the Torah (and, for Christians, the Bible) primarily, though not exclusively, on the basis of faith. In order for faith to be rationally justified, Jews and Christians maintain two things. First, that the existence of God – in one shade or another, either as the Creator, the Good, Heaven, Truth, Love, or a combination of these and others – *can* be known by all, such that all who *want* to know God can know Him. Second, those who want to know God are open to hearing His voice, and so when they read the Torah or Bible they can hear God testifying to them, saying, in effect, 'these are my words.' The testimony of God (a person who exists) to the reader (another person who exists) is a form of knowledge by acquaintance – what the French call *connaître* – and this knowledge is what Jews and Christians mostly mean when they talk about 'faith.' Thus, when Jews and Christians read Leviticus 19:28 – 'You shall not make any cuttings in your flesh on account of the dead or tattoo any marks upon yourselves: I am YHVH' – Jews and Christians claim to have gained knowledge: specially revealed knowledge, about an ethical command.[1] Consequently, on pain of both ignorance and impiety (i.e., ignoring the commands of a superior), neither Jews nor Christians are safe to ignore this passage about tattooing. However, few things in ancient writings, scripture included, are clear to modern readers and so the context needs to be unpacked.

Prior to the writing of Leviticus, Israel had been chosen by God to be a nation 'set apart.' It wasn't that only Israel could know of God's existence, nor that only Israelites could be reconciled with God after man's fall from grace (which will be discussed later); rather, Israel, as a 'pure' nation, was to be a sign to all nations of the perfect Holiness, Righteousness, or Justice that is God. Indeed, some non-Israelites were more pious and better than some Israelites: Abraham, the grandfather of Isaac (later named Israel), paid tribute to Melchizadek, the priest-king of a Canaanite city-state, and even Jesus is identified with this non-Israelite priest. Thus, the point of Israel being set apart was for it, as a nation, to reflect perfect doctrinal – and, from this, moral – purity.

Further, because the nations surrounding ancient Israel practiced either self-laceration (as a means to remember the dead, such as in Canaan) or tattooing (as in Egyptian fertility cults) as part of their impure religious teachings, Israel was forbidden to practice these. Indeed, because in nearby Mesopotamia being tattooed was also associated with being owned by a cult (Mesopotamian temple slaves were tattooed), there was a strong sense that Israel, as belonging to YHVH, ought not to be 'owned' by a lesser god and thus be associated with these unjust practices (unjust, of course, because to honor a lesser god over the greatest God is not to treat each as it ought to be treated). Israel, as a doctrinally pure nation, was to be the metaphorical bride-wife of YHVH, who is pure Righteousness or Righteousness itself.

Two things follow from this. First, nothing in Leviticus implies that tattooing *in and of itself* is immoral or unjust. Second, what is equally as clear is that, insofar as impure belief systems make tattooing a part of their practice, Israel is forbidden to engage in such practices: distinctions, it seems, need to be both visible and invisible. It is for this reason that Orthodox Jews, even to this day, see those who choose[2] to get tattoos as immoral or impious and hence usually forbid them, upon death, burial in a Jewish cemetery. For Christians, the case is a bit different. Because Israel was to be a *sign* of purity to all nations, the spirit, not the letter, of the law in Leviticus is what really matters: in other words, it's not obvious from the passages in the Old Testament that a person would necessarily be impious for choosing to get a tattoo. Nevertheless, there are still some passages in the New Testament that cause some Christians confusion over tattoos.

'You Are Not Your Own … Therefore Honor God with Your Body'

The majority of Christians throughout history have erroneously understood the prohibition against tattooing in Leviticus as being true to the letter for all time. Their mistaken understanding of this verse is reinforced by further misunderstanding another verse, this time in 1 Corinthians 6:19–20 of the New Testament, which reads: 'Do you not know that your body is a temple of the Holy Spirit, who is in you, whom you have received from God? You are not your own; you were bought at a price. Therefore honor God with your body.' Of course, there is nothing in this passage that explicitly forbids tattoos and thus would link them with impiety. In fact, if a person reads this passage properly – that is, from within its proper context – it is clear that God, via St. Paul, is talking about what happens when a man engages in sexual relations with a temple prostitute of an impure religion. Ink on one's skin is a red herring; the point, as in the Old Testament, is to preserve sanctity, and the argument for this is as follows.

God created the first man, Adam, and gave him authority over the entire planet. Adam was created in a just state, but, because he was given the faculty of free will, he was able to choose between justice and injustice: treating the greatest thing (God) as the greatest thing, or treating a lesser thing (such as Eve) as the greatest thing (God). Adam chose the latter and hence 'fell.' Because anyone who chooses to act unjustly even once can't enter into the presence of the burning purity that is perfect Justice or Righteousness (God), *all* who act unjustly even *once* are consigned, as the most ancient Hebrews,[3] Mesopotamians,[4] Greeks,[5] and even Japanese[6] knew, to the underworld or the land where the spirits of the dead dwell. Yet even if man can't save himself, insofar as God became man and dwelt among us as the Christ, He can do two things. First, he can represent all people since He has greater authority than even Adam: insofar as Adam, our first father, could pass on the curse of original sin (the disposition to prefer injustice to justice), the Christ, as the 'Second Adam,' can take all under His authority and pass on forgiveness of injustice by virtue of his authority. Yet, second, even this wouldn't be possible if the Christ weren't perfectly just or righteous; only because He is without injustice is He able to enter the presence of the Father so-to-speak and be in harmony with Him. And, insofar as people speak justly, confessing both that they can't save themselves (they can't remove all the

ADAM BARKMAN

stains of their injustice) and that the Christ can, these people, by the graciousness and authority of the Christ, can be accredited as just or righteous and hence be reconciled with the Father, who is perfect Joy. Thus, when 1 Corinthians says 'You are not your own,' it refers to those who have freely acknowledged the authority of God over all of what they are, including their bodies. Taking care of one's body as God has ordained bodies to be taken care of – here in respect to sexual matters ('The body is not meant for sexual immorality'[7]) – is an act of justice, and, because God is one's superior, it is also an act of piety. Nonetheless, there is nothing at all here that says getting a tattoo is a form of misusing one's body and hence acting impiously.

'We Must Not Injure Our Bodies: This Is the Beginning of Filial Piety'

Confucius lived around five hundred years before the birth of the Christ. As a self-confessed 'lover of the ancients,' he sought to align his teachings with the most ancient Chinese sages and to make their vague instructions more deliberate (hence, Confucianism is often called 'the deliberate tradition'). The teachings of these sages can be traced back to the beginning of Chinese civilization, around 2700 BCE, roughly a hundred years after the ziggurat of Eridu in Mesopotamia (a.k.a. the Tower of Babel) was abandoned. At this time, the first Chinese emperor, Huang Di, built a temple to the One Supreme God, known to the Han Chinese as Shang Di (later also called *Tian* or Heaven[8]). There never was, nor is to this day,[9] an image made to represent Shang Di since He is beyond all representation. This was the beginning of Chinese religious practice and the subject with which the sages of the ancient world were most concerned.[10] Thus, when Confucius complied the *Classic of History*, which describes the oldest accounts of the Middle Kingdom, he is careful to note not only that Shang Di is the Supreme Lord on High but also that 'It is virtue that moves Heaven'[11] and that 'His will extends everywhere;'[12] we are told,

> But Shang Di sent down calamities on the Xia Dynasty. The ruler of Xia had increased his opulence. He would not speak kindly to the people, and became utterly immoral and foolish. He was unable for a single day to bring himself to follow the path marked out by Shang Di.[13]

Mencius, the second greatest Confucian after the Teacher himself, thus perfectly agrees with the ancients when he writes that 'It is by the preservation of one's heart and the nourishment of one's character that man is able to serve Heaven.'[14] Shang Di or Heaven – God, we can say – was the source of true morality and justice, and the goal for the ancients, as for the earliest Confucians, was to look to Heaven to discern how to act on earth. Piety, then, was 'the root of all virtue.'[15]

Of course, Confucians, just as much as Jews and Christians (and many others), saw the scope of created reality not merely as an ontological hierarchy between God and man but also as a hierarchy taking into account differences of age, gender, ability, character, rank, and so on. On the top was Shang Di and below him were those belonging to the created heavens (lower-case 'h') – the *shen* or nature spirits and the *zu xian* or the spirits of the blessed ancestors[16] – and below these were those belonging to earth. First and foremost, the just emperor and then a myriad of hierarchies encompassing gender, age, ability, character, and rank distinctions. Piety, as the form of justice concerned with treating a superior as a superior, ought to be shown first and foremost to Shang Di and then, down the ranks, to one's father.

Confucius' *Hsiao King* or treatise on filial piety is the text often cited when discussing the impiety of tattoos. The piety discussed in this book is toward one's father, though, since to honor one's father is to honor the way of Heaven,[17] Heaven itself is honored when fathers are honored: 'In filial piety there is nothing greater than the reverential awe of one's father. In the reverential awe shown to one's father there is nothing greater than the making him the correlate of Heaven.'[18] In this vein it should be pointed out that even minor acts of injustice – minor when comparing one's father to God – offends Heaven and brings about trouble:

> Shang Di will pour down calamities on those who do evil. We must not neglect to do small acts of righteousness because it is by the accumulation of these that the nations celebrate. We must not neglect to avoid acts of unrighteousness because it is by the accumulation of these that an entire generation is corrupted.[19]

This, then, leads us to the relatively minor, though still vitally important, question as to whether getting a tattoo was, or, more importantly, ought to have been, considered an act of impiety according to Confucius and early Confucians.

In the *Hsiao King*, Confucius remarks, 'Our bodies – to every hair and bit of skin – are received by us from our parents, and we must not presume to injure or wound them: this is the beginning of filial piety.'[20] Here we should immediately note two things. First, Confucius doesn't explicitly mention tattooing. And, second, injuring or wounding one's body is only a *prima facie* prohibition since to wound one's body to protect one's family or in service of the emperor would have been praised, not condemned, and even suicide to remove the shame of a misdeed plaguing one's family was, and still is, generally accepted by Confucians. So, why, then, have Confucians linked tattooing with injuring one's body and thus with dishonoring one's father?

Racism is the likely explanation. Because the Han Chinese tended to look down on the ethnic minorities in their kingdoms, and because many of these minorities practiced tattooing (such as in Quanzhou and Taiwan), tattooing was associated with uncivilized peoples. Because of this, if a son were to get a tattoo, he would, in effect, shame his father by linking himself, and thus his father, with what the Han Chinese thought were lesser peoples and lesser practices. Moreover, because the minorities living in Han kingdoms were treated as inferior peoples, they couldn't get the best jobs and so were often forced into criminal activities. Tattoos, inferior people, and criminals were thus linked in the minds of the ancient Chinese and so it was easy for Confucians to interpret their master's prohibition against wounding one's body as a prohibition against tattooing.

But notice this: just as much in Confucianism as in Christianity, tattoos themselves aren't really the problem: the problem is what they are associated with and the subsequent embarrassment they can cause one's parents; if tattoos weren't associated with lower status or immoral people (criminals), then it's not clear that they would be a source of shame to one's parents. Indeed, legend has it that the mother of the famous Chinese general Yue Fei tattooed on her son's back the words 'serve the country loyally,' which suggests that getting a tattoo for the right reasons – namely, out of pious obedience (as Yue Fei submitted to his mother's needle) or as a reminder to be pious (as the words on Yue Fei's back implore) – may have had some legitimacy in ancient China and so among the earliest Confucians. Of course, just as much for a Confucian as for a Jew or a Christian, if one's superior (one's father, in this case) thought that getting a tattoo was a sign of disrespect, then, insofar as the son or daughter owes the father respect in this matter – that is, insofar as they are still under the father's authority – they must not get a tattoo, for to get one would be considered impious and unjust and thus an offence against Heaven itself.

The Christian Confucian Confusion

In this chapter I have agreed with Christians and Confucians that piety (i.e., the justice shown toward one's superiors) is indeed admirable and proper, yet I have disagreed with what many Christians and Confucians have understood piety to look like, particularly in respect to remaining free of tattoos. I have argued that neither the Bible nor the works of Confucius allow us to say that tattoos in and of themselves are bad, and, indeed (though, I didn't argue it) could be good, not only for aesthetic reasons but also, as we saw with Yue Fei, for didactic purposes. Nevertheless, because justice is more important than both aesthetics and mere reminders to be just, if one finds oneself under a *legitimate* superior who has, in that relationship, a *legitimate* claim to one's obedience, then to disobey the moral or non-moral commands of that superior would be impious and unjust.[21] Thus, if a child living under the roof of a Christian or Confucian parent forbad that child from getting a tattoo (or from dying his or her hair, getting a piercing, and so on), then it would be impious of the child to disobey: as Confucius says, 'When a youth is at home, let him be filial.'[22] However, when the child moves out and is no longer under the authority of the parent (I don't say, no longer owes the parent respect and certain duties), then the child (the woman or man) may legitimately opt for ink: Heaven, very likely, doesn't have a problem with this.

NOTES

1 Deuteronomy 14:1 and 1 Kings 18:28 re-enforce this command.
2 Of course, if a Jew is tattooed against his or her will, as when the Nazis branded six million of them, such Jews are not considered impious or unjust.
3 Philip Johnston, *Shades of Sheol: Death and Afterlife in the Old Testament* (Downers Grove, IL: InterVarsity Press, 2002), p. 77.
4 See '*Nergel* and *Ereshkigal*' and '*Adapa*,' in Stephanie Dalley (ed.), *Myths from Mesopotamia* (Oxford: Oxford University Press, 2000).
5 Thus, in book eleven of Homer's *Odyssey*, even the noble Achilles dwells in the underworld.

🦅 ADAM BARKMAN

6   In the *Kojiki*, the sacred text of Shinto, the land of *Yomi* is explained to be 'an underworld, … the habitation of the dead, … the land whither, when they die, go all men, whether noble or mean, virtuous or wicked.' See *Kojiki* I.ix.

7   1 Corinthians 6:13.

8   Zheng Xuan, a scholar of the Han Dynasty, comments, 'Shang Di is another name for Tian. The spirits do not have two Lords.' *Historical Records, Han History, and Zi Zhi Tong Jian*, Sima Qian, Historical Records, vol. 28, book 6, p. 624.

9   Even to this day, the Temple of Heaven complex in Beijing has no image of Shang Di in it.

10 Scholars, of course, continue to debate the origins of China and its religious practices, and so it's possible to get different interpretations, even radically different interpretations, of these. For example, compare Chan Kei Thong's *Finding God in Ancient China* (Grand Rapids, MI: Zondervan, 2009) with David Noss' *A History of the World's Religions*, 12th edn. (Upper Saddle River, NJ: 1999).

11 *Classic of History*, The Book of Tang, The Counsel of Great Yu, paragraph 21.

12 *Record of Rites*, Confucius, Xian Ju, verse 29.

13 *Classic of History*, Chronicles of Zhou, Duo Fang, III.

14 *Mencius*, vol. 13, Jin Xin Zhang, part I.

15 *Hsiao King*, chapter 1.

16 Supreme among the blessed or virtuous ancestors are the virtuous sage-emperors who have died: 'King Wen lives above, his virtues shine in heaven. Though our Zhou nation is old, Shang Di's Mandate is still with us. The Zhou nation was not established when the time of Di's mandate had not arrived. King Wen's soul is active and he lives in the presence of Shang Di' (*Classic of Poetry*, Da Ya, Anecdotes of King Wen, King Wen, verses 1–2).

17 *The Doctrine of the Mean*, book 1, chapter 1.

18 *Hsiao King*, chapter 9.

19 *Classic of History*, Book of Shang, Instructions of Yi, paragraph 8, verse 2.

20 *Hsiao King*, chapter 1.

21 Although some imagine that Confucius and the early Confucians accepted absolute obedience to one's superiors, this is simply not true. Obedience is owed only when the command is either moral or non-moral, never when it is immoral, since an immoral command is a command against God or Heaven, who has greater authority than fathers and emperors. 'He who has a moral duty,' Confucius insists, 'should not give way even to his master' (*Analects*, book 15, chapter 35).

22 *Analects*, book 1, chapter 6.

CHAPTER 18

CONFESSIONS OF A TATTOOED BUDDHIST PHILOSOPHER

Uh, Because I Am a Buddhist

I was already a middle-aged philosophy professor when I got my first tattoo. Soon I began collecting many largely Buddhist images on my body. Why was I doing this? I had admittedly been attracted to Buddhist practice and theory for years, and had even managed to teach a course in Buddhism every now and then in addition to the standard Western philosophy courses I normally teach. But why *tattoos*? After all, tattooing is not generally commonplace in traditionally Buddhist countries, and yet tattoos of the Buddha and other Buddhist-inspired images are quite popular indeed, at least in the West.

A few years ago, I was visiting a friend in Hollywood, California, and had joined an exercise class at a local gym there. I emerged from the shower after the workout, and a Tibetan man asked me about my tattooed armband, which is the popular Tibetan Buddhist mantra '*Om mani padme hum*' (translated as 'The jewel is in the lotus') written in Sanskrit around my bicep.[1] 'Why do you have this on your arm?' he asked. Standing in front of this gentleman utterly naked, I managed to stammer

Tattoos – Philosophy for Everyone: I Ink, Therefore I Am, First Edition.
Edited by Robert Arp.
© 2012 John Wiley & Sons, Inc. Published 2012 by John Wiley & Sons, Inc.

out, 'Uh, because I am a Buddhist,' followed by a weak grin. He returned a bemused smile and slowly walked away. That mantra adorns prayer wheels, flags, and jewelry in Tibetan practice. It is *sacred* for them, since it is the mantra of Avaloketisvara, who is like the patron Bodhisattva of Tibet. But to have it tattooed on the body seems a bit alien to the Tibetans. I wondered whether my displaying this and other Buddhist tattoos might seem to trivialize the significance of the images in some way.

My encounter with the Tibetan man encouraged me to become more mindful of my tattooing practice. Admittedly, part of the reason I got tattoos was aesthetic; I just plain like them. But, at the same time, many of us who get tattooed take it very seriously. Images are chosen with great care and deliberation. Tattoos should have meaning. Of course, Buddhist tattoos do have meanings related to the tradition, but what precisely do my tattoos say about my relationship to Buddhist practice? Is the practice of tattooing consistent with or at odds with Buddhist principles? I was aware of the tattooed and tattooing monks in Thailand, but this practice too seemed somehow vaguely un-Buddhist, since it was mixed in with ancient pre-Buddhist animistic practices that struck me as downright superstitious. I knew, for example, that many people who went to these monks to get tattooed were criminals who believed the tattoos offered protection from knives or bullets.[2] What does this have to do with the teaching of the Buddha? Naturally, in spite of my misgivings, I hoped and still hope to travel to Thailand to receive one of these tattoos myself! Perhaps I misunderstood these *Sak Yant* tattoos, however. Still, the whole business of a *Buddhist* tattoo seems puzzling.

In order to investigate whether there is a tension between Buddhism and tattoos, I'd like to look at the whole business of tattoos from the standpoint of what the Buddha (also known as Siddhārtha Gautama, c. 563–483 BCE) called the 'Three Marks of Existence,' which are 'impermanence,' 'no self,' and 'suffering.' The Buddha contended our everyday existence is necessarily marked – one might say, 'tattooed' – by these three characteristics. He thought that human beings must recognize the seemingly harsh truth of the Three Marks in order to be on a path to liberation and a satisfying life. Since the Three Marks of Existence can provide the basic thrust of the Buddha's teaching (what the Buddha and Buddhists call the *Dharma*), I want examine the extent to which getting yourself tattooed is consistent with Buddhist theory and practice. I hope to show that not only is tension between Buddhist teaching and tattoos merely apparent and not real, but also that tattooing can be a deeply authentic Buddhist practice.

Impermanence and Permanent Tattoos

One of the things that attracted me to tattoos is their relative permanence. I once heard that a tattoo is like jewelry you can't take off or lose, jewelry that lasts *forever*. Now, obviously my tattoos are not really permanent, because I am not permanent, but they come close. This is why it's good to make your tattoo choices, artwork, artist, and so on very carefully. I thought about my first tattoo for years before getting it. It was a Chinese dragon that covered the outside of my left calf. Some other broadly Asian tattoos followed: a large a tiger on my right calf to balance the dragon on the left; a crane and snake doing battle over most of my right arm. These were my pre-Buddhist tattoos. I do sometimes teach classes in Asian philosophy, and these images have significance particularly for Yin/Yang philosophy and Daoism. And, while I do like Chinese art, the images also fit in nicely with my favorite hobby, the practice of Asian martial arts. But, when my love for tattoos evolved into getting Buddhist tattoos, it was different. I took Buddhism seriously in a way that I hadn't other sorts of Asian philosophies that I had taught. I don't mean that I adopted Buddhism as a religion, but rather I looked at the Buddha as someone rather like Aristotle (384–322 BCE) or Epictetus (55–135 CE), both of whom outlined a practical philosophy aimed at some of the most fundamental problems in the human condition. It made sense to me, and I began to practice meditation and look more closely at the teaching of the Buddha. It soon struck me that *Buddhist* tattoos are a pretty strange if not contradictory idea. After all, from the standpoint of Buddhism, everything in ordinary experience is explicitly impermanent, and indeed one of the principle causes of dissatisfaction – of suffering – lies in looking for permanence when none in fact is to be found. Obviously, if you can never find something lasting, the continual attempt to have something last is bound to lead to frustration. So, isn't getting a tattoo an effort to have something 'forever' and thus, from a Buddhist perspective anyway, self-defeating? Soon after I had the Tibetan Buddhist mantra tattooed as an armband around my left arm, it occurred to me to have the image of Bodhidharma (fifth–sixth centuries CE), the legendary Indian monk who brought what was later known as Zen Buddhism to China. A short time later, I had the face of the Buddha tattooed on my left bicep. I did all this with enthusiasm for the teachings of the Buddha; I was beginning to wear my enthusiasm on my sleeve. Someone could get a tattoo of, say, Immanuel Kant (1724–1804) or Bertrand Russell (1872–1970) out of enthusiasm for those philosophers, and it wouldn't be obvious from the fact that the person had got the tattoo whether they understood these philosophers or not. But I was continually plagued with the thought that my doing this actually showed I hadn't really grasped the significance of the Buddha's teaching on impermanence. Rather than internalizing the teaching of the Buddha, I had got some 'Buddhist' ink.

Before determining whether the very idea of getting tattoos conflicts with this central Buddhist doctrine, let's consider what exactly the Buddha's teaching on impermanence is supposed to be. The central idea is this: whatever arises, ceases. Anything that has a beginning will, inevitably, have an end. Everything we experience through the senses will eventually cease to exist. Our health, job, relationships, and family eventually all will cease to exist. The same appears to true of us. Of course, this observation may appear to be depressing, but from the Buddha's perspective it is only depressing if we have expectations of permanence when there is none. If we were fine with impermanence, we'd be a lot less miserable. Bart Gruzalski tells a story that illustrates this point well:

> Suppose Sara, an adult, has lived her entire life next to a northern California beach and has daily experienced the tides, which rise and fall an average over five feet where she lives. Imagine that she takes her eight year old nephew, Richard, who has never even seen the ocean, to the beach. When they reach the beach, it is low tide. Sara and Richard together build a large beautiful sandcastle only a few yards from the wash of the waves. After the tide turns and begins coming in, it obvious to Sara that their sandcastle will soon be completely washed away. Precisely because she knows the inevitable force of the rising tide almost as well as she knows anything from experience, we can understand how it would be hard for her to be attached to the longevity of their sandcastle. Richard, however, has a radically different experience. We can imagine him wanting the sandcastle to remain standing and that he struggles to protect the sandcastle from the incoming tide. Of course it is hopeless. Sara knows this, but Richard suffers as his efforts to protect the sandcastle from destruction begin to fail.[3]

This story is a good example how knowledge and ignorance condition our desires. Sara grasps the impermanence of the castle; Richard does not. So, Richard has a strong desire to save the castle, which is of course frustrated. Sara has no such desire or frustration. But the fact is that most of us *already* know that our lives, relationships, and the rest are impermanent, and it seems as if the bare awareness of this impermanence, while understood, is painful nonetheless. It's rather like we know it but not deeply. And so, we can become attached to people, things, and of course our own health and lives such that when any of these are lost we experience pain and a deep sense of loss. The Buddha's teaching is about having a deep awareness of this mark of existence; if we have this, we eliminate much attachment and frustration.

Are tattoos then a vain attempt to find permanence in a world of impermanence? Well, that depends on the motivation of the person getting tattooed. In that respect, getting a tattoo, Buddhist image or otherwise, is not much different from any other activity. We can invest ourselves fully into whatever we value the most and suffer greatly when it's gone. Or we can value our health, relationships, and the rest precisely because we understand that they *are* impermanent. Obviously tattoos are not literally permanent. But they do last a lifetime, typically. So, perhaps tattoos could be a momentary distraction from the fact of impermanence. Do they encourage a fantasy of permanence? Maybe, but if you pay close attention to the tattoos themselves you notice that with time tattoos change, like everything else. Of course you can always get an older tattoo 'touched up' to make it look as good as new. But to do so would to begin with require the awareness that it is fading.

From what I've outlined so far, the most you can say about tattoos and impermanence is that tattoos are not intrinsically any better or worse than other things or activities that human beings engage in. Getting a tattoo in that sense is no different from building a sandcastle. But this leaves open the question of why, from a Buddhist perspective, one should get a tattoo at all. After all, the Tibetan Buddhist practice of creating sand *mandalas* (intricate works of art) ends with a ritual in which the newly created art is swept away, specifically to symbolize impermanence. That practice, which seems so counter to the notion that good art should last forever, appears to be much more in keeping with the teaching of the Buddha than does tattooing. But Tibetan Buddhism does in fact have long-lasting Buddhist art, as do other traditions in Buddhism from around the world. The various Buddhist *stupas* and statues, and Tibetan Buddhist *tangkha* paintings have outlasted and will outlast any tattoo of mine. As compelling as the sweeping away of the sand *mandala* is, it is unique to that particular form of Buddhist art. The other forms serve to convey parts of the Buddha's story and message, to encourage meditation and so on. Buddhist tattoos can do much the same. Here's what I tried to do with mine.

Beneath the image of the Buddha's face on my left bicep is the Wheel of the Path. It is a traditional and ubiquitous Buddhist wheel with eight spokes, representing the Eightfold Path of Buddhism. The Buddha taught that the human condition is characterized by suffering or dissatisfaction (more on that below), and that the cause of this suffering is craving, clinging desire, which, as the sandcastle example demonstrates, is conditioned by ignorance. The solution to all this is elimination of ignorant desire, which comes through following the Eightfold Path (wise or right understanding, attitude, speech, action, livelihood, effort, mindfulness, and concentration). A discussion of the Eightfold Path goes well beyond the scope of a chapter on tattoos and Buddhism, but suffice it to say that the reason this image is on my forearm is the same reason the image appears on Buddhist temples and in Buddhist art so often: it serves to encourage the practice that Buddha taught. So, I thought it might be nice to add a lotus flower next to the wheel on my forearm. In Buddhism the lotus flower symbolizes enlightenment. My thought was that, by placing these images on my forearm, I would actually see them most directly whenever I sat in a meditation posture. Has it helped? It's hard to tell, but the intent seems consistent with the practice of most Buddhist art generally. So, if there is genuine Buddhist art that is long lasting and serves in some way as a teaching tool for Buddhist practitioners, I see no reason why tattooing could not be a genuine Buddhist art as well. Tattoos need not contract the Buddha's teaching on impermanence and can encourage Buddhist goals.

'No Self' and Body Art as Self-expression

One of the cool things about getting a custom tattoo is that no one else has it. If you work in a creative way with a good tattoo artist, the tattoos on your body can be a part of your own personal expression. They separate you from all others. I feel that my own tattoos are distinctive of me alone. While they are Asian and largely Buddhist, they are not done in the traditional Japanese style, though I love that style. I wanted images that spoke to an ancient and venerable tradition that I respected deeply, but I wanted them to be *mine*. After all, the images on my body that I have claimed encourage Buddhist practice could have been works of art in my home or office. In fact, I have Buddhist works of art in both places. But why place them on *me*? One of the fundamental teachings of the Buddha is 'no self.' The very idea that I have an enduring, substantial self is a kind of psychological illusion. And it is an illusion that Buddhists believe leads to much suffering:

> According to the teaching of the Buddha, the idea of self is an imaginary, false belief which has no corresponding reality, and it produces harmful thoughts of 'me' and 'mine', selfish desire, craving, attachment, hatred, ill-will, conceit, pride, egoism, and other defilements, impurities and problems. It is the source of all the troubles in the world from personal conflicts to wars between nations. In short, to this false view can be traced all the evil in the world.[4]

Doesn't the practice of distinctively marking one's body contradict this Buddhist teaching? That is, doesn't having distinctive tattoos reify the notion of an enduring self. Of course, I could say that this depends upon what motive one has, just as in the case of the doctrine of impermanence. However, in this case, my motive at least is to have tattoos that are unique to me as well as being personal expressions of mine. So, let's clarify exactly what the 'no self' teaching says.

When the Buddha spoke of 'no self,' he was contending that there is no permanent enduring substance that is you or me. This view was radically different from some other spiritual and philosophical traditions of his day, but he thought it was crucial. All the self amounts to is a somewhat unified collection of physical and psychological processes. While it's certainly useful to conceive of these processes as a distinct and enduring self, the Buddha thought it was a kind of illusion. After all, the combined physical and psychological processes that make up a person are themselves always undergoing change. The Buddha divided these into five interwoven processes. First you have body, and its processes, which is continually changing. Second, there is feeling (pleasure, pain, and neutrality). Third, there is perception (the ability to perceive things as different objects). The fourth is called 'mental formations' and refers to our various mental activities – thinking, imagining, and willing. And, when you look within to try to find your 'self,' it is as if no one is home. You find nothing other than these processes. The great Empiricist philosopher David Hume (1711–1776) arrived at much the same conclusion, as have many contemporary thinkers, independently, of Buddhist teaching.[5] The concept of the self, then, is a sort of useful fiction, according to the Buddha. But, if not recognized as a fiction, it can be the source of attachment and therefore much unpleasantness. Direct recognition of

JOSEPH J. LYNCH

'no self' is at the heart of the Buddha's teaching. Liberation depends in part on letting go of the fantasy of the self.

Naturally, it seems subjectively to us that we have or are selves, even though no particular region of the brain houses an ego or self. To say that the self is fictional might be misleading. The same analysis of the self can apply to cars, computers, or, in one classic example, chariots. The chariot is not identical to any of its parts; when one looks for the essence of the chariot, one finds none. The chariot exists as a functional interrelationship of its parts. There is no chariot beyond that. Chariots did exist, of course, but the idea is that there is no substantive essence to them. But what applies to chariots applies equally well to the self; but it's difficult to let go of this idea, to be sure.

While I find the Buddha's 'no self' doctrine to be plausible, I am not trying to argue for it here. The question is, can that view be reconciled with going out of one's way, as I have done, to get custom tattoos? Does getting tattoos promote the illusion of substantive, independent selfhood? Again, the tattoos themselves are no different from other things we might possess. You don't have to believe in an enduring permanent self or soul to choose furniture, artwork, or a vehicle that suits your particular taste. Nonetheless, any of our possessions can reinforce a deep sense of self, of 'mine,' if you let them. And tattoos are possessions that you can't really give away as you can jewelry or any other possession you have. I have often wondered what it would be like to be a monk, with my head shaved, wearing the same sort of robe as every other monk (which would cover all my tattoos), all appearances of my individuality stripped away. My guess is that it easier to internalize the 'no self' teaching under these conditions. Still, the 'no self' teaching itself does not preclude individuality *per se*. To the contrary, the various processes that make up an individual are likely to all have conditions that produce distinct individual persons, even if those persons are not enduring selves. The famous analogy of the chariot illustrates this point clearly. Even though there is no chariot beyond the functional parts of the chariot, it doesn't follow that there are not unique chariots. I imagine there were. It's the same thing with us. I can accept the idea that what I think of as my 'self' is nothing beyond a collection of psychological and physical processes, and still believe in my own uniqueness as a person. In fact, the many early Arhats – or 'Worthy Ones,' who were the followers of the Buddha, and who also were said to be enlightened beings – having experienced nirvana, nevertheless had various distinctive and often impressive personalities. Neither they nor the Buddha himself saw any conflict between this and the teaching of 'no self.'

Okay, so maybe getting tattoos does not commit me to a substantive view about the reality of selves or souls. But tattoos could perhaps promote an attachment to one's own individuality, which in practice could amount to the perils of selfhood that concerned the Buddha. I could easily have the attitude 'Look at me, the guy with all the cool Buddhist tattoos.' That unfortunate attitude can be a problem not only about anything one possesses but also about distinctively Buddhist practices: one can egoistically practice meditation, go to retreats, practice generosity, and so on. Buddhists have long recognized that one can have unfortunate motives for otherwise praiseworthy actions. So, Buddhist tattoos too could be a potential trap for clinging to a false notion of selfhood, but they need not be that. After all, tattoos have signified, and continue to signify, different things about the tattooed. Tattoos are sometimes used to indicate membership in a larger community. Gang tattoos are like this. These tattoos seem to broaden the notion of selfhood beyond one's individuality. You are not just an isolated individual; you are a part of a greater whole. If the tattoos in question are Buddhist, they also can transform the conception of self of the person who has them. Buddhist tattoos have the potential both for attachment and reification of selfhood and for promoting awareness of 'no self.'

Suffering, the First Truth of Both Buddhism and Getting Tattooed

I have tried to show that getting tattooed does not, or at least need not, contradict the basic Buddhist teachings of impermanence and no self, in spite of initial appearances. In fact, Buddhist tattoos can be a tool for the realization of both of these concepts. The doctrine of suffering is a bit different. The Buddha taught that there is suffering, and if you get a tattoo you definitely suffer. Those of us who get tattooed recognize the reality of suffering and indeed willingly submit to it. Tattoos hurt! And some tattoos hurt more than others.

A few years ago, I decided to get a double-*vajra* tattooed onto my lower abdomen. In Tibetan Buddhism, the double *vajra* indicates the law of the *dharma*, or basic truth of the human condition. I liked that idea, and I thought the image looked very cool. By this time, I had several tattoos on my arms and legs and was confident that I could easily endure the pain. Well, I could barely last thirty minutes at a time! And upon each

JOSEPH J. LYNCH

return visit I was more and more medicated, until finally I slept through the final touches. I needed help on that day (I also needed help getting home in my medicated state). But even those other pieces of art placed on friendlier parts of my body caused at least some discomfort. And then there's the discomfort of the healing process – the tenderness, followed by the itching, and so on. What, if anything, does the discomfort have to do with the Buddha's teaching on suffering?

The Pali word, *duhkha*, can be translated as 'suffering' – but it could also mean dissatisfaction, stress, anxiety, or just plain frustration. In order to broaden our notion of just what suffering is, the Buddha characterized *duhkha* in different ways. First, there is the suffering resulting from pain. That's the most obvious connection to the experience of being tattooed. Much of the pain in the human experience has some instrumental value, and in a broad sense getting tattooed is rather like this. I want the tattoo, and I must endure some unpleasantness in order to get it. Then there is suffering resulting from change. Here again the failure to grasp the impermanence of phenomena can lead to despair. I remember my exhilaration just after getting my first tattoo at the large colorful Chinese dragon on my left calf. It took four hours, and I was so relieved that the pain of being drilled by needles had come to a merciful end. When I saw the dragon brightly decorating my leg I was beyond delighted. But that joy only lasted for a short while before fading. In fact, it quickly led to a kind of urgent desire to get another tattoo as soon as possible – my left leg appeared to me to be now pathetically bare.

Finally, there is suffering resulting from being in a conditioned state. My enjoyment of my tattoos or anything else depends upon my now having relative good mental and physical health. But it's pretty obvious that these conditions can be altered. If I were to get a terminal illness, it seems doubtful that the images on my body would provide much comfort. And, if I were to lose my mental faculties, it's entirely possible that I might not recognize that I even have tattoos (or family or friends), much less appreciate them.

The Buddha also distinguished physical suffering from psychological or dispositional suffering. The latter two have to do with grief, despair, and not getting what you want as well as getting what you don't want. While a lot could be said about tattooing and psychological and dispositional suffering, the most obvious connection to suffering for tattoos is at the physical level. On the face of it, anyone who gets a tattoo comes face to face with the physical aspect. The Buddha primarily had in mind old age, sickness, and death, however. It seems the only way you can avoid the first of these three is to bring on the last rather early. Otherwise, we are all bound to face these. Someone might get tattoos as a distraction from these unpleasant realities, but from a Buddhist perspective the mere experience of the physical pain is itself a reminder of the fragility of our existence. The Buddha never recommends suppressing pain or negative impulses. Rather than trying to run away from these experiences or acting on them in harmful ways, the Buddha suggests that one learns to be mindful of them. The Buddhist practitioner can learn to embrace the pain of the experience of getting tattooed, the healing process, and the rest, as a kind of meditative practice. The pain itself can become the object of meditation as one simply pays attention to the sensations without trying to push them away.

One of the highest values in Buddhist practice is compassion. And any experience of pain has the potential to increase one's compassion toward others, because that experience itself connects you to every other suffering being. So, the physical aspect of suffering presents serious opportunities for Buddhist practice. Of course, if you are getting the Heart Sutra tattooed on your ribcage, it might be tough to meditate impartially on that sort or agony or use the pain as an opportunity for compassion for suffering beings everywhere. If you're like me, you opt for prescription painkillers instead. Still, the opportunity is there.

Mindfulness of Ink

Mindfulness is at the heart of Buddhist practice. It is what all that meditation is supposed to be about. Indeed, right mindfulness is a part the Eightfold Path. That path is supposed to be the way to end suffering; it is the way to enlightenment. The Buddhist practice of mindfulness includes attention to the breath, paying attention to bodily positions and activities, being aware of feelings and thoughts, and more. A Buddhist can be mindful of her ink as well. I have been trying to argue that an appropriately mindful approach to tattoos can make them a good Buddhist practice. I must admit that perhaps the sweeping away of sand *mandalas* by Tibetan lamas makes a more powerful point with respect to impermanence, and the practice of some of the Thai Buddhist faithful of being tattooed with invisible ink might better express a sense of 'no self' than does most Buddhist art. Still, I am neither a Tibetan lama nor a Thai monk. I'm just a tattooed Buddhist philosophy professor. And it seems to me that, while tattoos clearly hurt, they don't have to hurt Buddhist practice at all. In fact, they can be a distinctive kind of expression of the teachings of the Buddha.

NOTES

1   The mantra is usually translated as 'The jewel is in the lotus,' though it has multiple symbolic meanings. It is the mantra of universal compassion, associated with the Bodhisattva, Avaloketisvara, who is rather like the patron deity of Tibet. Good introductions to Buddhism include Thubten Chodron, *Buddhism for Beginners* (Ithaca, NY: Snow Lion Publications, 2001); Huston Smith and Philip Novak, *Buddhism: A Concise Introduction* (New York: Harper-Collins, 2003), and the relevant chapters of Huston Smith's classic work, *The World's Religions* (New York: HarperOne, 2009). Also take a look at the information found at http://www.buddhanet.net.

2   Colin Hinshelwood, 'Thailand's mystic tattoo ceremony,' *CPAmedia.com: The Asia Experts* (http://www.cpamedia.com/articles/20080724_04).

3   Bart Gruzalski, *On the Buddha* (Belmont, CA: Wadsworth, 2000), p. 63.

4   Walpola Rāhula, *What the Buddha Taught* (New York: Grove Press, 1974), p. 51.

5   See David Hume, *An Enquiry Concerning Human Understanding*, ed. Peter Nidditch (Oxford: Oxford University Press, 1979); Derek Parfit, *Reasons and Persons* (Oxford: Oxford University Press, 1986); and Daniel Dennett, 'Why everyone is a novelist,' *Times Literary Supplement* 4459 (September 16–22, 1988): 1016, 1028–1029. also see Sam Harris, 'What scientific concept would improve everybody's cognitive toolkit?' (2011, http://www.samharris.org/site/full_text/the-edge-annual-question-2011).

CHAPTER 19

AN ATHEIST AND A THEIST DISCUSS A CROSS TATTOO AND GOD'S EXISTENCE

The Belief in Jesus Christ, and Other Religious Beliefs and Disbeliefs

During my high school and college years, as well as one year for my M. A. in philosophy, I was studying to be a Roman/Latin Catholic Christian priest for the Archdiocese of Chicago, Illinois. That's nine years total, from 1984 to 1993. I would have had to study four more years at the theologate in the Chicagoland area to become an actual ordained priest, but decided that I wanted to start a family eventually and, well, the rest is history. I left the seminary in 1993, taught high school religion classes for three years, met my future wife in 1995, got married in 1996, went to grad school at Saint Louis University to study philosophy shortly after that, got my philosophy Ph. D. in 2005, taught philosophy classes at two universities, did a post-doc, worked as government contractor, and here I am now with a wonderful wife and two equally wonderful girls.

While I was in the seminary, I hung around with two good friends – call them Rick Anderson and Bill Drake – who were both pretty sharp

Tattoos – Philosophy for Everyone: I Ink, Therefore I Am, First Edition.
Edited by Robert Arp.
© 2012 John Wiley & Sons, Inc. Published 2012 by John Wiley & Sons, Inc.

guys who studied a lot of Christian philosophy and theology. In 1988 they decided to get matching tats on their arms of a cross, to symbolize their Roman/Latin Catholic Christian faith since, according to Christians, Jesus Christ was God in human form, and Jesus died on a cross crucified by Romans (c. 33 CE in Jerusalem). Christians also believe that Jesus Christ rose from the dead three days after being crucified to allow the possibility that any human who believed in Jesus and followed his commandments would be able to be with God in some heavenly place after s/he died. Further, along with Eastern Catholic Christians, Roman/Latin Catholic Christians are types of Catholic Christians, and all Christians believe that Jesus Christ, God the Father, and the Holy Spirit are actually three manifestations on one God.[1] So, Christians, along with Muslims and Jews, are monotheists, and monotheists are theists, or believers in a god of some kind (see Figure 19.1).

Now, Rick and Bill actually designed the cross tattoo together, and Rick had the tattoo placed on the deltoid area of his right upper arm, while Bill's was placed on the same area of his left arm. They felt like proud Christian rebels displaying their tattoos at swimming parties and on the beach during a time when tattoos were still looked upon by almost everyone as surprising, scandalous, stupid, or any combination thereof. I recall Rick's mom saying to him, 'Why the *hell* would you do that?' when she saw his cross tattoo the first time at a summer pool party. She followed that up with an exacerbated and disappointing-sounding, 'Jesus Christ!' Rick then said sarcastically, 'That's very observant of you, mom. It's supposed to represent Jesus Christ since it's a cross,' to which she responded, 'Don't be a smart ass!'

Since then, Rick and Bill have had numerous conversations about faith, religion, and the existence of god(s) while in my presence.[2] While Bill's faith in the Christian god has strengthened over the years, Rick's has gone away, to the point where Rick sympathizes with the general worldview of the atheist.[3] Interestingly enough, Rick actually regrets having the cross tattoo and often thinks of covering it up or removing it, while Will has added embellishments to his cross and has even gotten more Christian tattoos to symbolize his deep faith in a god. In this chapter, I present a dialogue consisting of a conversation that Bill and Rick had one time regarding a few arguments for and against the existence of some god or gods. I personally witnessed this conversation and, in essence, I'm going to be like Plato (c. 428–348 BCE), who wrote down many of the conversations he witnessed between his mentor, Socrates (c. 469–399 BCE), and other interlocutors.[4] Bill would consider himself a

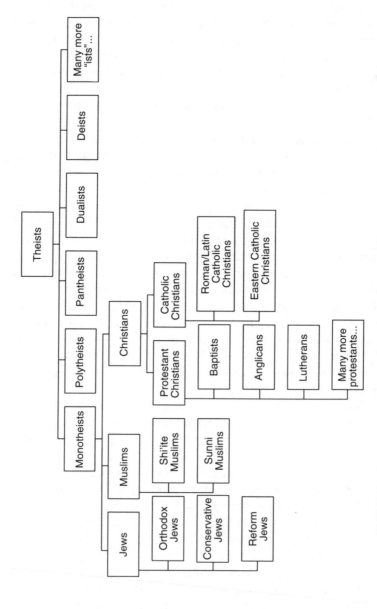

FIGURE 19.1   One classification of Roman/Latin Catholic Christians. Created by Robert Arp.

monotheist in general, and a Roman/Latin Catholic Christian particularly – as I have noted already – while Rick would consider himself an atheist and a secular humanist. Before we begin, look at Table 19.1, which summarizes many of the basic beliefs and disbeliefs in god – numerous 'isms' with adherents out there in the world – complete with examples drawn from history and present-day famous folks, groups, and religions of the world.[5]

Tattoos, Tea, and Testing Faith

About a year after graduating from college, Rick, Bill, and I met at a coffeehouse for some tea in Washington, D. C. to catch up on what we'd been doing for the past year – we were big tea drinkers. We had gone our separate ways after graduation: I was finishing up my M. A. in philosophy in Washington D. C. at The Catholic University of America, Rick was finishing his first year of law school in the L. A. area, and Bill was teaching at a private high school in the Chicagoland area. After the hugs and general 'How's it going? What are you up to?' stuff, things took a more serious turn…

William 'Bill' Drake (WD): Guys, check out my new tattoo of Jesus on my shoulder. Rick, did you ever get any more tattoos?

Rick Anderson (RA): No. Believe it or not, I kind of regret having this cross tattoo on my arm.

WD: What? Why?

RA: Well, I'm not a believer anymore.

WD: That's kind of a shock! What do you mean? What happened to your faith?

RA: I've become convinced that ghosts, gods, demons, devils, and all that paranormal and supernatural stuff is a bunch of baloney. I consider myself more of a secular humanist now.

WD: Well, I'll agree with you on the paranormal stuff, but the Christian God is in a different category altogether. He created you and all that exits, Mr. Humanist!

RA: I don't see how the Christian God is in a different category, really. You can't sense or 'test' for this god with the scientific method, either directly or indirectly, like you can with other entities and forces at work in the universe. So what makes you think this god exists?

TABLE 19.1   Beliefs and Disbeliefs in God(s).

Belief	Definition	Example
Theism	From the Greek *theos*, meaning 'god'; the belief in a god or gods. The gods of theists are usually understood to be at least kinds of divine, spiritual, or supernatural forces or causes, but many of these gods are understood by theists to be personified beings (with minds and wills) that are powerful enough to be feared, adored, praised, worshipped, and appeased.	Adherents to religions such as Buddhism (only a few sects), Christianity, Daoism, Hinduism, Islam, Judaism, and Sikhism are theists. Socrates (c.469–399 BCE), Plato (c.428–348 BCE), and Aristotle (384–322 BCE) were theists in their own ways. All of the great medieval Christian philosophers – for example, St. Augustine (354–430), St. Thomas Aquinas (1225–1274), and Francisco Suárez (1548–1617) – were theists too.
Monotheism	From the Greek *mono*, meaning 'one', and *theos*, meaning 'god'; the belief in one god. Usually this god is understood to be at least an all-powerful, all-knowing, all-just, and all-good supreme being, and creator/source of all that exists in the universe.	Adherents to religions such as Christianity (whose one god is triune – i.e., one god in three 'persons': Father, Son (Jesus Christ), and Holy Spirit), Islam (whose god is called 'Allah'), and Judaism (whose god is called 'Yehovah,' 'Adonai,' or 'Elohim') are monotheists.
Polytheism	From the Greek *poly*, meaning 'many', and *theos*, meaning 'god'; the belief in many gods. Usually, there is an entire pantheon of gods for some particular polytheist.	Adherents to religions such as Buddhism (only a few sects), Daoism, Hinduism, and Shintoism are polytheists. The Ancient Greeks, Romans, and Egyptians were polytheists, too. Recall gods such as Apollo, Athena, Hera, Poseidon, Zeus, and other gods of the Greek pantheon from Greek mythology.

Term	Definition	
Dualism (theological)	From the Greek *duo* and Latin *du*, meaning 'two', the belief in two gods or principle forces at work in the universe: one that is good, harmonious, unifying, positive, and generative; and another that is bad, disharmonious, discordant, negative, and destructive. Usually the dualist believes that these two gods or forces are necessary in order to maintain a kind of balance in the universe.	Adherents to religions such as Daoism (only a few sects), Manichaeism, and Zoroastrianism (in its early form) are dualists. For early Zoroastrians, Ahura Mazda is the good god and source of all that is good, while Angra Mainyu is the evil god and source of all that is evil. The *yin* and *yang* – existing as polar opposites generating energy and life in the universe – are dualist ideas central to Daoists, and most people have heard of these two forces. The ancient Greek philosopher Empedocles (c.490–430 BCE) thought that love and strife were the ultimate sources of existence and change in the universe.
Pantheism	From the Greek *pan*, meaning 'all'; and *theos*, meaning 'god'; the belief that god and the universe are one thing, or that all things in the universe are manifestations of god in some way.	The writer John Toland (1670–1720) and the philosophers Zeno of Citium (334–262 BCE) and Baruch Spinoza (1632–1677) are famous pantheists. Pantheism can also be found in the early writings of the Daoist thinker Lao Tzu (sixth century BCE).
Deism	From the Latin *deus*, meaning 'god', and prominent especially during the Age of Enlightenment, the belief that god is a first cause, first mover, and source (like a clockmaker) who has designed, created, caused, and set in motion the universe, but then has nothing to do with the universe after that.	Montesquieu (1689–1755) and Voltaire (1694–1788) were deists. Thomas Paine (1737–1809) was a deist, too, as were many of the Founding Fathers of the United States of America, including Benjamin Franklin (1706–1790). Unitarianism has been strongly influenced by deism, and many present-day Unitarians would consider themselves deists.

(continued)

TABLE 19.1 (cont'd)

Belief	Definition	Example
Anthropotheism	From the Greek *anthropos*, meaning 'human,' and *theos*, meaning 'god,' the belief that gods are really just deified humans. Also, usually the anthropotheist believes that certain humans are not only the most important things in the universe but also that these certain humans can achieve divine, god-like status while existing on Earth, and are, at root, divine, god-like beings.	Members of the official Church of Satan started by Anton LaVey are anthropotheists of a sort, using Satan as a mere moniker – LaVey's brand of Satanists, interestingly enough, don't believe in the existence of Satan. In L. Ron Hubbard's Church of Scientology – which has celebrities such as Tom Cruise, Katie Holmes, and John Travolta as adherents – the concept of a thetan has an undertone of anthropotheism in this sense.
Agnosticism	From the Greek *a*, meaning 'without,' and *gnosis*, meaning 'knowledge,' the belief that it is not possible to know whether a god (or gods) exists or not.	T. H. Huxley (1825–1895) – Charles Darwin's 'Bulldog' – was a professed agnostic, as was Darwin (1809–1882) himself later in life. Brad Pitt, Zac Efron, and Annie Lennox are also known to be agnostics.
Atheism	From the Greek *a*, meaning 'without,' and *theos*, meaning 'god,' the belief that a god (or gods) does not exist. Atheists are almost always adherents of Scientism, Naturalism, and Secular Humanism, too (defined below).	Barack Obama, Sr. (1936–1982) was an atheist, apparently, as was science fiction writer Arthur C. Clarke (1917–2008). Film directors James Cameron, John Landis, and Steven Soderbergh, as well as Family Guy creator Seth MacFarlane, Ronald Reagan, Jr., and, of course, Richard Dawkins, are all atheists, too.

Scientism	The belief that the worldview and methods of natural science are the most accurate and most appropriate interpretation of reality. Scientism is usually understood to be an epistemological (how we come to know things) position.	Anyone – and there are probably millions of folks – who agree with the title of this article written by Sholto Byrnes from the *New Statesman*: 'When it comes to facts, and explanations of facts, science is the only game in town.' See http://www.newstatesman.com/200604100019.
Naturalism	The belief that only natural entities, properties, laws, and forces that can be perceived, tested, and controlled directly or indirectly exist, and that gods, ghosts, paranormal activity, and anything else that is super-natural does not exist out there in reality. Whereas scientism is usually understood to be an epistemological position, naturalism is usually understood to be a metaphysical (what exists out there in reality) position.	Anyone – and there are probably millions of folks – who agree with this claim from John E. Jones, III relating to his final decision in the controversial Kitzmiller versus Dover (2005) creationism case: 'naturalism is a "ground rule" of science today which requires scientists to seek explanations in the world around us based upon what we can observe, test, replicate, and verify.' See http://www.pamd.uscourts.gov/kitzmiller/kitzmiller_342.pdf.
Humanism (secular)	The belief in scientism, naturalism, and other secular beliefs and forms of practice as appropriate ways to understand reality and solve problems, as well as pursue matters concerning ethics, politics, and overall human fulfillment. Humanists specifically reject all forms of divinity, religiosity, and supernaturalism, and are dedicated to debunking pseudoscience and superstition.	Paul Kurtz, founding president of the Council for Secular Humanism, is a humanist (obviously!), as were John Lennon (1940–1980) and Charles M. Schulz (1922–2000), apparently. Bill Maher is a humanist, too. Many humanist ideas can be traced back to, and found in, the ideas of August Comte (1798–1857), father of sociology and positivism.

WD: Well, first off, to think that the scientific method is the only way to know reality assumes from the start that a being like the Christian God doesn't exist, which it's unfair to do in any discussion, and is kind of myopic, too.

RA: I'm not being unfair at all; nor am I being myopic. It's the theist who needs to prove that god exists, not the atheist or agnostic. After all, atheist, agnostic, and *theist* alike believe that natural things that are testable through the scientific method exist, right? So, it's the theist who wants to add this extra supernatural being – some god or gods, and other stuff – and the burden of proof is on the theist, therefore, to prove that such a being or beings exist.

Unmoved Mover and Uncaused Cause

WD: Fair enough. I think Aquinas' proofs for the existence of God still are viable, so let's start there.[6] The first two proofs – the proof from motion and the proof from causation – can really be combined and go something like this: Premise one is that we see around us that things are moved and/or caused, and nothing can move or cause itself. We're talking about every entity involved in any action, process, or activity in the universe. Every thing that moves or is affected *has to be* moved or affected by something else. Further, if we ask, 'Well, what moved or caused that?' 'Well, what moved or caused that?' 'Well, what moved or caused that?' over and over and over and over again, eventually nowadays almost all people would agree that the ultimate answer we come to is 'the Big Bang.' So, we can trace all motion and causation back to the Big Bang, really, since the generally accepted, and scientifically based, answer to the question 'What *ultimately* moved/caused the universe?' is 'the Big Bang.'

Take the tattoo artist who put the cross tattoos on our arms: we can ask what moved/caused him to be in that tattoo parlor and what moved/caused him to be able to work on our arms, and the answer would have to do with a combination of vast amounts of other processes, activities, events, people, and materials. Then we can ask what moved/caused all of those *other* processes, activities, events, people, and materials, and so on, and so on, and so on. Eventually, and ultimately, after all of our 'Well, what caused that? OK, got it. Well, what caused that? OK, got it. Well, what caused that? OK, got it. Well, what caused that?' questioning we'd get to the final answer of 'It's the Big Bang! That's what ultimately

ROBERT ARP

caused the *entire universe* of processes, activities, events, people, materials, and everything in it!'

So far, so good. Now, Aquinas' second premise is that it's impossible for this series of motions and causes to continue backwards infinitely without some ultimate source of the motions/cause, since, then, there would be nothing to move or cause anything, and *right now* there would be nothing moved or caused, which is absurd and plainly false. So, with our tattoo artist, for example, he's obviously able to do his work, which means that tracing motions and causes backwards from him has to lead to some ultimate source of his tattoo work. Same with the Big Bang itself: something had to put in motion, or cause the Big Bang. In fact, almost everybody in the scientific world buys this, and that's why scientists, researchers, and other thinkers are looking for, and speculating about, the cause of the Big Bang itself.[7]

Premise three, however, is that the thing that moved or caused the Big Bang – as well as the entire series of motions and causes in the universe – must itself be something *outside of*, or *utterly other than*, (a) the Big Bang, (b) the series of motions/causes that comprise the universe, and (c) any one of the things in the series. So, the source, mover, or cause of the *natural phenomenon* of the tattoo artist, his inks, his trade, his being able to breathe, his parents, the Earth, the universe, and so on – as well as of the Big Bang and subsequent motions and causes – has to be something *wholly unlike* this natural phenomenon of the Big Bang and any natural phenomena in the universe.

The conclusion, then, is that there must be a wholly *supernatural thing* – meaning a thing that is 'outside of,' or 'other than,' or 'unlike' any natural entity, force, law, movement, or cause – that itself must be *unmoved* and *uncaused* by anything natural, but yet is the ultimate source of the entire series of motions/causes that is the natural universe and all of its natural workings. And that supernatural thing that is the unmoved mover and uncaused cause of all that exists we can call 'God.'

To use an analogy, if you had an infinite string of train boxcars or dominoes set up, they would never get moving or cause one another to fall down without something that is different from one of the boxcars or dominoes itself – namely, a train engine for the boxcars, or someone's hand for the dominoes. The engine or hand is like God, while the boxcars or dominoes are like the infinite series of motions/causes that comprise the universe, including the activities of the tattoo artist who put the tattoos of the cross on our arms.

I find this to be a convincing argument, obviously, and it helps to give a kind of ultimate explanation of how and why things exist.

RA: I think that Aquinas' argument is an impressive piece of philosophizing, no doubt, and I appreciate that he was a believer who was trying to make sense of, and ground, his belief in rational argumentation. However, the argument seems to suffer in at least two ways.

First, I don't agree with the third premise that an infinite series cannot move or cause itself. Why can't the infinite series move or cause itself and be its own source of movements or causes? Sticking with your analogy, if we think of the train of boxcars or dominoes as always having been moving or causing one another to fall down – as we both agree upon by virtue of what is meant by 'infinite' in this sense – then why do you need an engine or a hand in the first place, or even ultimately? The infinite chain is *its own source* of motion and/or causation for itself. I can conceive of the boxcars and dominoes moving and falling on some kind of a slope, with a previous boxcar or domino in the infinite chain itself being the source of motion or cause for the next, in an infinite manner – this one moved/caused this one, which moved/cause this one, which moved/caused this one, which moved/caused this one, which moved/caused this one, and so on, in both directions of the infinite chain.

And, if I'm right about this, then we come to my second problem with the argument: the conclusion is false and unsupported by one its premises. One need not conclude that the source of motion and cause in the universe is something wholly outside the universe itself – some supernatural god. I'm a naturalist, and I think naturalism is the right way to approach reality, so we should be looking for natural causes of the universe, not fantasizing about supernatural ones that really don't exist anyway.

WD: But Rick, the slope you mention in your example is something other than the boxcars and dominoes, and it is necessary – even in your own example – to get the boxcars and dominoes moving. So, you do admit that something other than the boxcars and dominoes is necessary. I can adjust my analogy a bit then, and I will maintain along with you that a slope is necessary; but this slope, then, is what I call God.

Interaction of the Supernatural and the Natural

RA: Wait a second, for me the slope is just another natural cause, while for you it's a supernatural cause – what you are calling 'god.' Again, I see no need for positing a supernatural cause, and ask you, 'Why can't any cause of the universe – even some ultimate cause – be wholly natural?'

Here's another problem to think about if you want to posit this supernatural being as a cause for natural things. By your own admission, you maintain that this god is wholly other than, radically distinct from, and utterly unlike, the natural universe, right?

WD: Yes.

RA: Well, if that's true, then how in the heck does this being that is wholly *super*natural interact with anything that is natural? There seems to be an interaction problem here. It's easy to see how natural forces, laws, principles, entities, and whatnot causally affect other natural forces, laws, principles, entities, and whatnot. Everyone agrees, for example, that gravity acts on trees, making them fall to Earth, that viruses infect cells, and that my brain and nervous system cause my hand to pull back from fire, and everyone agrees that gravity, trees, the Earth, viruses, cells, brains, nervous systems, and hands are all natural things being causally affected by other natural things.

Now throw a supernatural being into the mix. How exactly does this supernatural being interact with gravity, trees, the Earth, and so on? Further, how *can* such a *super*natural being interact with natural beings, again, given that this supernatural being is wholly other than, radically distinct from, and utterly unlike any and all natural beings? If you say, 'Well, it's a mystery how god interacts with nature,' then I say that this is not much of an explanation at all and our conversation stops dead. Even if you say this god acts as an unmoved mover, uncaused cause, and/or source of the universe of natural things – as you have said – I still want to know exactly how this kind of being does it! I mean, your analogies to trains and dominoes only go so far and only do so much work here. They're analogies that help people understand, but I want the kind of precise, exact, satisfactory explanation that you find with a scientific explanation. Who wouldn't?

WD: There's plenty of supposedly natural causation where one just plain can't get a precise, exact, satisfactory explanation, and I would submit that God's interaction with nature is like one of these. For example, it's a complete mystery how beliefs, thoughts, wills, and desires of a conscious mind like that of a human being's – which seem to be on their own level, plane, or realm – interact with the brain and nervous system to cause something as simple as the raising of my arm. However, most would acknowledge that this does indeed take place, that a mind does interact with the body, and yet that the mind seems to be radically distinct from the body.

RA: I agree that the human, conscious mind is an incredibly mysterious thing. But there's a big difference here. With the mind interacting with the body, even though there are mysteries now, no one seriously expects there to be a supernatural explanation at work. In fact, researchers are making great scientific strides and have satisfactorily explained most of the brain's workings. Why should we think that the hardest problems related to the conscious mind – beliefs, thoughts, desires, and so on – *won't* be solved someday by this same scientific work?

The 'Three Ms'

WD: Well, besides the unmoved mover and uncaused cause arguments, I think that what I'll call the 'three Ms' – mind, meaning, and morality – are things that science just cannot explain, and we need God as an ultimate source and explanation of these. So, that the three Ms exist shows that there is a God.

Let's start with mind. You're right. There is an interaction problem, and it is amazing that the conscious mind is able to move the body. I think the only plausible explanation of this is that God created the conscious mind the way it is and assists in moving the body. I mean, if all other natural explanations aren't working and do not fit the evidence, then I think we can posit a supernatural cause as an explanation.[8] I'm not saying that we use this supernatural cause willy-nilly; we can be rationally responsible in our use of God as an explanation. I believe that human brains evolved just like evolutionists, naturalists, and other scientists and researchers think it did. But the emergence of the conscious mind – which is not only able to move our bodies, make us believe and feel, and cause us to ponder the existence of God with a sense of wonder, but *also* is something wholly different in kind from the brain and body – could only have happened with the help of God 'divinely intervening' at a certain point in human history and putting conscious mind in humans.

RA: Let me stop you there. Exactly how did this God divinely intervene to bring conscious mind into existence? This was my point before.

WD: I don't exactly know the *how*, but at least we have the satisfaction of knowing the *that*.

RA: But don't you see that this kind of supernatural explanation actually stops any meaningful discussion as well as the search for legitimate explanations? If some god becomes the answer, then people get lazy. God talk actually is counterproductive to humans flourishing and understanding!

ROBERT ARP

Meaning

WD: Hang on. I'm not saying that we stop looking for natural explanations for natural events. Of course we should continue doing that! I'm saying that natural explanations can only get you so far. This leads us 'naturally' – no pun intended – into a discussion of meaning in human life, which is my second M of the three Ms. The God I have in mind is a Christian God who is an all-powerful, all-knowing, all-just, and all-good supreme being, and creator/source of all that exists in the universe. God creates us freely because he loves us and wants us to be with Him eventually in a heavenly place. He gave us the scriptures, prophets, theologians, and his only son, Jesus Christ, to show us how we can lead our lives with the goal of getting back to Him in heaven. Thus, this understanding of God gives us meaning to our lives. 'What's it all about,' you might ask? Why are we here? Why something rather than nothing? The answers to these questions, again, have to do with the fact that God created us to be with him, if we choose to. This gives me – and millions of others on the planet – a sense of meaning, purpose, and comfort.

RA: Well, being a secular humanist, I have plenty of things that give my life meaning.[9] There's a common misconception that atheists, agnostics, and other kinds of unbelievers live meaningless lives. This need not be true. One could live one's life without any meaning, like some existential nihilist. But, that's not me, and that's not what humanists believe. The difference between you and me is that I believe humans make *their own* meaning, choose to fulfill their own plans in life, and even make up a being like god as part of trying to better themselves.

In fact, let me take the gloves off completely now and say that your god is really just a fiction of your mind that represents all of the good, noble, true, and righteous things that you and other humans desire to be. God is not real, it's a fictional ideal! And I find it amazing that so many people have died throughout the centuries for this made-up ideal. No, I take that back: I do understand how one could die for an ideal that never has or will exist, as plenty of idiotic folks have done this throughout human history. And I know that plenty of people have murdered, raped and pillaged, tarred and feathered, and tortured and deceived others in the name of this god as a cover for their own selfish, evil, dastardly deeds. But c'mon, man! Wake up and grow up! God is a nice, neato, nifty, non-existent, made-up thing.

WD: No need to get offensive here with the 'wake up' and 'grow up' comments. But nice alliteration!

RA: Sorry, dude, but the truth hurts.

WD: Are you finished with your insulting rant?

RA: Yup.

WD: Why did you get that cross tattoo, by the way, if this is how you feel?

RA: I was a kid who just took it for granted that a god and all that stuff was true. Then, like I said, I *woke* up and *grew* up through college, and came to see that Christianity is full of myths just like any other mythology in human history.[10] Again, sorry dude, but the truth hurts.

Morality

WD: OK. Getting back to the discussion, morality is the final M of the three Ms I want to talk about. When you take a look around at all of the evil perpetrated by people in the world – some of which you just mentioned with murder and the like – you can't help but think that these evil-doers will get what they deserve. In fact, there are plenty of evil-doers who go through their lives and die, never having paid for their crimes. Likewise, there are folks who are do-gooders who die never having received their just desserts either. So, to ensure that evil-doers get punished and do-gooders get rewarded, there has to be a God who metes out that justice.

Further than this, a God who will in fact punish and reward people actually keeps people in line in this world. I have heard many Christians, and other people of other faiths, say that they 'can't do it alone' and that they need God's grace and assistance to help them to make the right decisions, especially during tough times. Also, without a God who knows every thought we have, people would be more inclined to act in evil ways. Knowing that God is out there watching your every move and knowing your every thought keeps a person from committing all kinds of horrendous evils. I would argue that those folks you mention who have done evil in the name of God were not really in a true relationship with God in which they knew that God was watching their every move; otherwise, they wouldn't have done such horrible things!

RA: Regarding your first point, the cold, hard fact is that evil-doers die unpunished and do-gooders die unrewarded, and that's all there is to it. Just because you and others want there to be justice does not mean that there actually is some god out there – as well as a hellish existence for punishment, and a heavenly existence for reward – that really exists! It's wishful thinking and, again, part of the fantasy that some just, parental kind of being will be there to make things right in the end. We have to work hard here and now, in this reality, to make sure evil-doers and do-gooders get justice. In fact, the crazy belief that there is some afterlife and a god, or even some kind of 'messiah' who'll save people eventually, has actually kept people down, made them complacent in the face of oppression, and allowed them to be walked all over, as well as murdered, raped, stolen from, and so on by other a-holes in this world – many of these a-holes being religious folks![11]

Regarding your second point, there are plenty of secular ethical positions out there that require a good, hard, honest investigation of conscience when making an ethical decision that will affect others. I don't need some god scaring me into doing what's right. In fact, your god scaring folks into doing what's right makes people out to be like little kids who begrudgingly do what's right … or else! This child-like motivation for action is akin to a child-like belief that we need some fatherly or motherly being to understand reality, make sense of our supposedly purpose-driven life, and other baloney that really just hinders folks from flourishing in life.

WD: Wow! You sound like an anti-theist! Is there no good that can come from a belief in God or religion?

RA: I guess there have been plenty of cases of 'good coming out of evil' when we think of how religious belief has created some of the greatest works of art around the world, or how someone has changed their life around completely and truly does good now because of a personal experience of being 'saved.' And, of course, we were in the seminary studying at a Catholic university, and Catholics have undeniably played a big part in fostering education as well as free thought throughout the centuries. But could we *have had* – as well as *have* – such goods in life without some god? I think we've reached the point where we can now. We can move forward doing great things without a god anymore. I mean, no one seriously believes in the Greek gods anymore, so why believe in one god, or two gods, or three, or more, anymore since we've come so far in our understanding of nature from a natural perspective? I'll repeat myself: why search for supernatural explanations for a natural universe? Why not stick with what has been working for the past few hundred years now – namely, the methods and ideologies of modern science?

WD: Well, I'd say something like, 'I'll see you in hell, Rick' but you'd probably laugh at the thought.

RA: Yup. One final point needs to be addressed while I am still thinking of it. Even if you're right that this god is an unmoved mover or uncaused cause, how is it that he all of a sudden is this all-knowing, all-good, thinking, and willing being who 'wants' us to be with him in heaven? Even the word 'him' has connotations of a knowing and willing being closer to a person, rather than some force or source that is wholly lacking in *person*-ality. The unmoved and uncaused stuff makes your god out to be the god of the deist, really. And you need a whole other set of arguments to make the 'move' – pun intended! – from unmoved mover to loving creator!

WD: You're correct, and we need a different kind of argument for the God who is knowing, willing, loving, and so on. I will say this much, however. Earlier you mentioned that you appreciated that Aquinas was a believer who was trying to make sense of, and ground, his belief in rational argumentation. If we start with the Christian God of the Christian scriptures, who – as we're told in the first few lines of Genesis – created the world and saw that it was good, then we can interpret this to be consistent with the unmoved mover and uncaused cause kind of God, can't we? All we need to do is recognize that, theologically and religiously, God is creator, while, philosophically and rationally, God is unmoved mover and uncaused cause.

In his famous proofs, Aquinas' final proof for God's existence has to do with a God who has intelligently designed the universe and its workings, and William Paley (1743–1805), Oxford philosopher Richard Swinburne, and a whole host of other philosophers, theologians, and researchers have put forward versions of an argument from design.[12] It's here, with the argument from design, where I would try to respond to your critique of God as a mere 'force' or 'source.' God can be conceived as a knowing and willing *and* a moving and causing being without a problem. But there's probably been enough philosophical bantering – Rob's eyes are glazing over and my tea is getting cold.

NOTES

1   Good introductions to Catholicism include Richard McBrien, *Catholicism* (New York: HarperOne, 1994); Gerald O'Collins, *Catholicism: A Very Short Introduction* (Oxford: Oxford University Press, 2008); and Lawrence Cunningham, *An Introduction to Catholicism* (Cambridge: Cambridge University Press, 2009).

2   Philosophy of religion is the branch of Western philosophy that investigates questions surrounding arguments for god's existence, arguments from religious experience, the problem of evil, attributes of god, the question of miracles, the intersection of faith and reason, science and religion, and religion and ethics. Good introductions include Charles Taliaferro and Paul Griffiths (eds.), *Philosophy of Religion: An Anthology* (Malden, MA: 2003); Brian Davies, *An Introduction to the Philosophy of Religion* (Oxford: Oxford University Press, 2004); William Rowe, *Philosophy of Religion: An Introduction* (Belmont, CA: Wadsworth, 2006); and Louis Pojman and Michael Rea (eds.), *Philosophy of Religion: An Anthology* (Belmont, CA: Wadsworth, 2007).

3   Good introductions to atheism include Julian Baggini, *Atheism: A Very Short Introduction* (Oxford: Oxford University Press, 2003); B. C. Johnson, *The Atheist Debater's Handbook* (Amherst, NY: Prometheus Books, 1981); George Smith, *Atheism: The Case Against God* (Amherst, NY: Prometheus Books, 1989); Christopher Hitchens (ed.), *The Portable Atheist: Essential Readings for the Nonbeliever* (New York: DaCapo Press, 2007); and Richard Dawkins, *The God Delusion* (New York: Mariner Publishers, 2008).

4   Good introductions to Plato include Julia Annas, *An Introduction to Plato's Republic* (Oxford: Oxford University Press, 1981) and Julia Annas, *Plato: A Very Short Introduction* (Oxford: Oxford University Press, 2003).

5   Good introductions to the religions of the world include Lewis Hopfe and Mark Woodard, *Religions of the World* (Upper Saddle River, NJ: Prentice-Hall Publishers, 2008) and Huston Smith, *The World's Religions* (New York: HarperOne, 2009). See also the *A Very Short Introduction* series, which has books on all of the world's major religions.

6   See St. Thomas Aquinas' own words in his *Summa Theologicae*, First part, a, Question 2, Article 3. There, Aquinas lays out five proofs for the existence of a god. See also Joseph Owens, *St. Thomas Aquinas on the Existence of God: The Collected Papers of Joseph Owens*, ed. John Catan (Binghamton, NY: SUNY Press, 1980).

7   See, for example, William Lane Craig and Quentin Smith, *Theism, Atheism, and Big Bang Cosmology* (Oxford: Clarendon Press, 1993) and Maurizio Gasperini, *The Universe Before the Big Bang: Cosmology and String Theory* (Berlin: Springer, 2010).

8   For more on a responsible kind of faith, see Alvin Plantinga and Nicholas Wolterstorff (eds.), *Faith and Rationality: Reason and Belief in God* (Notre Dame: University of Notre Dame Press, 1983) and C. Stephen Evans, *Faith Beyond Reason: A Kierkegaardian Account* (Grand Rapids, MI: William B. Eerdmans Publishing Company, 1998).

9   See the information on the Council for Secular Humanism's website: http://www.secularhumanism.org. See also the American Humanist Association: http://www.americanhumanist.org.

10 See Anthony Duignan and Tom X. Chao, 'The top 10 intelligent designs (or creation myths),' *Live Science* (December 19, 2004, http://www.livescience.com/11316-top-10-intelligent-designs-creation-myths.html).

11 See James Haught, *Holy Horrors: An Illustrated History of Religious Murder and Madness* (Amherst, NY: Prometheus Books, 1999) and Charles Kimball, *When Religion Becomes Evil: Five Warning Signs* (New York: HarperOne, 2008).

12 For more on the Design Argument for God's Existence, see Michael Ruse, *Darwin and Design: Does Evolution Have a Purpose?* (Cambridge, MA: Harvard University Press, 2004) and William Demski and Michael Ruse (eds.), *Debating Design: From Darwin to DNA* (Cambridge: Cambridge University Press, 2007).

NOTES ON CONTRIBUTORS

ROBERT ARP, PH. D., has taught and published in many areas of philosophy and ontology in the information science sense. He also has done a lot of work in the philosophy and popular culture realm, and has regularly flashed his half smiley face, half skull tattoo (located on his right arm, thank goodness!) to make a point about the distinction between appearance and reality in 'introduction to philosophy' courses.

JENNIFER BAKER, PH. D., admires people with virtue and writes about them as much as she can. She once expressed her wish to be cool enough to get a snake tattoo and was told, 'Get the tattoo, and then you're cool enough.' Contemplating how thoughtful that line has kept her so busy that she never got the damn snake tattoo!

KIMBERLY BALTZER-JARAY, PH. D., is an independent scholar (for absolute clarity, she is an 'independent scholar' meaning without university employment rather than supremely wealthy) whose area of expertise is early phenomenology and existentialism but who has interests in just about every area of philosophy. She even likes Kant, and she often admits that fact out loud, in public. She is president of the North American Society for Early Phenomenology, and author of the blog *A Tattooed Philosopher's Blog: Discussion of the Type I Ink, Therefore I Am*. The first

Tattoos – Philosophy for Everyone: I Ink, Therefore I Am, First Edition.
Edited by Robert Arp.
© 2012 John Wiley & Sons, Inc. Published 2012 by John Wiley & Sons, Inc.

philosophical tattoo she got was of Jack Skellington; it takes up most of her mid and lower back. She explains its significance by saying that she has an affinity with Jack – she is always asking metaphysical questions (what else is out there, what's the essence of this, and so on), and she, too, doesn't understand Christmas.

ADAM BARKMAN, PH. D., is Assistant Professor of Philosophy at Redeemer University College. He is also the author of *C. S. Lewis and Philosophy as a Way of Life* and *Through Common Things*, and is the co-editor of *Manga and Philosophy*. After playing the video game *Breath of Fire* he wanted to get a red star tattooed on his forehead, and after seeing the movie *Gladiator* he wanted 'SPQR' on his arm, but wisely (that's what philosophy's for, after all) he decided to wait a few months to see whether his feelings changed. They did.

THORSTEN BOTZ-BORNSTEIN, PH. D., is a German philosopher trying to be slightly funnier than Kant. Being attracted by everything that is virtual, stylish, playful, and dreamlike, he has been drawn toward things Japanese for a long time. He has found much of the desired dreamlike atmosphere in classical Japanese and Chinese philosophy, but has also elaborated on profound parallels between the design of the new Mini Cooper and traditional Japanese pottery, and provided philosophical reasons why some Asian subjects tend to use the English language as a 'linguistic air guitar.' The continuation of his research takes place in a setting not less unreal than Japan: Kuwait.

FELIPE CARVALHO, PH. D., is a philosopher whose main interests tend toward perception and perceptual experience in all its forms. Although he has mainly worked and published in that domain, his dating a tattoo artist for over two years has led to a growing interest in the unexplored domain of tattoo art and its relations to philosophy and aesthetic/bodily experience. It has also led, of course, to many new tattoos.

KEVIN S. DECKER, PH. D., is actually a series of tattoos on various bits of philosophy professors across the world. On the left shoulder of Professor N. M. from Sweden he's co-edited *Star Wars and Philosophy* and *Star Trek and Philosophy* (Open Court, both with Jason T. Eberl), as well as *Terminator and Philosophy* (Wiley-Blackwell, with Richard Brown). On the right outside thigh of Dr. E. A. C. in New Mexico, he's authored chapters on philosophy and popular culture focusing on James Bond,

Stanley Kubrick, *Avatar*, and *Doctor Who* (among others). According to the tattoo on the right buttock of Professor L. R. in Hertfordshire, U. K., he is an Associate Professor of Philosophy at Eastern Washington University.

JUNIPER ELLIS, PH. D., is Professor of English at Loyola University, Maryland, where she teaches courses that include tattoo literature (and former students give her classes credit for their new body art). She is the author of *Tattooing the World: Pacific Designs in Print and Skin* (Columbia University Press, 2008).

RACHEL C. FALKENSTERN is a Ph. D. candidate at Temple University, where she is writing her dissertation on Hegel. She is an adjunct lecturer in philosophy at Hunter College, CUNY, where she also received her B. A. in Philosophy. She hopes her parents don't read this and think she would ever even consider getting a tattoo!

KYLE FRUH is A. B. D. in the Philosophy department at Georgetown University, where he has taught courses in bioethics, ethical theory, environmental ethics, personal identity, and agency and responsibility in *The Wire*. He is writing a dissertation that deals with the problem of overly demanding moral duties by developing a theory of sacrifice and its place in moral life. He is pretty sure that this last line is where a clever quip about tattoos should go.

JONATHAN HEAPS has a B. A. in philosophy and communications from North Park University in Chicago, Illinois and an M. A. in philosophy from Boston College. He is currently pursuing a M.A. in theology at Boston University, writing on the category of transcendence and philosophy of education. Since the age of eighteen, Jonathan has continued to acquire high-quality, custom tattoos and hopes to continue for the rest of his life. He has waded into these philosophy and popular culture waters before, producing an essay on advertising as formative practice that included an extended Paris Hilton example.

NANCY KANG, PH. D., is Postdoctoral Faculty Fellow in the Humanities at Syracuse University. She has written widely on ethnic studies, feminism, philosophy, film, and literatures of difference. While generally afraid of needles, she has no problem discussing other people's use of them in various cultural contexts.

WENDY LYNNE LEE, PH. D., is professor of philosophy at Bloomsburg University of Pennsylvania. In addition to her work in philosophy of language, feminist theory, animal welfare theory, and environmental philosophy, she enjoys her life as a mom, Leftist political agitator, union activist, marathon runner, and companion to fifteen rescue animals who share her home – including a rather large iguana and two parrots. She loves her tattooing, and finds it to be the greatest first-day-of-class icebreaker ever.

JOSEPH J. LYNCH, PH. D., is a philosophy professor at California Polytechnic University-San Luis Obispo and editor of the online journal *Between the Species*. He has been attempting to have the entire contents of his courses on Asian philosophy and Buddhism tattooed onto his body. While he considered using his ink as visual aids in the classroom, he continues to follow the maxim 'Never get a tattoo you can't cover up in court.' Hence, the tattoos remain obscured during lectures. One student got a glimpse of part of a tattoo on Lynch's arm during office hours and asked, 'Now that you are a professor, are you going to have that tattoo removed?' He replied, 'Why would I? I just got it two weeks ago!'

NICOLAS MICHAUD teaches philosophy at the University of North Florida. He still has been unable to bring himself to get a tattoo because of his fear of pointy objects. When his students ask him when will he finally suck it up and get one, he distracts them with questions such as 'If I get a tattoo, am I the canvas, am I the artist, or am I the artwork itself?' While they chew on the gristle of thought, he runs away, quickly.

DANIEL MIORI is a physician's assistant practicing in palliative care in Buffalo, New York. He is also clinical adjunct faculty member at the University at Buffalo's medical school as well as a member of the ethics committee at Millard Fillmore Gates Circle Hospital, where he works. After having coasted through college-level philosophy courses, his medical experience brought him to the understanding that there are few areas where the importance of philosophic contemplation is as profound as in healthcare.

MARK ODDEN is a photographer and visual artist, having worked on various projects in the fine arts and design fields. His interest in aesthetics – what most of his philosophic work focuses on – is best represented by the

Banksy-inspired painter tattoo on his left calf honoring his grandfather, who first taught him to draw and paint.

ROCKY RAKOVIC is the Editor of *Inked* magazine, an award-winning international publication that focuses on the culture, style, and art of the tattoo world. Since he took over *Inked*, newsstands have moved the magazine from the tattoo section to the marquee rack, where it sits next to *Vanity Fair* and *GQ*. He has represented *Inked* on *LA Ink*, *NY Ink*, and *CBS News*. Along with *Inked*, he is a Contributing Editor at *Playboy*. He hates tramp stamps, but loves Forever stamps.

TANYA RODRIGUEZ, PH. D., professes philosophy at John Jay College (CUNY). In her classes, film and popular media become portals into deep philosophical questions (answers forthcoming).

CLANCY SMITH is completing his Ph. D. in philosophy at Duquesne University. He has published and presented numerous essays on pragmatism, phenomenology, and the philosophy of memory. The epitaphs and arcane symbols tattooed into his skin – testaments of solidarity to friends past and present – are examples of how unchanging ink is nevertheless constantly being reinterpreted through memory. It doesn't hurt that they look pretty cool, too.

CHARLES TALIAFERRO, PH. D., is a professor of philosophy at St. Olaf College and the author or editor of seventeen books including *The Image in Mind* (Continuum). He has also contributed to popular culture and philosophy books on cannabis, James Bond, Harry Potter, and Superheroes. He plans on getting a tattoo of his much beloved dog, Tiepolo, who has attended his philosophy classes and seminars for ten years, letting everyone know that love is (or should be) all around.

EMILY THOMAS, PH. D., is a post-graduate researcher at the University of Cambridge. Her interest lies in metaphysics, particularly the philosophy of time and fundamentality. She is currently writing a thesis on contemporary monisms that examines (among other things) the way in which British neo-Hegelian arguments have infiltrated contemporary philosophy. Outside philosophy, her main interest (or, mild obsession) is backpacking, and by her early twenties she had backpacked to all seven continents.

SIMON WOODS, PH. D., is Co-director of the Policy, Ethics and Life Sciences Research Centre (PEALS), University of Newcastle (U. K.). PEALS is an ethics think tank involved in research, teaching, and public engagement on the ethical and social implications of the life sciences. Simon has a longstanding interest in medical ethics and the societal challenges of new biotechnologies. Simon holds bachelor's and doctoral degrees in philosophy, and over the past ten years he has pursued a career of teaching and research within bioethics. His recent research concerns the ethical and social implications of early human development research, medical nano-technology, and translational research for rare genetic disorders. Although Simon has no tattoos or body modifications, he does count the tattooed among his close friends and colleagues.